DABCHICKS AND DOODLEBUGS

memories by Jane di Marco

ISBN: 978-1-916732-50-6

Published By: -

i2i

PUBLISHING

i2i Publishing. Manchester.
www.i2ipublishing.co.uk

Contents

Chapter 1 – Early Days

I was born (or so I was told) on January 12th, 1932, at 12 Alexander Square, my grandmother's house in Chelsea, demolished later in the London Blitz. The next sixteen years were spent at Starborough, between Edenbridge in Kent and Lingfield in Surrey.

Later, of course, I realised that I had a very privileged upbringing, but at the time, life just was. The only really unhappy times were when my nanny left when I was four, and when, three times a year, my brothers went back to boarding school. My Welsh nanny was gentle and loving. She was sent to England quite young, during the Great Depression, and must often have been homesick. My mother dismissed her summarily when she discovered she was pregnant, but of course I didn't understand why she had gone. Later, my mother relented enough to take me to visit her and her baby, after she had married and moved to Lingfield. At that time, and indeed all through her life, pregnancy before marriage was the ultimate sin for my mother. This has certainly affected my own attitude to sex, but I hope my own children have not suffered too much from this.

After nanny's sudden departure, my mother must have hurried to find a replacement as she had no experience of mothering. She had no role models, as she had been brought up entirely by a nanny herself. What a strange world it was for the upper classes and what a lot of joy they missed out on by not looking after their own children. My mother had firm ideas though, including a horror of spoiled children. The only way I suffered from this was over the matter of a teddy bear. I wasn't much interested in dolls, and I longed for a teddy bear. One April Fool's Day, my mother called up the back stairs, "Jane, a lovely teddy bear has come for you by post," only to follow this with, "April Fool." I'm sure she didn't realise how cruel that was, but she never did give me a teddy. In fact, I didn't have one until many years later, when my daughter Rachel gave me Walter, who sits on the pillow on the other side of my bed. As the nose and mouth of a teddy are hand sewn, each one is unique. I remember my brothers going to Harrods, walking along the line and scrutinising each face before choosing one for their little brother, Simon. My favourite toy was a black Scotty dog, but as he had heavy feet to make him more walkable, he was not very cuddly. I did have a teddy hot water bottle, but he only came into action when I was ill.

Not long after my nanny left, my governess, Miss Smith, arrived. She was tall, and seemed austere and a little frightening, but I soon warmed to her. I think children instinctively know who they can trust, but it may be different for those who have had bad experiences. Miss Smith had the same bedroom as nanny had had, on the other side of the nursery, and I knew I must never go into her room. Life was much the same, with meals in the nursery and lunch brought up from the kitchen by the nursery maid by the back stairs. The big difference was that now I had lessons. I enjoyed reading, but I hated practising writing. The immediate challenge was learning to tell the time. My mother promised that if I could tell the time by Christmas, they would give me a watch. Miss Smith worked hard with me for the next few months and by Christmas I could just about manage it, though I was not always sure about the bits between the quarters. I had my watch though, just before my fifth birthday.

I enjoyed nearly all the lessons. History, with a marvellous book called *A Box of Dates*, which had rhymes for all the kings and queens of England, incorporating their dates as well. Thus, 'Alfred, of the toasted bun, His reign began eight-seven-one'. Geography, with maps and names of countries, capitals, rivers and mountains. I must have liked arithmetic and Miss Smith coaxed me on to maths, so by the age of ten I could do differential calculus, though without really understanding what was happening. So, I have to thank her for my love of maths and, indeed, for my love of learning. We never did any science though, and her efforts to teach me the piano at five were a dismal failure. My inability to draw or paint must derive from Miss Smith's attempts to get me to paint, say, a sweet pea. Not an appropriate activity for a young child! Later, at ten, I asked to learn the piano and have played ever since, though not well. In my very old age, I might try some drawing or even painting.

In her gentle, quiet, undemonstrative way, Miss Smith must have given me crucial self-confidence as well as an inquisitive mind. Although she never gave me outward signs of affection, I knew instinctively that she was always 'there for me'. When I became a mother, I had to work out mothering skills for myself. I think my children, now parents themselves, have forgiven me for all the deficiencies.

I had time to roam, and lots of space in which to do it. There were yards, garages, and a most interesting assortment of outhouses; the harness room, which had a distinctive smell of leather soap, but which later made me feel guilty about not cleaning Sunshine's bridle often enough. Next, the little apple shed with slatted shelves and a delicious smell. Only perfect apples and pears could be stored, carefully separated from each other. The governess cart was kept next door, and then came the potting-shed, full of all sorts of interesting objects, and smelling mostly of wood and sawdust. I found a leather covering for a pony's hoof, from the times when lawn mowing was done by ponies. Last in the line was the engine room where oily pistons whirled and rumbled, on the days when Gunner came to work them. We were not on mains electricity, so we had to make our own. Fires were coal or wood, and I usually had chilblains in winter. We had no fridge either, and when I was old enough I would bicycle a few miles down the road to the Hamiltons' and bring back a large thermos of ice.

After the yards, there was a huge kitchen garden, where Pysing reigned supreme. He was head gardener and was usually to be found in the big greenhouse, making sure of a regular supply of grapes for my mother. The hard work was done by Bob, the son of a local farmer, who was always ready to chat and give me cigarette cards. I've still got several books of cards, mostly Players. In the far corner of the kitchen garden, I had a sandpit where, in the afternoons, I saw an aeroplane flying over. It was probably the regular flight from Croydon to Paris.

I was always intrigued by aeroplanes. One afternoon, when we were having tea in the nursery, we heard an aeroplane close overhead, and when it landed in the front field we rushed out to see. Two men emerged, one tall, the other short. My parents had heard the noise and were there too. The men apologised and made some sort of explanation about turning back from the coast due to fog and recognising the house and moat as having once belonged to an aunt. They asked to look round, but my father had suspicions and only took them round some of the garden. Some weeks later his suspicions were vindicated; Miss Smith read in the paper about a robbery in Derbyshire, (her home county) where a man had enticed a wealthy widow out to dinner and his accomplice had robbed her home. There were photos of the two men: our air invaders. They'd asked me if I wanted to see inside the plane and of course I'd said yes, but was pulled back. Would they have kidnapped me, I wonder?

I had a wooden swing, hung from twin oak trees on the little lawn by the moat. At first it had two ropes on each side, making it very stable, and I could get up to a good height and then jump down. Presumably because of wear and tear, the two ropes were replaced by one on each side and the next time I was about to jump, the swing turned over and my head hit the tree roots at the bottom. Amazingly, I was unhurt as my jawbone was so strong, but I think my mother saw the crash from the window and must have been concerned. Later, a trapeze was added and I had fun with that. I also climbed any reasonably accessible trees, mostly limes.

Clearly, I was something of a tomboy. For exercise I had two hoops, a small iron one and a big wooden one. With two people, you could arrange for the iron one to go through the wooden one. With my brothers, I played bicycle polo on the gravel with the result that I had more or less permanently cut knees. In the summer I wore shorts, except on special occasions and Sundays, when I went to church at Dormansland with my parents.

Sunday School had not been a success, so I went to 11 o'clock Matins. It was not exactly exciting, but I didn't mind going. The sermon seemed long and boring until my brothers told me of the alphabet game, which helped. The alphabet game entails listening for a word beginning with A, then B etc. One appears to be listening intently!

I enjoyed the music, and soon knew the Canticles off by heart. The hymns were good, especially when one of the men in the choir got redder and redder in the face. Would he explode? The hymn, 'Nearer and nearer draws the time, The time which shall surely be', affected him strongly.

In the holidays, whenever horses were mentioned in the psalm, Michael and Peter would look across the aisle to the Hamiltons and grin. The Hamilton family, with their numerous animals, especially horses and ponies, were great friends. I once met this old man with a withered arm, who was General Sir Ian Hamilton, one of Kitchener's generals, whose nephew of the same name was our friend. Any connection with Kitchener was interesting to my mother; he had been her godfather, was cousin to both my grandparents, and often stayed with them when he was in England.

He was referred to in the family as Cousin Herbert. In the summer of 1916, he invited my grandmother to tea and my teenage mother was told to 'disappear'. My grandmother apparently asked him, "Herbert, where are you going?" to which he replied, "Edie, I can't possibly tell you." Next day, he boarded HMS Hampshire and the rest, as they say, is history. He may well have been in love with my grandmother, and there is at least one photograph which would seem to endorse this.

Chapter 2 – The Moat

As a child, I took the moat for granted. It was just part of the garden, but always interesting. The island had been originally a wooden Saxon castle, perhaps built in Surrey to rival one in Kent. In medieval times it was rebuilt in stone, then flattened by Cromwell in the Civil War. At least this was what we were told. We, that is Michael, Peter and I, didn't worry about the history. For us it was a marvellous playground. At the back, the moat narrowed to allow access by a wooden bridge. Hundreds of trees meant that years of leaf mould created a soft surface, ideal for burying bodies. When a duck died, a shoebox would act as a coffin and we would enjoy enacting elaborate burial ceremonies.

My mother had exotic ducks which she ordered from Peter Scott in East Anglia, including American Widgeons, Pintails and Tufted Ducks. These were especially fun to watch, as they disappeared under the water for ages, and you didn't know where they'd come up. The Pintails tried to copy them, without much success. I've always enjoyed watching birds but I've never wanted to become a 'twitcher'. Just watching the behaviour of pigeons, or gulls, or the differing characteristics of tits, gives me pleasure. I'm lucky in having good eyesight, and can easily spot a heron or a buzzard, or recently, a kite, while driving.

I'm not much good at identifying birdsong, though I love listening to thrushes, as each bird has a slightly different song. As a child, I collected birds' eggs, very carefully, and laid them out in cotton wool. People would be horrified now, but then it was normal and there were many more songbirds around.

I heard that when my parents first went to Starborough in 1930, there were no rooks nesting on the island. A few years later though, there was a flourishing rookery and the sound of rooks cawing still makes me nostalgic. There was also talk of the island being haunted. In the fifteenth century, the castle was owned by a Lollard family and there was a story that the Roman Catholic lover of the daughter had come to a sticky end.

Had the haunting kept the rooks away, and had the coming to the house of a happy family expelled the haunting? An interesting thought. This story of the lover intrigued us as teenagers, and when Starborough was the venue for the Church fête, Peter, our cousin Kenya and I made a side-show of it. Peter, dressed formally, greeted visitors at the bridge and brought them up to the cobwebbed ruin of the little seventeenth century pseudo-castle. As they approached, Kenya, wrapped in a sheet, rushed across the entrance and disappeared. As Peter related the gory story of the severed hand, I released a cardboard one down to the window from the roof, and then dragged chains overhead. After that, I had fun howling from the roof, and the sound must have carried clearly across the water. What the faithful members of the church made of it, I can't imagine, but it was by far the most enjoyable fête I can remember.

Other years, I had been asked to entertain by dancing the Sword Dance, with a borrowed kilt from the Hamiltons, and two of my father's real swords. It was tricky doing it to bagpipes though, as the piper couldn't keep strict time. I obviously liked being a show-off whenever I got the chance, but at home I was mostly subdued. This may have been because my mother was such a strong personality and it was difficult standing up to her.

Spring was a very active time for life on the moat. The special ducks didn't breed, but besides mallards, there were dabchicks and moorhens, and dominating everything, swans. Mother duck had to make sure the swans were not around before bringing her family round the corner. The male swan, in breeding time, would kill anything smaller if they got too close, but luckily there were plenty of hiding places.

My father had populated the moat with brown and rainbow trout, and weekend visitors could fish from the lawn. There were eels too, as well as frogs, toads and sometimes grass snakes swimming across. Michael was surprised to find he'd caught an eel with a bit of red carpet as bait. Later, both brothers exercised their fly-fishing skills on holiday in the Highlands. Michael, in his nineties, still sent me postcards from Glen Etive reporting on fishing conditions and how many salmon he had caught. One of their teachers was my godmother, Cousin Bea, who was a champion fisherwoman. As for swimming, when someone tried to teach me in the moat, I was so disgusted with the squidgy mud between my toes that I refused to go in again. I was scared of water, and although in middle age I forced myself to learn to swim, I have hardly ever immersed myself in water, other than in a clean, warm bath.

One very cold winter, the moat froze over completely, even the narrow bit under the bridge. The poor ducks tried to keep some free water by swimming frantically around in smaller and smaller circles, but it was no use, and the foxes came over the ice and caught them. One day a specialist ice racer arrived (I think he was Dutch), circuiting the moat with wide strides, looking like a huge spider. I think he must have escaped from Nazi occupation and was practising for post-war traditional races along the Dutch canals.

Once, when the ice first appeared, as the youngest and lightest, I was sent out to test the safety. As I got near the middle, I heard deep growling noises, and cracks spread out all round. I was terrified, and ran back towards the landing stage, taking a huge leap to safety. Days later, with safety affirmed, we all ventured on the ice. I borrowed my mother's skating boots, and pushing the old bathroom chair in front, tried to teach myself to skate. Given the opportunity, I think it could have been a wonderful sport for me, having so much in common with dance.

Among other stories about the castle was one about an underground passage to Lingfield, some three miles away. Ursula Thorpe was one of my mother's many friends who came to lunch. Often they brought a son or daughter with them, and it was assumed we would be friends. One day, Jeremy came with his mother and we had great fun on the island, searching for the underground passage. Years later, after the war, I met up with Jeremy at teenage parties given by mutual friends, and was once introduced to his godmother, Megan Lloyd George. As a young man, Jeremy was brilliant – a great orator and the life and soul of parties. His mother, Ursula, was a Tory and sometimes they would share political platforms in amicable disagreement. His behaviour much later was truly tragic.

During the war, the island was used to store Molotov cocktails, some kind of grenade, probably for the Home Guard, and so was out of bounds for us. Other wartime activity, though, provided more than enough interest. A sad thought is that the moat, a large square of water, may have provided guidance for German bombers on their way to blitz London.

Chapter 3 – Family and Friends

Because I didn't go to school when I was younger, I had virtually no friends. Later on, at boarding school, it was difficult too, as my contemporaries in the dormitory were different from those I did lessons with. Those I did make friends with didn't live anywhere near home, and after schooldays our lives diverged, both geographically and culturally. As a result, I have many acquaintances, people I like and admire, and a few with whom I share cultural interests, but very few 'buddies'. I envy those women who meet up in a group with shared memories.

As a child, I was not aware of isolation. It was just life. I was delighted when my baby brother Simon arrived when I was twelve, but I'm not sure I should have coped well with a sister near my age. I would have sensed a rival, especially for my father's love. This, though undemonstrative, I could feel to be strong, especially when, as a young adult, we would have friendly, serious discussions. These my mother never took part in; she would retire to her desk in the drawing room and write letters.

I did have a rival in Jane Hardy, who came during wartime to share lessons with Miss Smith. I resented the fact that she had long legs and could run faster than me. In other ways I could hold my own. We had a special card game which we played early in the morning. One evening, I did a rather mean thing, by so arranging the cards that next morning I was bound to win. We managed to get along, but were never real friends. Perhaps my standard for friendship is unnecessarily high, or I am a bit of a 'loner'. I am always interested in people though, and enjoy listening to their stories and lives, so that when I'm with people I am rarely bored, except at noisy parties with no opportunities for real conversation.

My brothers Michael and Peter were friends in a special way. They teased me, of course, but never unkindly. When they decided to test the efficacy of dock juice on nettle stings (we had lots of nettles) by squeezing dock leaves in a vice, it was of course I who offered to go out and test the juice. I didn't mind getting stung; I was just glad to be part of their experiment.

There were three black days in the year; those when the brothers went back to school. Michael and Peter were very different, in looks, in character and in their academic and sporting abilities, but they remained close friends all their lives, until Peter sadly died in his late seventies. They called each other Deanie, and used a special language. Peter enjoyed making up words, in the manner of Lewis Carroll, such as 'mimsy', being a mixture of 'flimsy' and 'miserable'. Very fortunately, they married wives who also became friends, and for many years as a foursome they would share fishing holidays in the Highlands. Peter was both academic and a natural sportsman, but Michael never appeared in the least bit jealous of his younger brother. In fact, playing tennis, Michael was often on the winning side, through perseverance and solid concentration. Peter would play brilliant strokes, but with little consistency. Neither seemed to worry much about winning, though I think winning was quite important to Yvonne, Michael's wife, who had been to Roedean and was a competent player.

Whilst Michael and Simon were each at various times regular soldiers, Peter must have found National Service very unsettling. I think Michael helped him out once, when he forgot some important duty. It was only in the army, under compulsion, that Peter's sporting ability came to the surface. He became, in fact, the hurdling champion of BAOR (British Army of the Rhine), but he never spoke of it. Peter had no idea what he might do after Cambridge. He thought of journalism, and may have fantasised about penning witty articles for *The Times*. Our father acted to bring some realism into his fantasies, and arranged a meeting with a leading editor. Accounts were related of standing for hours in the rain, or reporting on endless boring meetings, so his thoughts of journalism quickly evaporated.

Peter arrived at teaching more or less by accident, and ended up as a much-loved, but exhausted, house master at Repton. Peter in love was difficult to live with. He had met Mariel in the summer, but she was unable at first to respond to his overtures, and my mother and I watched helplessly as he spent the holidays sighing and groaning. Then the situation changed, and it was Michael who engineered the vital meeting, resulting in a wonderfully happy marriage. It was heartbreaking when Peter died, and I still keep coming across ideas, jokes and birdwatching experiences that I want to share with him. He was an excellent linguist in both French and German, and was once hauled off the train at Calais after insisting he was Maurice Chevalier. He gave frightening impersonations of Hitler, his face turning red with passion, and he would send my pony, Sunshine, galloping frantically up and down with his convincing imitations of foxhounds.

Peter would get very angry when people praised our mother, as he knew that our father was the truly great person. He said that our mother cheated at Racing Demon, a card game that we often played, and in later life he made sure that he was never alone in the room with her, as he might not be able to control his anger. Although never made explicit, it was clear that anger should never be expressed at home. I grew up thinking that anger was wrong, and had to work out for myself how to manage its power. Our rebellions had to be muted.

My brother Michael, when over ninety, was able to tell of the terrifying insistence, when he was thirteen, that he should go down to formal dinner in the dining room with our parents, instead of friendly nursery supper. I don't think our parents had much idea about bringing up children, though each had been a rebel when they were young. My father was apparently so mischievous that he was sent away to boarding school at six. My mother, sent away to boarding school in her teens, forged letters supposedly from her mother saying, for instance, "I don't want my daughter to learn..." As a result, her education was somewhat deficient and I think she was trying all through her life to fill in the gaps. She was clearly intelligent, as well as being extremely attractive, with excellent social skills, and was a Surrey County Councillor and Chairman of the Juvenile Court at Oxted. She must also have loved and deeply respected my father, and was able to resist having an affair with a Canadian officer in the war.

This was a particularly exhausting time for my father, working in the City and never knowing each morning whether the office would still be standing. Often in the evening he would be out as captain in the Home Guard, doing his best for morale. It was, after all, only just over twenty years since the last war, in which he had fought. He had contracted polio in the trenches, and was told he would be in an iron lung for the rest of his life. Being basically strong and very determined, he managed to recover enough to lead a normal life, though with the loss of some muscle, notably in the stomach, arm and leg. Somehow, he managed to play tennis with a jerky serve, winning points with accurate placing, and he enjoyed teaching the boys golf. One of his great sporting pleasures though, he had to give up. I think I was out riding with him for the last time, when he realised that riding without sufficient tummy muscles was too dangerous. With the help of a brace, he kept upright but any infection that involved coughing was difficult to cope with.

My father developed, with friends, a successful bill broking business in the City; he was churchwarden and church treasurer, and the very epitome of a gentleman. His wisdom, gentle firmness and strong ethical standards helped restrain my mother's over-exuberance and her desire to use the black market in the war to help with shortages. His sense of fairness and clarity of thought would have made him an excellent judge. He was expecting to go to Oxford, but the war intervened, and afterwards, as soon as he recovered, he had to earn a living. But he never complained. Like most of his contemporaries, he was only too aware of being lucky to have survived. I have a photo of him by Baron, taken in the London office of Jessel Toynbee; there is a ghost of a twinkle in the eye, and the elegant hand is prominently displayed. Though he died nearly fifty years ago, his spirit still feels near and I only hope I have inherited some of his wisdom.

I never felt close to my mother. Perhaps we were too alike (though not in looks). I must have been a terrible disappointment to her. She was no doubt hoping for a daughter who would be a social success and marry well, (preferably into the aristocracy). Instead, I read maths at Cambridge and married a penniless curate. She could never accept my first husband John, and, rather unfairly, never expressed love towards our children. More happily, she loved and accepted her daughters-in-law and their offspring. In her very old age, around a hundred, I was glad to have the chance to get closer and be able to sit quietly with her, gently stroking her hand.

I never knew my grandfathers. My mother's father Joe had died when my mother was fifteen, having his appendix out on the kitchen table, as he refused to go into hospital. My mother missed him dreadfully. She was the youngest, and specially close to him. By all accounts, Joe was an old-fashioned, benign country squire, riding round, even on Christmas Day, to check that all was well with his tenants. He loved horses, refusing to have anything to do with cars, unlike my Toynbee grandfather who wanted one at once. Walter Toynbee had married my grandmother Florence, in a sort of friendly family arrangement. His brother had married Florence's sister, and when Florence was freed from being hostess for her father, and Walter needed a wife, it seemed like a good idea. It appeared to be a happy marriage, and they quickly had two sons, my father being the younger.

Florence was acutely deaf when I knew her, but a lively character, who recited *The Hunting of the Snark* with a forceful brio and a twinkle in the eye. My mother said that she deliberately slashed a portrait of herself by Sargent, so that my mother wouldn't feel obliged to hang it. Whether this is true or not, it would fit her character as she would have hated any fluffy romantic portrayal of herself. Apparently she sold all her jewellery and gave the proceeds to the Red Cross in WW1. She was brought up in Biddulph Grange, which must have been fun with all those intriguing mini-gardens, and she had married and left before the fire that destroyed the house. Through the National Trust, the wonderful garden can now be enjoyed by everyone, though I imagine that my great-grandfather Robert Heath was too busy making money to appreciate it.

My Granny Monins was very different, and also fun to be with. To me, she was a sort of silvery character, playing the piano and always interested in what we were doing. She once sent me a bar of chocolate (a most welcome present in the war) to my school address. Unfortunately, due to her flowery handwriting, 'Lydney' had been misread as 'Sydney', and the chocolate had travelled halfway round the world and back before I could enjoy it. In the holidays, she would summon Michael to her bedroom, where she sat regally in bed after breakfast, and got him to read her the latest stock market figures. She had many admirers, including retired generals and admirals, who asked her to put money into their enterprises, and she wanted to know how they were prospering. I think few of them did, and her affairs, after her death, consisted of masses of small investments of very little worth. Men loved her, which naturally she enjoyed, but she remained faithful to her Joe and never married again. She was amazingly healthy in her eighties, and only died after being run over by a police car in Chelsea.

Chapter 4 – More Family

My father's brother Jack had survived the war with two MCs and a Belgian Croix de Guerre, but was no doubt affected by it in other ways. He succumbed to Aunt Una on a cruise, perhaps on the rebound, having earlier fallen violently in love and been rejected. Aunt Una was a strange woman, strong but unsympathetic. My mother was sure they never slept together. Later, Violet appeared on the scene, supposedly a cousin of Una, and a ménage à trois, with Jack, Una and Violet, was apparently established. In the thirties, Jack had been ordained and was a curate in Cirencester; he may have been the last hunting parson in Gloucestershire. He loved horses and was brilliant with animals. He later abandoned his priestly ministry and became a farmer, with a pedigree herd of cattle. Later still, he became a judge at horticultural shows. Aunt Una bred dogs. Jack and Una never visited us, and it must have been sad for the brothers not to meet. Perhaps the antipathy between my mother and Una had something to do with it. They were always kind to me though, and my brother Michael was very helpful to their adopted daughter throughout her troubled life.

My mother had one brother, John, who with his American wife Peggy, hosted pre-war family Christmases at Ringwould, my mother's childhood home, between Dover and Deal in Kent. The house was near the church, having once been the rectory, and I would wake on Christmas morning to the wonderful sound of bells. As the youngest, I was treated with great kindness, but had to endure the tedious business of Christmas lunch. My shoulders were about the same level as the long, white cloth; I didn't understand what the grown-ups were laughing and talking about, and I longed to get back and play with my presents.

I was far too young to appreciate the bitter hostility between the sisters-in-law, my aunts Adela (my mother's eldest sister) and Peggy, which reached its peak later after John was killed in a car crash. Aunt Peggy was a Carter (whether related to the president I don't know), and in the thirties my parents had been invited to Miami. At the beach, the wives took turns in looking after the children, and when little George Bush misbehaved, my mother slapped him. She told us this when Bush became President. After a failed second marriage, Peggy married Victor Robartes, the last surviving male from Lanhydrock. On a visit to the now National Trust house, I was taken aback when I saw a photo of Peggy on the desk. She was always kind to me, and sent me dresses in the war when we had clothes rationing. She was also brave, continuing to drive the tractor in the fields near the Kent coast while German dive-bombers took pot shots at her.

Uncle John was eccentric, like his father Joe, who would arrive late for dinner, pick up plates and start juggling with them. Uncle John had fought in the Great War, but, like many of his contemporaries, was appalled at the thought of another war. Had he lived, his political views might well have proved embarrassing.

Among other eccentricities, he was reputed to have buried some family silver on a little Scottish island, and after his death, Aunt Eleanor, as a spiritualist, was asked by her sisters to discover the whereabouts of the buried treasure. Needless to say, no information was recovered. Perhaps one day it will be found, and classed as treasure trove. One year he brought my brothers a boomerang from Australia. They were trying it out on the front lawn when, luckily, I saw it just in time and ducked as it whizzed past me.

The three sisters, Aunts Adela and Eleanor and my mother, were very different, though all tall and good-looking. Adela was thoroughly regal, a viscountess and a patron of the arts in London. In her Chelsea house she also provided safe lodging for daughters of friends. There were strict rules on hours, and on the flushing of the ancient lavatory. She was one of the very few people that my mother was afraid of, and in their old age there was real enmity between them. I had tea with my mother and Adela in Chelsea, sitting between the sisters; Adela turned to me with, "ask your mother if she would like some more tea." I could have knocked their heads together. Was Adela jealous of my mother's happy marriage, I wonder? She was kind to me though, even when I told her she was a naughty old woman for saying my mother was not to go to her funeral.

Aunt Ellie was completely different. Married to a shell-shocked Anthony, who stated openly that he preferred horses to people, Ellie was a spiritualist and eccentric, playing the flute from the bedroom window at night, and cycling the Shropshire lanes in her nightie. She was blonde, unlike her sisters, and enjoyed, along with my father, teasing Adela when the sisters were both staying with us. They were all strong women and lived long lives, my mother until a hundred and two. Perhaps it was just as well that they lived a distance from each other. Do siblings with strong personalities grow further apart as they get older, I wonder? It wasn't true for my brothers Michael and Peter.

On the other side of the family, my father's double first cousins, Bea and Freda were also strong and eccentric. Michael and Peter were once invited to tea with them in London. "Gunters," said one to the taxi driver; "No, Fullers," said the other. The two boys wondered whether they would ever get their tea. Bea lived in London, Freda in Oxford. Their beloved young brother Geoff had been killed in the war, along with most possible husbands for them. They were both passionate women, and much of their frustrated love was poured out on us.

Bea was my godmother, and a great lover of ballet. She was wealthy, and could afford the best seats in Covent Garden, so that, in the thirties, I saw the Ballets Russes, and later the beginnings of British ballet. A great surge of joy would thrill through me as the lights slowly went down and the curtain rose, and Cousin Bea's enthusiasm made it all the more wonderful.

In the summer of 1940, Michael, Miss Smith and I went to Cornwall for a week, to help Michael's convalescence from mastoid. Fellow guests in the little Polzeath hotel were a group of young adults, friendly and high-spirited, who danced on the sands. At the next visit to the ballet, (probably then at Sadler's Wells because of the war), Robert Helpmann was dancing Hamlet. With great excitement I exclaimed to Cousin Bea, "That's Bobby!" She was very surprised until I explained that we had met him, along with, as it turned out, Frederick Ashton, Margot Fonteyn, Beryl Grey, June Brae and others. Bea kindly passed a note round, and we were invited backstage at the end. I remember grubby, white-tiled walls, and Robert Helpmann sitting high up, streams of multi-coloured sweat pouring down his face, with adoring females crying out, "Bobby, darling, you were marvellous!" I just turned and fled.

Cousin Bea loved Scotland, often staying with Peter Fleming and his wife (the actress Celia Johnson), and was, for a time, Scottish fly-fishing champion. There was a huge stuffed salmon framed above the hall door of her London flat. I have a photo album of her world trip in 1911, including one of her in India with a mongoose on a lead. Bea loved life: ballet, music, racing, bridge, good food and drink. In her last years she would read to blind fellow residents of the care home. She had an almost childlike delight in life. When we went to the zoo, she brought honey to feed the bears. I rode on an elephant, and there was great excitement when the first panda appeared. It was always fun with Cousin Bea.

Freda was quite different, and spent her time and money on charitable work. Before the war, Miss Smith, Peter and I stayed in her seaside cottage at Charmouth. I didn't mind the damp smell and primitive conditions; it was lovely just being able to run barefoot across the sand. In her old age, Cousin Freda would drive into Oxford, wearing her ancient straw hat, and expecting to park wherever she wished. She had become well known in the city, and a small street in the Hinksey district, Toynbee Close, is named after her.

Of my generation, only my brother Peter seemed to have inherited our grandfather's and uncle's eccentricity. He was a competent juggler, and indifferent to many social and political conventions. Our cousin Fanny inherited her mother Eleanor's psychic sensitivities; she knew exactly when her son Richard was in trouble in Africa, and told me once of a most horrifying nightmare. She had felt herself viciously attacked by evil spirits, which made me re-think my ideas of evil. Fanny was a person suffused with goodness, so what was the meaning of that nightmare? Some modern writers, such as Rupert Sheldrake, are reminding us of psychic realities that many people seem to find unsettling. Are we perhaps in danger of ignoring these, in favour of safer 'certainties'? Are we becoming more boringly conformist? I believe, and sometimes say to my grandchildren, that it is the lateral thinkers, those who think 'outside the box', who will save the world.

My cousin Henry Kitchener (great-nephew of Herbert) had a formidable brain, but was chiefly a philanthropist, and funded much innovative research into subjects including the effect of diet on prisoners, and vegetarianism. He was much involved with the Ryton Organic Garden near Coventry. He kept a low profile, and his many kindnesses were known only to a few.

Chapter 5 – Pets and Ponies

There were always dogs around at Starborough, and being half a mile from the nearest road, it was easy for them to roam freely. In spite of precautions, Dinah, a black labrador, managed to produce puppies regularly. Her most marvellous puppy was Bonzo. His father was a lurcher, and Bonzo was very fast, as well as being a good jumper. He had a curly black coat, with a white 'shirt front' and white on the tips of his paws and tail. My little dog Melia was also a mongrel, quite small, half Pekingese, but without the squashed nose. She had black rings round her eyes and a curly tail. Both dogs were very intelligent and great friends. Melia would nudge Bonzo awake to go hunting. Melia, being small, would go into the copse to ferret out a rabbit, which, when it emerged, Bonzo would chase and catch. A very effective partnership. They teased each other too. I'm not sure Melia enjoyed being spun round by her tail, but she could retaliate by lying low and pretending not to notice Bonzo stalking her. When he sprang forward she would take two steps backwards so that he missed. Watching them together was always fun.

My mother adored Bonzo. When he cut his tongue on barbed wire and had to be put down, she was heartbroken. I was away at school when Melia had to be put down, as she was carrying puppies that were far too big for her small frame. With modern veterinary skills, both might have been able to survive, but perhaps the death of a loved pet can help children to cope later with the deaths of friends and family. I've always been a dog person rather than a cat one, and dogs seem to sense this. Coming towards me, they start wagging their tails, as though picking up 'pro-dog' vibes.

Ponies were also an important part of my childhood. I must have learnt to ride early on, as there is a photo of me, aged three, on Trixie, an old moorland pony. I think I rode in a show then, without a leading rein, so I must have been quite confident. Later, Miss Smith and I would take the bus up to Crockham Hill where I had riding lessons with Miss Rogers. A line of us rode through the woods on Limpsfield Common with Miss Rogers at the back. She was strict, but kind. "Knees in, Jane," I would hear, and immediately grip the saddle more closely.

Then my mother, or possibly my grandmother, bought Sunshine from Miss Rogers, as she was thought too dangerous for a riding school. She was a very beautiful pony, chestnut with mane and tail like spun gold, but with a difficult, even vicious, temperament. Several times I felt she was trying to kill me, either by charging or by rearing up suddenly. I didn't tell anyone about this. Presumably the adults thought I could cope. We had many battles of will, which I usually won, but there were also some near disasters. The worst concerned Harry. He had come with his mother to lunch (he, of course, shared nursery lunch) and my mother said that Harry would like a ride on Sunshine. I don't suppose he thought that at all, but we children were so polite in those days that we seldom contradicted the grown-ups. Poor Harry.

Perhaps he didn't want to appear wimpish in front of me. Anyway, Miss Smith and I saddled up

Sunshine and took her out to the field, and Harry got on. Sunshine realised at once that he was a nervous rider, and promptly cantered round and then swerved suddenly; one of her favourite tricks. Harry fell off, but caught his foot in the stirrup. Miss Smith and I had to watch as his head was dragged along close to Sunshine's hooves. We didn't dare do anything in case she swerved again. I couldn't breathe until she stopped and we could rescue poor Harry. It must have put him off horses and riding for life.

Sunshine regularly deposited nervous riders onto rhododendron bushes, and she and I were banned from Sam Marsh's Edenbridge Horse Show after she bolted, causing chaos among the gathering of ponies behind. I think she had once belonged to a circus, which might have explained some of her challenging behaviour. My experiences with her meant that later I really appreciated the offer of a well-trained pony to ride in gymkhanas. During the war, we tried Sunshine in a governess cart, of which, most appropriately, Miss Smith took charge. She submitted to the harnessing but, instead of progressing at a brisk trot, she adopted a slow canter, creating a sick-inducing sensation in the passengers. The experiment ended when she repeatedly bolted whenever an army lorry appeared, and army lorries were common on the roads in wartime. I enjoyed going to the blacksmith in Dormansland though, with that special smell of sizzling hot iron being tried on the hoof. Luckily, Sunshine seemed to enjoy it too, as she always behaved well at the forge.

When I outgrew Sunshine, I took over Minnie, who had been Peter's pony. She was a Welsh cob with large feet, and had been beautifully trained by our Uncle Jack. She made opening gates easy and was very comfortable to ride, but there were two things to beware of. One was her propensity for bucking, the other was her habit of nipping your backside when putting your left foot in the stirrup for mounting. You quickly learned to tighten the right rein. She was willing to jump solid obstacles, but refused to perform at a gymkhana when a fake wall blew down in front of her. She certainly had character.

When we moved to Fawke Common near Sevenoaks, before we found a field for her, she was so furious at being put in a stable that she broke down the door. I had a key to nearby Knole Park, and Minnie and I had good rides along the various avenues. I fell into disgrace one dry summer by riding Minnie over one of the golf course greens. An enraged greenkeeper rushed towards me, telling me to get off, but, as I explained, after apologising, Minnie's big hooves would have made much more damage by turning round. I can't think why I did it, perhaps by accident, certainly not on purpose.

Our house was in the middle of a wood, and in April 1950 there was a freak snowstorm. The snow stuck so heavily on the trees that small branches broke off, and we woke to what sounded like gunfire. It stuck on the telephone lines, and the huge poles on the main road were snapped in half like matchsticks. The roof of a garage in Sevenoaks collapsed under the weight. By mid-day the sun had come out, and the whole scene was calm and beautiful.

My parents had personal contacts with Knole. Charlie Sackville, who was then old and had been friendly with my grandmother, sometimes came to lunch, accompanied by his American ex-actress wife Ann. The car was decorated with a huge Sackville crest. For a return luncheon visit, the parents were instructed to arrive ten minutes early, as it took the aged butler five minutes each way to travel from the Sackville apartment to the front door. All social contacts stopped though, after an incident concerning a teenager. This lad was involved in some minor crime at Knole, perhaps stealing lead, and my mother, who was Chairman of the Juvenile Court, put him on probation. Ann Sackville was so incensed by this, that she struck my mother off her visiting list. Ann was one of a long line of exotic wives captured by male members of the Sackville family, and recorded by Charlie's cousin Victoria Sackville-West. For her, Knole had been a much-loved home, and she was heartbroken at not being able to inherit it because she was a woman.

My experiences of Knole were long before tourism became popular, and I'm glad I got to know it in quieter times. It was one of the first non-fortified mansions in England, and stands squarely, but not at all pompously, in its enormous park. Inside it is packed with objects of historical interest, and is now well managed by the National Trust.

I've always loved horses and ponies, despite unnerving experiences with Sunshine. Smoky was a grey, half-Arab pony and a brilliant jumper, and I was asked to ride him in various gymkhanas, mostly with good results. One year at the Bridport Show, though, we failed badly. The take-off ground before most of the jumps was very muddy and slippery, and I just didn't want to take part. In general, I'm happy with racing and cross-country, but less now that I know of the cruelty involved. Wherever a lot of money is involved, I'm afraid there is increasing cruelty, even in racing. As for the white Spanish stallions, what cruel constraints must be used to make them perform such unnatural antics?

Perhaps things were more natural for horses when Lingfield racecourse re-opened after the war, when it had been a prisoner-of-war camp. I had a moment of glory when once I caught a horse there. We were by the water jump when a horse pecked on landing. The jockey fell off and the horse galloped away. As it came back and was approaching a gap in the hedge, I ran over and put my arms out to catch it, ignoring the policeman's shout of "Let it go!" I realised that it wanted to be caught, and led it back to the rather shame-faced jockey.

Chapter 6 – War

Noon, on Sunday 3 September 1939. Someone (Mrs Spender-Clay I think) had brought a wireless into church, and everything stopped for us to listen to Chamberlain's announcement. I was seven, and it was only gradually that I came to realise how life would change.

Some weeks later, looking out of the nursery window, I saw a long procession of square, box-like, browny-green cars coming up the back lane. A platoon of Princess Patricia's Canadian Light Infantry had arrived to be billeted on us. Apparently owners of large houses were given the choice of either handing over the house (as hospitals or for housing troops), or having soldiers billeted on them. My parents had chosen the latter. The officers were given the spare bedrooms, and the rest of the platoon were to sleep in the attic. My mother made it clear that boots should be left at the bottom of the back stairs.

When my mother heard that two of the men were lumberjacks, she asked if they could fell a large, dead fir tree by the moat. They worked all day with a double saw, and the tree fell in exactly the right place between two rows of young apple trees. Captain Rosser was very dashing, and I sensed that my mother found him attractive. He had brought a Dalmatian (spotted dog) with him (how on earth did he manage that?) and would take it for long walks. The Canadians didn't stay long. They must have been part of the abortive Expeditionary Force, but I never found out what happened to them. Information is difficult to get, because they were not British. Captain Rosser must have survived, as he kept in touch and became a godfather to Simon. After the war, General Crerar sent us a box of maple syrup candies; my first experience of maple syrup.

The next troops to arrive were those of a tank regiment under Guy Crittall. Our big garage was requisitioned as a Royal Electrical and Mechanical Engineers (REME) workshop, as tanks were being prepared for action in the desert. My mother grumbled about the damage that turning tanks did to the gravel. Guy Crittall was kind to us girls (Jane Hardy was with us at the time), and wrote us bits of silly verse. I don't think he was at all suited to army life, but that must have been true of thousands in the Forces. He sent me a wooden camel from the desert, along with more verses.

I was away at school when the anti-aircraft gunners were around, but at home for much of the time when the barrage balloons were trying to catch the doodlebugs. The balloon crew near the drive asked if I'd like to go inside. Of course, I said yes, and climbed the ladder to the middle part, which was full of ordinary air and just smelled rubbery. While I was inside they had a call to send the balloon up, but luckily one of the crew remembered I was inside. As it happened, on that occasion the balloon cut loose and didn't come back. The doodlebugs I found much more frightening than bombs, because of their unpredictable behaviour, and the fact that you could see them, like evil demons. At night I would hear the 'dum dum' noise, and watch the horrible black jerky object as it made its way towards London. Sometimes the light would go out and the 'dum dum' noise would stop, and I would hold my breath. It might glide on, or it might drop with a big explosion. One time we were in the garden when one came over close and stopped. We all dived down, but I looked up. At the explosion, I saw the rear windows in the house bend out and go back. "Don't be silly, Jane," I was told. Later, of course, we learned about the effects of blast, and the windows certainly rattled more afterwards. My poor father was driving back from the station, saw the doodlebug coming down, and thought it must have landed on the house. I remember his getting out of the car, with a white face and shaking legs.

On the borders of Kent and Surrey, we witnessed many dogfights overhead in the Battle of Britain. I remember Miss Smith calling out to me, "Get in the summerhouse, Jane," as shrapnel was raining down. My mother refused to be done out of her tennis, and at least once played in her warden's tin hat. Sweeping the court later, I did find some bits of shrapnel, and added them to my 'black museum'. This was an old shoe box, and contained various bits of war debris, many of them messy. At the doodlebug crater, which we had rushed to on our bikes, I picked up an interesting bit of oily, twisted metal. Then a warden appeared and said it had to be sent to London, as it had numbers on it.

Before the doodlebugs, I only felt frightened occasionally. During the Blitz, some German pilots (presumably not Nazi sympathisers) unloaded their bombs in the country, and at night I would listen to a 'stick' of bombs getting nearer and nearer. Would the next one hit us? Out of the bathroom window one morning I saw a crater in the field. "Nonsense, Jane," I was told. But it was there, quite near, and it stayed for years, a large and increasingly muddy hole. I became very aware of different plane sounds, and one day, down the lane, I heard a Hurricane's engine stop and saw it fall into the field and burst into flames. Even now, seventy years later, I listen anxiously when I hear a small plane overhead. A friend of my parents rushed out to his field when he heard a Heinkel landing, grabbing his WW1 revolver to take the crew prisoner. As it happened, they were only too relieved to be alive, as there were unexploded bombs inside, and a Spitfire had blown the undercarriage off.

Although we were in the country, we got used to air raid sirens and the parents thought of turning one of the stables into a shelter. My mother arranged for chairs, rugs, books and packs of cards, but soon found that the upheaval of getting out to the stable, about two minutes' walk from the house, just wasn't worthwhile and in the end very few bombs landed near. Blackout was strictly enforced though, and the drawing-room was out of bounds after dark, as was the billiard room. One night, Michael forgot and turned on the light. He felt very guilty when, shortly afterwards, there was a distant explosion. Apparently some sheep were killed at Marsh Green. My father was on the committee of Edenbridge Hospital and often met injured airmen, both Allied and German. Badly burned airmen went to the specialist hospital at East Grinstead, where they were treated by Dr McIndoe, the Australian surgeon. Going to East Grinstead with Miss Smith, we would pass the hospital (I always looked out for the snake curling round the pole outside), and sometimes an airman would get on the bus. I found it difficult not to stare at the horribly disfigured face, and it must have taken great courage for him to venture out in public on his own.

Petrol rationing meant car travel was strictly limited, and only slow at night, as lights had to be dimmed. My mother had an allowance for shopping in Edenbridge. I liked the post office with its big posters. 'Careless Talk Costs Lives' was my favourite, with a smirking Goering sitting in the back of the bus. 'Dig for Victory' was one of the less interesting ones, but they gave me something to look at while my mother was at the counter.

I was puzzled as to why she had to go to both the post office and the bank to get money. The only interesting thing in the bank was the toy lifeboat with a slot in the top for donations. I looked forward to visiting the grocer, with the huge wooden counter and wonderful smells. There were interesting things to watch; sugar being poured into a paper funnel; cheese being cut with a wire, and the bacon slicer, with the pieces placed carefully on a sheet of greaseproof paper. While ration books were handed over, and bits cut out with scissors, I liked reading the names on the little drawers on the wall behind the counter.

When we got to the butcher, he had to come round to the driver's window for the order, as my mother couldn't stand the sight of raw meat. Bread and milk were delivered, and we had plenty of fruit and vegetables from the kitchen garden. When runner beans were in season, we tried to preserve them for winter and I helped with slicing and then storing them in large stone crocks with salt between the layers. Fruit was preserved in Kilner jars. I don't think there was much jam-making because of sugar rationing, but perhaps it was in the war that beet sugar started being produced in Britain. Many years later in Edinburgh, I joined the 'sugar campaign', encouraging the use of Caribbean cane sugar, and the phasing out of the beet.

At school we had 'orange jelly', which was made from carrots. We now realise that the brilliantly worked out food rationing in the war made for better health for everyone. The privileged indulged less in cream, butter, sugar and meat, and the poor, for the first time, had enough nourishing food. I'm told that, when the government saw war looming, they imported huge quantities of tea, feeling that public morale might not survive if the 'cuppa' was not available. Even now, I still find it hard to leave food on the plate, and I scrape the butter dish thoroughly.

We were, of course, very fortunate at home in having a flourishing kitchen garden. The summer of 1940, the Battle of Britain summer, produced a bumper harvest of plums and greengages. Trees were bent down with the weight of fruit, and if there were tin hats lying around, we would fill them with plums. One of the household was taken to hospital with suspected scarlet fever, which turned out to be plum rash. We had chickens, and surplus eggs were preserved in 'water glass'. We had no refrigerator because of not being on mains electricity, but we did have a huge walk-in larder facing north, with a slate shelf.

Petrol was allowed for church, as our parish church of Dormansland was several miles away. A new Sunday ritual was inaugurated; my mother, in her Sunday best, would raise the bonnet and remove the distributor. This was, presumably, to prevent the car being used by an enemy. Other preventative measures were introduced, such as turning signposts round, and removing names from railway stations. As these were only dimly lit, travelling by train at night meant carefully counting the number of stations passed.

Carrying your gas mask also became routine. One of my mother's jobs as warden was fitting gas masks to the housebound. Two sisters lived nearby, in a lonely house down a long drive. I would visit them with my mother before the war. Everything in the room seemed dark red, except for a little glass-covered table which was low enough for me to see the collection of interesting objects inside. When my mother went to fit the gas masks, their wigs began to slip. I think my mother enjoyed relating this, but at the time it must have been acutely embarrassing, as the sisters were very private people.

Because of sugar rationing, the sweet ration was meagre. I would hoard some, to curry favour with the brothers in the holidays. They must often have been hungry; it's well known that teenage boys have 'hollow legs'. It was while cycling to Marsh Green to get my sweet ration, that I had the most frightening war experience of all. I looked up as a German plane appeared low overhead, and I could see the bomb-aimer's goggles looking down at me.

Once, Jane Hardy and I acted as informal spies. The Home Guard were doing an exercise, with our house as the focal point. One side were attackers, the other defenders, and they wore appropriately coloured ribbons. Jane and I walked down the drive, where defenders were hiding behind rhododendron bushes. We pretended not to notice them, and when asked by the attackers, further down the drive, if we'd seen anything, we said no. They protested about us later when they were 'captured', but we thought it was fun. My father, as captain, was often out with the Home Guard in the evening. With his frail body, he must often have been exhausted after a day in London, but he was determined to do as much as he could for the war effort. The Home Guard no doubt had its ludicrous side, and *Dad's Army* was a brilliant drama, but the effect on morale was important. It enabled men who were not able to join up to feel they were doing something positive to help.

I am so grateful to my parents who, through the agonising summer of 1940, never imparted their fears to me. I was unaware that they had debated as to whether to send Peter and me to Canada. The torpedoing of a ship carrying children put a stop to that. As a child, I watched the boarding up of the river bank and the felling of the tree where the kingfisher perched. Concrete boulders appeared on the bridge, and strange brick 'pillboxes' in the field on the other side. I was upset about all these changes, as I loved walking down the lane to the river, but I was too young to realise the full implications. We were, in any case, on 'the wrong side of the line'. But my mother, despite her fears, had the insight to take me to see a train due to come through Edenbridge Station with rescued troops from Dunkirk. I watched the exhausted, grizzled faces trying to smile, and bits of ragged clothing held out of the windows. I was left with a vivid memory, but again without realising the menace that lay behind it all.

There were fundamental changes on the domestic front, quite apart from the threats of war and the presence of soldiers. Dorothy, our cook, was called up, and gradually the whole household structure collapsed. The housekeeper, butler, chauffeur and nurserymaid, as well as the cook, all left. Many middle-class women took to cooking, but my mother apparently never even considered it. No doubt her aversion to red meat had something to do with it, and food, apart from necessity, never seemed to play an important part in my parents' lives.

As household members left, familiar faces were replaced by a succession of strange individuals. There was a 'butler' who my brothers said looked like a convict, which was not surprising as he had been in prison. He would often go down to the local pub in the evening to play the piano, and he seemed friendly and likeable. Unfortunately, he also had a drink problem, and as the level in the whisky bottle dropped sharply my parents couldn't cope, and he had to go.

Unusual, and sometimes frightening, people arrived in the kitchen. I was once chased out by a witch-like individual with an umbrella. Eventually Miss Smith volunteered to cook simple, plain meals. I don't know what happened after she left, but my mother never learned to cook. She did just manage scrambled eggs, following instructions in Philip Harben's book *The Way to Cook*. I still have that copy, published in 1945. By a strange coincidence, some years later I was teaching maths to his daughter.

My mother was determined that one lawn should be mown (there was, of course, no petrol for mowers). So, she decided to mow the rose garden by hand, dressed only in her petticoat. I was on guard in case anyone came up the drive.

On a positive note, wartime Christmases were much more fun than those at Ringwould. Our great friends the Hamiltons would come over for tea, followed by charades. Both my parents loved acting, and somehow there were plenty of bits and pieces for dressing-up. As well as horses, ponies and goats, the Hamiltons kept pigs, and Helen went round the neighbourhood with Griselda, the highland pony, in the old cart, 'pig-bucketing' – collecting waste food for the pigs. She would drive her father Ian to the station in the cleaner cart. They were often late, and the stationmaster would hold the train when he heard Griselda's galloping hooves.

Chapter 7 – School

I was really excited at the prospect of school, though desperately sad to be saying goodbye to Miss Smith. I knew about sadness from when my nanny left, and from the regular times that my brothers went back to school, but I didn't see the grown-ups expressing emotion. It just wasn't done. Nobody cried. When I cut my knee, (which happened often), I had to 'be brave, like a soldier'. Afterwards, I kept up correspondence with Miss Smith and she told me about her new charges, but it was only years later that I really appreciated what she had done for me.

Meanwhile, in the late summer of 1942, the sadness was mitigated by all the preparations for school. The idea of a whole set of new clothes was thrilling. We went to Harrods for the uniform (it was that kind of school) which included a coat and skirt in bright, emerald green, and was packed in a box with tissue paper, giving off a delicious smell. Apart from a small suitcase for the first few days, everything else was packed with a list into a trunk and was sent PLA (passenger luggage in advance). On arrival, the unpacking was supervised by a senior girl, and books were carefully scrutinised. Were they worried about pornography, or seditious material?

I arrived, with my mother, on the platform at Paddington, amid a sea of emerald green. I wasn't scared, only bewildered, and parting with my mother was not traumatic as we had never been close. We were to change trains at Gloucester, before arriving at Lydney. The school had been evacuated from North

Foreland to Lord Bledisloe's mansion of Lydney Park. He and Lady B sometimes paid a visit from the Dower House, no doubt to check on possible damage. An enormous portrait of Lord B in ceremonial robes hung by the main staircase.

The head of the school was Miss Gammell, an enlightened Scotswoman known as The Gam, so that, although still maintaining a few pre-war trappings, we had a remarkably liberal education. I owe a great deal to The Gam, and we became good friends. Once, in my last year, I was with her when she spotted, out of the window, some difficult parents arriving and asked me to deal with them while she climbed out of the window onto a balcony, effectively disappearing. No doubt I learned some useful diplomatic skills.

In 1942, the school was more of an establishment for young ladies and among the few annual prizes it had one for deportment. It sounds old-fashioned, but has been of great benefit to me during my life, especially during five pregnancies. I still try to sit upright, and use a properly designed chair. Perhaps now, with so much back pain around, it might be time to give deportment more consideration? The only other prize was the Improvement Prize given to the girl whose work had improved in the most subjects. This was really good, as it prevented the 'brainboxes' from getting all the prizes. Academic excellence was considered reward enough. Another of The Gam's principles was that there should be no 'extras', i.e. no girl should be denied an activity because of cost.

Pianos were everywhere; in the bedrooms, the corridors and the dining room, piano sounds rang out. Anything from stumbling travails of Grade One, to sophisticated Beethoven sonatas. The two piano teachers, Prof and Miss Churchill, couldn't have been more different. Prof was very small, with tiny fingers to match; she was an Austrian refugee who had, apparently, as a child prodigy, played with the Vienna Symphony Orchestra. She was only strict with regard to finger nails. If they were too long you were sent to your room to cut them. Miss Churchill was tall and stiff, and insisted on severe articulation of the fingers, which I found very hard.

Once a year, the two teachers collaborated by playing *Scaramouche* on the grand piano in the drawing-room. I was never gifted at piano, but with hard work and determination I managed Grade Six, which meant I could play for Evening Service. At Lydney, this took place in the hall and on the staircase.

Miss Pike, a remnant from pre-war days, still wore a long, red velvet evening dress, but things were changing fast. Most of the staff were refugees. One English teacher was an Australian philosopher, and when we tried, as a silly stunt, to read from under the sofa, she just took no notice. A very wise response, and one which may have coloured my own reaction to bad behaviour when I became a teacher myself. I tended to ignore mischief-makers, and concentrate on those who were working.

The Pollaks, husband and wife, were, I think, from Czechoslovakia. Mrs P became school secretary, Mr P taught art and fencing. He had a sabre scar on each cheek, and was a brilliant fencing teacher. Gillian Sheen, a few years senior to me, won gold at the Melbourne Olympics. Mr Pollak was kind, but he would stand no nonsense. If you made a stupid move, he would 'de-foil' you, so that you had to run down the steps to retrieve the weapon (fencing lessons took place on the terrace). I was not brilliant, but was good enough, with another old girl from the school, to inaugurate at Cambridge the Oxford v Cambridge Women's Fencing Match.

Mr Pollak also taught art, a subject that was a disaster for me. Perhaps it was the legacy of Miss Smith's attempts to get me to paint a watercolour of a sweet pea. Finally, Mr P said, "I think it is better, Jane, if you do not come to art classes," and that was that.

It was wartime, and after breakfast we cleaned our bedrooms; basins had to be immaculate, taps polished, beds neat with hospital corners, and, of course, not a mite of dust anywhere. They were inspected each day by Frances, who listed the results on the noticeboard. At the end of term we took our mattresses outside (or threw them out of the window), and beat them. Working in pairs, we shook out the blankets. This was before the arrival of duvets.

To ensure health, we had a spoonful of cod-liver oil after breakfast, followed by a large peppermint. One Sunday, a whisper went round that the roast was horse. As many of us had ponies at home, the experiment was not repeated. Sometimes, I think we ate whale. Instead of marmalade, we got used to 'orange jelly', made from carrots. At Lydney, we had a week off lessons in October for potato picking. It was hard work, but good to be out in the fresh air, and perhaps earn some pocket money.

Apart from sport, The Gam insisted on a mid-morning run. If you were in the team, you cradled a lacrosse stick as you ran. We often practised Scottish country dances on the terrace during morning break. After supper we had to walk round the house, and it was then, armed with a torch and a basic star book, that I learned to recognise the main constellations in the dark, wartime skies. We played rounders on a hilly field, skirting round cow pats, and grass terraces became tennis courts. Wartime restrictions meant rationing of baths, and we became experts in 'strip washing' which took place at the basin behind a screen. Personal hygiene was a worry, and the arrival of Odorono deodorant was a huge relief.

At about twelve or thirteen I must have been quite athletic, as I remember somersaulting over a line of kneeling girls, with the line gradually being lengthened. I was small for my age then, and formed the top of the 'pyramid' when we appeared at local fêtes. I was also the Dormouse in *Alice in Wonderland*, getting very hot and sweaty in a furry boiler suit.

The Gam was keen on cultural education. She organised a 'music circle', whereby local people would be invited to the school, (presumably for a fee) to classical concerts. I remember sitting close to the piano for a recital by Clifford Curzon. A leading soprano once suddenly stopped singing when she realised the elaborate chandelier was affecting the sound. The concerts took place in the drawing room, with much of the furnishing still in place.

My earliest experience of concerts must have been going to *Hiawatha* in the Albert Hall with my grandmother before the war. The lights went down, and 'Indians' in costume rushed down the aisles, making a hollering sound. I felt really sad when Famine and Fever stalked around the wigwams in a pale ghostly light. Later, also in the Albert Hall, I was deeply moved by the *St Matthew Passion*, conducted by Sir Malcolm Sargent, with a massed chorus. There was a long lunch interval, when we went out to Kensington Gardens. On a lighter note, I fell deeply in love with the hero in *Desert Song*. We always sat in the same two seats, inherited from a relative who had been an original investor, and once we had John Ireland and Vaughan Williams sitting behind us. I worried about what expression I should have on my face, when my profile was between the conductor and the composer.

Among other benefits of the school was the tennis coaching by Mr Cooke, who had a Wimbledon past. He was very tall, and when I complained that it was easy for him to serve, he just knelt down and delivered a few faultless ones. His coaching must have been exceptional as, although a small school, we did well in the regional championships. I became quite good at singles, but was never much use at the net in doubles.

Besides fencing, tennis and music, the school, of course, provided the best academic education it could manage in the circumstances. From Mademoiselle I learned to pronounce 'eu' almost correctly. She could be really fierce and rap your knuckles with a ruler if she felt you weren't trying hard enough, but was truly kind underneath. Is it true, I wonder, that at secondary age, children learn better with a teacher who is not too 'soft'? I met Mademoiselle sometimes in the holidays, as a friend, when I discovered her true nature.

After School Certificate, which I took at fourteen, I concentrated mostly on maths and history. I disliked the history teacher, so maths predominated. When university seemed a possibility, I was sent to study once a week with a professor at Reading University. I found him quite unnerving, but he seemed to think I had ability and engaged me to check the answers to exercises in a book he had written for students. At the time, I did have a facility for what was called analysis, and it was that that enabled me to gain a place at Newnham College, Cambridge. I enjoyed the bus ride along the A33 from Basingstoke to Reading and back, as the school had by then moved to Sherfield-on-Loddon, near Basingstoke.

The Sherfield mansion was similar to Lydney in general layout, but was much larger, and as it belonged to the school there were no restraints. At Lydney, The Gam used to collect the tiny gold beadings from the skirting boards, so she could glue them back before we left. Pictures had stayed on the walls, and in the Pink Room we were amused by a semi-clothed *Fatima the Fair Sultana*. Some of the bedrooms had amazing wallpapers with huge exotic birds and flowers. I don't think I'd come across wallpaper before. The Park, too, provided an adventure playground. We played happily among the Roman remains, without really appreciating them.

We had jobs to do, including collecting wood and sawing it into 'billets'. We kept away from the deer in the autumn, but heard the baying of stags in the rutting season. The winter of 1946/47 was very dramatic. We took our book sacks and put on wellies, trudging through the snow to the town to get food. The deer struggled and then mostly starved, as there were no helicopters or other means of providing food. We even made an igloo, but with several of us inside it started to drip. It may have been that winter that the Severn flooded and then froze, and we were able to skate along the fields.

Life at Lydney was exciting, but there were drawbacks. There were no facilities for science, and even after the move to Sherfield, it was a few years before proper labs were installed. I therefore went up to Cambridge to read maths with virtually no physics. That was one reason for my dismal failure, the other being that I had probably reached my 'ceiling' in maths.

In one direction, Sherfield-on-Loddon was near enough to Basingstoke for some of us to join the Basingstoke Choral Society. Crammed tightly on the stage for Haydn's *Creation*, we opened our scores to *Representation of Chaos*, and had to restrain our laughter. In the other direction was Stratfield Saye, and I would sometimes cycle over for 8.00 Communion in the chapel, feeling, I'm sorry to say, disgustingly virtuous. My teenage piety lasted for many years, and was probably a factor in my falling in love with John. A young, glamorous curate proved to be irresistible.

Chapter 8 – Skye and Sadness, Deb Days and Student Years

Although I seem to be lacking in Scottish blood, I had an important Highland connection in my godmother Sheila Macdonald, who in 1949 invited me to Portree for the Skye Ball. I learned some interesting facts; I must not play the piano on Sunday, as the cook was a 'Wee Free'; you only put salt on your porridge, never sugar. When Harry Macdonald needed a new kilt (from Jenners in Edinburgh), it had to be put in the sea for a few days to acquire a suitably weathered look.

When it came to the Ball, much of the day was spent on the thorny question of the plaids to be draped over the balcony in the town hall. Should there be two Macdonalds and one Mcleod, or two Mcleods and one Macdonald? There were still faint echoes of the enmity between the clans which had brought burnings and bloodshed two centuries before. In the end, one plaid of each clan was draped. Thanks to my Scottish headmistress and school, I was well versed in Scottish dancing, and although possibly the only woman not wearing a sash, I was able to dance like a native.

After Portree, I was invited by a schoolfriend to join their family party at Sligachan. Without quite realising what was involved, I agreed to go rock-climbing in the Cuillins with her father, Malcolm Douglas-Hamilton. Perhaps at seventeen I was lacking in imagination, or just naive, as the climbs were not for beginners. Later, I read that they were used in training for the Alps. Somehow I survived, traversing Sgùrr nan Gillean, going up the King's Chimney, and arriving at the ridge on top. After a scree run down, the amazing day ended with a pony ride along Glen Brittle. Round the fire, in the evening, Malcolm's nieces, the Mackintosh sisters, who were keen skiers, suggested to their uncle, who was then MP for Inverness, that he might develop Aviemore as a skiing centre. How right they were.

The autumn of 1949 brought great sadness. I was sharing a room in a crammer's establishment near Cambridge with Judith, who'd been a friend at school. I was working towards Cambridge, Judith towards Oxford to read English. At night in our room, we had long conversations and discussions about life. Judith was serious about, 'To those to whom much is given, much will be required'. One evening she put her books neatly together, the pencil box on top, went upstairs and hanged herself in the bathroom. Her body was found next morning. In the general confusion and distress, I had no idea how to cope. I was only seventeen, and needed to talk about my feelings of guilt. What had I said to lead her to do this? Later, I heard that after leaving school she'd been treated in hospital for severe depression. She was a very special person, with so much to give, and it seemed a terrible waste of a good life. As a suicide, she was not even allowed to be buried in the churchyard. Hallowe'en has been a sad time for me ever since.

The summer of 1950 brought some contrasting experiences. From Monday to Friday in term time I helped at a small 'prep' school in Woking, run by two teachers I'd known from Lydney. It was a very gentle introduction to teaching, and helped me decide on teaching as a career. It was on a Monday morning in

June, as I caught the train from Sevenoaks along with my brother Michael who was going to the War Office, that I saw him turn a sickly shade of yellow as he opened his *Times*. He gulped, and said, "I think I'm going to be rather busy." As a junior subaltern he'd been given a minor job in the War Office, studying an obscure corner of the world. That morning, the headlines were screaming, 'War breaks out in Korea', and Michael's 'obscure part of the world' was Korea.

His life then became very interesting, including going to Downing Street each morning to mark up maps for the Cabinet meetings. At weekends, for some months, all the latest information on Korea was locked up, along with the silver, in our safe at home. Later, when Michael was on night duty at the War Office, a red alert arrived from the USA, saying that General MacArthur wanted to drop an atomic bomb on Korea. Attlee had to be told immediately, and next day he flew across the Atlantic to beg President Truman to restrain his impulsive general. After his experiences that summer, my brother Michael, a true-blue Tory, nevertheless always had great admiration for Attlee.

After four days of teaching, at the weekend I became a part-time deb. The London Season was already on the way out, but still hostesses met and shared lists of girls and suitable young men, of whom Michael was deemed a specially safe one. I enjoyed the dressing up (I've always liked long evening dresses), but the realities invariably proved disappointing. I became almost a professional wallflower, but with the exciting prospect of Cambridge in the autumn, it didn't worry me much. Friendly hostesses would give dinner parties for, say, six debs and six young men from the approved list. It was assumed that each young man would dance at least once with each of the girls at the dinner party, but often it didn't work out like that. Sometimes the men were competing for a particular girl who had a 'reputation'.

One evening, Michael saw me across the room and came over. He whispered that he'd seen some men who'd been turned out of the regiment (The Rifle Brigade). Invitations for that evening had been sent by two hostesses, giving plenty of opportunities for gate-crashing. He saved the evening for me, "Come on, Muffet, let's dance."

Debs were offered a free make-up by a leading cosmetic firm. I took up the offer, but was so appalled by the plasticising effect that I scraped it all off. The London Season should have included Presentations (at Buckingham Palace), but they were postponed because Queen Mary had died. I did in fact get 'presented' a few years later, when we curtseyed to the new Queen Elizabeth and Prince Philip. That was quite fun, because after the curtseys we were free to wander round the palace. At one point I realised I was at the back of the Throne Room with the famous balcony. I came face-to-face with a girl wearing an identical dress; I smiled and said "Snap", but she was not amused.

Thank goodness the long white dresses and ostrich feathers had been replaced by smart dresses with hats and gloves. My mother had taken me to Tunbridge Wells to buy the dress, pale blue silk, which was expensive and very boring and didn't suit me at all. I suppose I was not prepared to have a row about it, after the row we'd had a few years earlier. I'd bought a lovely off-the-shoulder, wine-coloured evening dress, and was away when it arrived home by post. My mother opened the box and expressed great disapproval. I think she thought any sort of red denoted 'dubious reputation', and that only pastel shades were appropriate for respectable young ladies. I loved that dress, and I was wearing it later when there was a photo of me in the *Tatler*, sitting under the Christmas tree with Douglas Hurd at the Tory Ball in Cambridge. In 1950, we were still riding on the exhilarating tide of the 'New Look' in clothes, after war rationing. Besides a somewhat utilitarian nightdress made out of blue parachute silk, I revelled in bright floral cotton dresses in summer, with neat waists and full skirts. In those days I had a small waist.

I was excited and amazed to be in Cambridge. One day, in the corridor, I was asked something by a kind lady who was so amused by my enthusiastic response that she invited me to Sunday lunch. It turned out she was Lady Bragg, wife of Sir Laurence, a famous physicist, and was herself a Newnham governor. Many years later, I became friends with her daughter. I was determined to try my hardest, and must have overdone the effort, as I developed boils in my first term and was told not to work so hard. Suddenly, I was with others much better at maths than I was, and I struggled to keep up. I enjoyed some lectures, including Fred Hoyle's on the dynamics of the Earth's movement round the sun, but I seemed to have reached my 'ceiling' in maths, exacerbated by my ignorance of physics. Luckily, I had an understanding supervisor who realised I was doing my best and would ask, "How's the tennis going?" I hated the idea of economics, and in those days history would not have been an option, so I battled on and at the end was allowed a degree. I hope perhaps that my experience of struggling made me a more sympathetic maths teacher later.

Newnham is divided into Halls, and I was in Peile, with a ground floor room looking out over the garden. There was no central heating, and I was too lazy to cope with the coal fire, so in the winter I would work in an overcoat. I was not very sociable, and once chased an unwelcome male intruder out with my fencing foil. The corridor at Peile was wide enough to practise fencing with Christine, who'd done fencing at school with me. We were able to initiate a challenge to Oxford, generously organised by the men's team at Fenners. Oxford, very magnanimously, accepted the challenge, and I think the match has become an annual fixture.

In the summer, there was tennis. My game improved after the Cambridge coach helped me with my serve, which I practised on my own on the Newnham courts in winter. Perhaps it was my hidden aggression that made me better at singles, which enabled me to beat the Oxford captain in 1953, giving me a Full Blue. She was reputed to have a bad heart, so I made her run as much as possible. She was a generous loser though, and didn't hold it against me. That year (1953), we were given superb seats at Wimbledon, above the players' stand, and I think that was the year we watched the marathon match between Drobny and Patty. They were each playing so brilliantly that it was impossible to think either of them a loser. In those days there were no tie breaks, and it was almost dark at the end, with crowds gathering from all around.

The principal of Newnham at the time was Dame Myra Curtis, a formidable woman. She was probably an atheist, as Newnham has an atheist foundation. Dame Myra was very angry when someone put up a notice about College Communion, but when she came to Peile for supper, she still insisted on a Latin grace.

It was through Peile that I met up with a distant and very erudite cousin Jocelyn. She had found a letter in her postbox addressed to Miss J. Toynbee, but realised, on opening it, that it was not meant for her. Jocelyn was Laurence Professor of Archaeology at the time, and one of the world's most revered classical archaeologists. It was to her that the authorities went when the Temple of Mithras was discovered in London. She and her sister Margaret, a historian, were sisters of Arnold Toynbee, but when I remarked on enjoying some of his philosophical ideas, she replied, somewhat waspishly, "Oh, all that waffle." She was a true scholar, and her great ambition, as a devout Roman Catholic, was to find the remains of St Peter in Rome. Sadly for her, she never did. In her old age she suffered from dementia, but when I took my son James, a budding archaeologist, to meet her, she was able, with a huge effort of will, to discuss Cambridge and archaeology quite lucidly for about twenty minutes. Then I saw the light fade from her eyes, and we left.

It should have been an exciting time to be at Cambridge, with Peter Hall and politicians like Douglas Hurd and Geoffrey Howe who were older and had done National Service, but I was too young and inexperienced to appreciate it fully. The politicians did ask me to stand as the first woman President of the Union, but I was sensible enough to refuse. A few years later, I married into a Liberal family and have been an enthusiastic supporter of liberalism ever since.

My brother Peter had also gone to Cambridge after National Service, and was in his last year at Magdalene. We met up for tennis and tea in the summer of 1951, along with another girl and Jim Millar. Jim, a Scots medical student, had become a good friend, and we both enjoyed Scottish country dancing. He invited me up to Aberdeenshire for the Aboyne Ball, and a party of us climbed Lochnagar. It was cold and wet (anoraks hadn't been invented), and I was grateful for a tot of whisky before the descent. Jim later became a doctor, but tragically died young of a brain tumour.

Another Cambridge friend was Geoff Weston. He'd been second-in-command of HMS *Amethyst* when she was shelled by the Chinese. When the captain was killed and medical supplies destroyed, he had to take command despite excruciating pain. When a film was made of the incident, Geoff was portrayed as an alcoholic. This was deeply upsetting to his family, and no doubt to him, though he never talked about it. He was a lovely person, and I think his shrapnel wounds led to an early death.

I had a dire experience of a May Ball, when the son of a friend of my parents (no doubt instructed by his parents) asked me to be his partner. He spent most of the night trying to explain his research on the effect of the moon on tides, whereas I was just longing to dance. It was a long night. What is it about British males and dance? (I have known just a few brilliant exceptions.) Also at Cambridge was 'Boz' Ferranti, who asked if I'd like to work at the new computer they were developing. This was 1951. I told him I wanted to be a maths teacher. It must, though, have been an exciting time for those interested in computer development.

Chapter 9 – Bridesmaid, Teacher, Bride

Michael was the first of us to get married, and naturally I was a bridesmaid. The dress was stiff, cream brocade with an ugly waistline. I determined that, if I became a bride, my dress would possibly have no waistline. When the time came, a London dressmaker made a beautiful princess-line dress in French lace, which John's sister liked so much that she borrowed it later for her own wedding. My bridesmaid's career started early when I was five, happy in a yellow taffeta dress with primroses in my hair. Next year it was a London wedding, entailing long sessions with a dressmaker, resulting in a hideous (I thought) stiff, powder blue dress.

I've never been smart or stylish, but clothes do matter to me. At Peter's wedding in Godalming our pretty blue broderie anglaise bridesmaids' dresses kept us cool on a stiflingly hot summer's day. I wore that dress later at a Hunt Ball in Northumberland. My sixth and last bridesmaid's dress was in peacock green satin. At that wedding in London, the bride's sister Meg and I knew we looked our best, and I dimly remember an interesting evening afterwards. As children, Meg and I had once crossed the lake in her parents' garden by clambering along the ironwork under the railway bridge. It hadn't occurred to me that if I fell in, I couldn't swim. Meg was great fun. After our marriages our lives diverged, but when we eventually met up again we could still laugh. By then we were each much involved with families, and Meg had become a talented painter of miniatures.

I first met John Whitley on a so-called Fruiting Campaign run by a Franciscan brother. Christian students from Cambridge were invited to camp at Wisbech to help families from London who had come to pick fruit. Female students looked after children while the mothers worked; the men took care of medical needs, consisting mostly of removing gooseberry thorns. John had started out intending to study medicine, like his father, but had switched to theology with a view to getting ordained. We met up again on a skiing holiday, and a few years later were engaged to be married.

Meanwhile, when I left Cambridge, there was such a shortage of maths teachers in 1953 that I got a job straight away, with no training, as head of maths at Channing School, Highgate, a private girls' school. I was only three years older than the sixth form girls, and was sometimes taken for a prefect and sent on errands, but I think I did a reasonably good job. My brother Michael once met a young woman who said I'd helped her a lot. In the summer term I also helped with tennis coaching.

One evening, as I was walking back up Highgate Hill from Archway Station, I heard footsteps behind and realised I was being followed. Turning round, I encountered a very black face. He was a Nigerian student, and was looking for some female companionship. There were few black students in Britain then, and hardly any black girls, so no wonder he was lonely. I had to think quickly. He seemed quite genuine, so I agreed to meet him for tea in a cafe in Camden High Street. By that time, I was engaged to John so I was able to show his photograph and explain my situation without, I hope, hurting his feelings. My friends thought I'd taken a foolish risk, but the poor man was in need of female friendship. I hope he found some.

My father's reaction, when he realised I was going to marry a penniless curate was, "But darling, you don't know how to cook," to which I replied, "But Daddy, I can learn." This I did by going to London, staying at Bishop Creighton House in Fulham, and attending the Gloucester School of Cookery. The most helpful thing I learned was confidence, actually getting my hands in the pastry mix. Though I've never really enjoyed cooking, I was able to produce enough decent meals for the family over many years. In London, I also learned dressmaking. There was a wonderful moment later that year when my father was admiring my dress and I was able to say, "I made it." I'd chosen the material from John Lewis where there seemed to be an explosion of beautiful fabrics at the time.

Preparations for the wedding were underway, but, because our parish church at Underriver was very small, my mother decided we should be married in St Nicholas, Sevenoaks. That meant I had to sleep in Sevenoaks for three weeks to qualify as a parishioner. A kind friend agreed to put me up, and I drove there each evening on my new Lambretta. My mother was slightly less apprehensive about it when I assured her that I had a helmet.

I was angry though, when I failed my scooter test in Sevenoaks having passed my car driving test several years earlier. For this I'd driven my parents' Austin 16, probably 1935 vintage, a beautiful old car with a purring engine, running board, footstools and tables. It had such a long wheelbase that I was allowed a five-point turn rather than a three-point one. The actual driving required double de-clutching both up and down, but road conditions were much easier then, with so little traffic. After we married, the Lambretta went up to Northumberland and John used it around the parish before we had our first car.

I thoroughly enjoyed our wedding, and the flags were flying in Sevenoaks as it was the Queen's birthday. My godfather, Rupert Riley, made the speech, which was short as he had a stammer. I wish I'd known him better, as I believe he'd had a remarkable life, including spying and driving a Riley car across America in some special race. We flew to Rome for the honeymoon; it was my first experience of flying and not entirely a happy one as my feet, trapped in new shoes, swelled painfully. I don't think planes were properly pressurised then, even though we only flew at about sixteen thousand feet. There was a marvellous pink dawn over Mont Blanc on our way back, before an unexpected delay at Heathrow. We were to fly on to Newcastle, and waited in a little hut for news.

As the day wore on, there were deliberations as to whether the train might be quicker, but eventually the pilot appeared, and we followed him to the little plane. He checked that everything was properly balanced before taking off, and after a slightly uneven flight we landed bumpily on the grass at Newcastle. This was our destination, as John was curate at Ashington, under Anthony Hunter. I arrived as a complete alien, but was given a truly heartwarming welcome, and I enjoyed Geordie friendship and generosity for over three years. Life in Ashington revolved around the three pits; there were some Cornish names from when Cornish tin miners migrated north, but in 1956 it was a tightly knit community, with anyone going south to college or 'marrying out' being felt as a threat.

Customs were strictly adhered to. Monday was washing day, when boilers in the back yards, fuelled by free coal, steamed away merrily. After mangling, the washing was hung out, but I soon discovered that if the wind was in the east, black soot from the pits tended to drift into our back yard. Luckily, after James was born, I realised that it was acceptable for nappies to be washed on other days as well. I bought a twin tub washing machine, the very latest in 1956 technology. It was filled by a hose from the sink, then emptied and refilled for rinsing. Not brilliant, but better than doing it all by hand.

You had to be careful with the wringer, though, when dealing with buttons. My worst laundry disaster was washing a pink bedspread along with John's white lawn surplice. The latter's shocking pink tinge never quite disappeared. After James was born, the women would joke with pithy phrases about pregnancies and there may be some truth in the sayings about contagion. (Six of my grandchildren were born within five years.) There was a ritual placing of silver in the pram, and the compulsory remark, "My, isn't he like his father?" I made several cultural mistakes, such as opening a bazaar while noticeably pregnant, but I think I was forgiven on account of ignorance. We misunderstood the invitation to 'tea', not realising that 'tea' meant the evening meal for the man returning from the pit. We tried not to be surprised when lamb chops were served along with the 'cuppa'. Afterwards we learned to accept with "Thank you. A cup of tea in my hand." A very different hospitality from that of friends of my parents who invited (or who were asked to invite) us to dinner. John was unwell, and when I arrived on the Lambretta they were aghast. A dinner guest without a car was unthinkable. Needless to say, the invitation was not repeated.

I never went down an Ashington pit, where I think the conditions were horrendous, but I did go down the more modern one at Lynemouth and emerged with a deep headache, perhaps to do with the pressure. The Ashington pits have long gone, and perhaps something of the precious community spirit went with them. Now, one hopes, new ways of being a community have emerged.

I cried when we left Ashington, but there was no time for regret with two small children and a third on the way. John's new job was a curacy at Chiswick, under an irascible Welsh vicar with a vicious ankle-biting corgi. He approved of me because together we could beat the churchwardens at tennis on Saturday mornings. The vicar would visit the grand houses along Chiswick Mall, and John would get to know families in the poorer back streets.

When a West Indian family had saved enough for a wedding, there would be a splendid party with girls dressed in brilliant colours, and much joy and laughter. The BBC used the church hall for rehearsals, and George Cole, involved in some long-running series, would come out and play with James in the interval. I've had a soft spot for him ever since.

There was nearly a ghastly tragedy on the day we moved from Chiswick. The removal men had left the gate open, and in an unguarded moment, James, with his baby sister, wandered out to the Great West Road. Soon after, they were brought back by a shocked and furious lorry driver. I think I was too shocked and horrified to thank him properly.

We were moving to Ware in Hertfordshire where John had been invited to be the vicar. At last, we had space. The vicarage had been built in the twenties, in the days of servants. There was a butler's pantry, where an early dishwasher was installed; a housekeeper's sitting-room (very useful for storing jumble) and, to the delight of the children, a back staircase.

Chapter 10 – Vicarage Life

At last, we had space, both indoors and outdoors. The garden was full of possibilities for children. A rope ladder led to a crude tree house in the beech tree; the slope on the lawn was good for rolling down, and there were plenty of mysterious dark corners. Some aspects were difficult for children, though. John had invited the Parochial Church Council (PCC) to the vicarage, and James, aged four, watched a procession of strangers, some with hats, coming up the drive. He stood at the front door, clenching his little fists, and called out, "Go away!" I whisked him off to the kitchen to explain that they would indeed be going away soon.

The congregation, mostly old, had a shock on John's first Sunday. There were no 'child-friendly' services then, so I had to take the three (all under five) to early Holy Communion. In the children's corner they spotted a small 'bishop's chair', and proceeded to re-enact John's Induction service. Things had to change, and soon there were family Eucharists and a flourishing Sunday school. Extensive post-war housing had brought many young families to the area, and we benefited from excellent new primary schools. At the time, the Hertfordshire primary schools were some of the best in the country, if not in the world. Our family was complete after two more daughters, and the girls all enjoyed their early experiences of school. It was a shock when we encountered a very different experience in Edinburgh.

Ware is a Trinity College Cambridge living, and former vicars had usually been retired academics, so the arrival of a young vicar with a family was something of a shock to some older members of the congregation. The head of the Mothers' Union expected me to take over. I had to explain that being mother to a young family, at three o'clock in the afternoon I was collecting children from school. It was also a surprise to some respectable ladies that I was not a Conservative.

The outstanding character around the church was Old Ben, the verger. He more or less lived in the church, polishing the pew ends with a duster and climbing a ladder to play hymn tunes on the bells. He had come to Ware from the east end of London with Allen & Hanburys, and was sometimes seen selling dubious herbal remedies from the vestry door, together with mushrooms from the fields. Once, when I was in church with Sarah and Kate, he introduced us to a visitor who looked suspiciously at the two little girls. They were then, and have remained, markedly different in looks. "Are these BOTH the vicar's children?" the visitor asked. I was never quite sure whether Ben had suspicions too. He died soon after his hundredth birthday.

The vicarage must have been on a well-trodden 'tramp route', as I was regularly giving out tea and sandwiches from the kitchen door. The recipients were mostly Irish, and called me 'sister', and presumably left some sign on the gate post, indicating hospitality. We did put up a homeless family for some weeks, but it turned out she was a drug addict and he was an alcoholic and they needed more help than we could give. Another needy character was Muncer. He wanted something to eat, but only in return for work, which was usually sweeping up leaves. He, and his rather unpleasant brother, lived in some squalor in the town, and had been repudiated by their respectable cousins. Their great dread was to be taken to the hospital up the road, as they remembered the building as the old workhouse. Some years we took them Christmas lunches, and a saintly lady in the congregation would visit regularly and attend to Muncer's ulcerous legs. At his funeral, with no mourners, John asked me to toll the bell. The respectable cousins kept away. I don't know what the brothers' history was, but they might well have been traumatised by WW1 and had no one to help them afterwards.

Another regular visitor was 'John'. By his haircut we guessed that he was frequently in and out of prison. He always asked for a job, before sandwiches and tea, and sometimes washed in the scullery sink with Lifebuoy soap. He was completely harmless, and one Christmas even stayed overnight in the housekeeper's sitting-room. By the end of the sixties, we had more aggressive visitors. Not satisfied with clothing or food, they wanted money, and things became difficult. It was a huge relief when Social Services had an agreement with a café near the station, and we could give out food vouchers.

I wanted the children to have pets, but our efforts were not very successful; the rabbit disappeared; the goldfish died, and the hamster ate holes in the velvet curtain. I would have liked a dog, but after the one next door was run over, we acquired a cat.

Unfortunately, Eskimo was not a nice character. An aggressive tom, we were woken by fierce fights in the night, and he was very greedy. We fed him well, but he put on a convincing act of starvation for a widow in the back lane. One Sunday morning on her way to choir, Kate found his body on the road. He had crossed over to the hotel kitchen once too often.

The Cold War in the sixties left us with anxieties and feelings of helplessness. The Civil Defence ran courses such as learning how to cook emergency meals for large numbers of people. We were told about protection from nuclear attacks, most of which would have been utterly useless, but I suppose the authorities had to do something to help morale.

Sometimes it was difficult to refuse requests for help. I was asked to help the wife next door with her driving, which was at times a terrifying experience, such as when we drove backwards, very fast, onto the A10. To express their gratitude, her husband, who was a director of Arsenal, invited us to an evening match. I think what impressed me most was the policeman patrolling the kerb, holding the parking space for his car. Unfortunately, Arsenal lost that evening, but I enjoyed the experience, especially the rose-perfumed boudoir for the women during half-time.

Even with a big family, there was still room for occasional visitors, and we became the centre for family Christmases. John's parents, Mary and Bompa, would bring a huge turkey, and various aunts and cousins would arrive for lunch, followed by present-opening and exhaustion. One year we were twenty-eight for lunch, including two babies. Once, about to reach screaming point on Christmas Eve, I retreated to the old henhouse for a short time to recover.

On Christmas Eve, after the turkey had been put in the oven for a long, slow cook and the children were asleep, a delightful peace would descend on the house. John would be at the Midnight Service, and I was left to play Mother Christmas with the 'sacks' (pillowcases). But before I started on my rounds I could sit at the piano and play 'Silent Night' and 'O Little Town of Bethlehem'. Precious moments. Years later, when we were no longer a clergy household, I was able to 'break the mould' by taking some of the family to Rome for Christmas. Now, I don't feel any Christmas obligations except worship. I've never been interested in the 'feasting' aspect, and the present-giving can become tedious, but it's good to meet up with family.

Another friend who visited was Nanny Marshall, a retired nanny who we'd met in Ashington. She was desperately lonely, her father having been the town doctor, and therefore not part of the ordinary mining community. She enjoyed relating experiences as a visiting nanny, and how, at Chatsworth, no nappies were allowed to be hung outside. It's a horrific thought that, as a teenage nursery maid, she had not been given enough food. Early under-nourishment may well have explained her shortness. She shrunk so much later, that she had to stand on two telephone directories to answer the phone. For many nannies, life must have been a succession of heartbreaks. They loved and cared for a baby, then, when it was old enough to return the affection, they had to leave.

With a large house, I needed help in keeping the vicarage reasonably respectable, and Mrs Hills was a godsend. Over coffee, I learned some of her history. As an illegitimate child whose mother couldn't keep her, she was fostered out many times, and although highly intelligent, was not allowed to go to grammar school. She longed for more education, but her husband felt threatened by it. Stability in marriage must have been the highest priority for her, and she never complained. Later, she became somewhat of a matriarch to a large family.

We engaged 'mother's helps' for a year each after the last two babies, as I thought there would be too much work for an au pair. They were both German, but very different. Inge was a superb cook, but seemed to have a chip on her shoulder. Karin became a good friend, and we kept in touch until she died. I have a cushion, a cardigan and Christmas decorations made by her, and Bertram and I visited her once in Switzerland.

As vicar of Ware, John helped to make history by convening a Consistory Court, an ancient ecclesiastical court that hadn't been used for centuries. A parishioner objected to the removal of pews to make space for a nave altar. She then withdrew her objection, but the Chancellor of the diocese was eager to test the Court's capability, and it was duly convened in the church, with John defending his case. Since then, Consistory Courts have become quite frequent, as have nave altars and the removal of pews.

I enjoyed being the vicar's wife and a mother, but there were bad times too. As a result of medication, John became very ill with depression and for a time was hospitalised, followed by extremes of manic and depressive behaviour which I found difficult to cope with. On one journey to Scotland, he insisted on so many stops that I became almost too tired to drive. By that time, together with my mother-in-law Mary, we had acquired a holiday cottage in Galloway, and a VW van, and journeys to Galloway became a regular summer activity.

Chapter 11 – Scotland

I had happy memories of Galloway from pre-war visits to Murrayton, a hill farm up the valley from Gatehouse of Fleet, the home of my mother's friend, Betty Murray Usher. Miss Smith and I, together with my dog Melia, would walk up the platform at Euston and ask the engine-driver, "Please would you stop at Gatehouse of Fleet?" Hours later, the Stranraer Express would clatter over the viaduct and grind to a halt at the tiny station high up in the moors. A car would be waiting to take us six miles down to the town, and then up the valley to the farmhouse.

I would wake to farmyard noises in the cobbled courtyard, and walk out on the moors among the sheep. It was all so different from home. I was a little frightened of Mrs Murray Usher, who was a large lady with a loud voice, but later became a good friend. It was she who, in the early sixties, alerted us to the sale of the cottage near Borgue. We were looking for a possible holiday cottage for the family, and I bought it jointly with my mother-in-law Mary. She and Bompa, who had retired to Edinburgh, would go down there at weekends, and we joined them for summer holidays.

Those Galloway holidays were wonderfully restful for me, as Mary did all the catering and Bompa oversaw any medical needs. He had been a much-loved and respected GP and obstetrician, and had been a huge reassurance to me during my pregnancies and subsequent births. After an accident he would know whether a hospital visit was needed, and over the years we became quite familiar with the friendly hospital at Kirkcudbright. When John mowed over a wasp's nest, and the furious colony swarmed on poor Tessa, the visit was urgent.

With the sea within walking distance, and the hills behind, there was always plenty to do. We climbed Cairnsmore of Fleet, explored the Water of Minnoch, failed to climb the Merrick owing to mist, and sailed the dinghy around Ardwall. The dinghy travelled on top of the VW van, adding to the complexities of packing, but it helped the children with the rudiments of sailing. On one hill walk James and I came across a sheep on her back. She struggled hard as we turned her over, but we felt instinctively that it was the right thing to do.

My favourite expedition was always up to Gatehouse Station, dodging the curly-horned sheep wandering across the road, and re-living childhood memories. By that time, the line to Stranraer had closed and no more trains rattled over the viaduct, but we could paddle in the Fleet and picnic on the grass, away from noise and traffic.

We left Ware when John had a new job in Edinburgh, and the move entailed far more complications than I had expected. The clergy flat had four bedrooms and one bathroom, which necessitated a strict routine on school days. The worst headache, though, was the Scottish educational system and culture. The reason for Kate's stomach pains on Wednesday mornings was that the headmaster of her primary school took the top class for arithmetic, and would administer the strap for unsatisfactory performance.

Other complications in the educational system, when they became apparent, meant that all five eventually ended up in the fee-paying system. This worked out well for the girls, but James suffered from an illiberal regime, and only survived thanks to the two teachers who recognised his thirst for scholarship. Soon after, Edinburgh adopted the comprehensive system, and a few years later I found myself teaching in one.

After years as a vicar's wife, and with now no obvious place in the life of the cathedral, I felt somewhat desolate. It never occurred to me to get a job, and I was still suffering from John's remark to a friend in Ware that, "Her job is me." Things changed later. Meanwhile, domestic life became easier when we bought our own apartment with plenty of space. Enough space to host a Ugandan Asian family while they waited for permanent council housing. They were delightful visitors, but became a serious culinary challenge for me as they were Jains, and therefore vegans. On the third day, the elder daughter (who spoke English) came to me saying that her mother (who didn't speak English) had suggested that she cook the evening meal for us all. Spicy, unfamiliar smells pervaded the kitchen, and we drank copious glasses of water, but it was the best solution. I went with the family and the social worker to the council estate, where they may well have been the first Asian families around, and we introduced them to the neighbours. We were overjoyed and greatly relieved to hear that they had become friends with the family below, and had even shared meals.

Holidays in Galloway stopped after Mary had a bad stroke and John decided he wanted sailing holidays. We bought a lovely French yacht (with a legacy from my father) and I tried to be an enthusiastic sailor. I felt a complete outsider at the Yacht Club, but I did enjoy sailing round the Western Isles, sitting in the cockpit with binoculars, watching birds. We could sail silently past seals basking on rocks without disturbing them. Once we were completely becalmed in an eerie white fog. Complete silence. Were we in the centre of some freak weather? Then the sail twitched, and gradually everything came back to life. We had an embarrassing moment in Tobermory Bay when our anchor chain dragged across those of other smaller boats, and a terrifying few minutes when Rachel's foot caught in the line and she was being dragged under water, but on the whole the experience that summer was good. It certainly gave Sarah a great love of boats and sailing.

Sadly, the boat was damaged in a storm off Granton harbour, and the next year John decided to have a sailing holiday in Greece. This turned out to be a far more dangerous adventure than we had bargained for. At the time, Greece was under the oppressive regime of the Colonels, supported by the USA, and our boat was American, flying a Stars and Stripes burgee (little flag), which explained the hostility we encountered. The real danger, though, was that it was built for the Baltic and flat-bottomed. When the Meltemi (storm) blew up we were nearly battered to pieces off the harbour wall at Paros. Then, as if by a miracle, a man in a white suit appeared and guided us to an anchorage in the middle of the harbour. His name was Apostolos, and on board during the evening he told us of the dire political state of his country. He could do this safely, as the boat was not 'bugged'. The storm continued, sinking boats in the harbour at Mykonos, so while John stayed to hand our boat back to the owners, I came back on the ferry with four children (Kate had had enough of sailing). So it was that I found myself with four children on the quayside at Piraeus, late at night, wondering what to do. Staying the night in a port with three teenage daughters seemed unwise, so we took a taxi to the British Embassy. A disgruntled young man appeared at the door and suggested a safe hotel, and soon the whole family was reunited in Athens.

James, now a teenager, had set his heart on archaeology and I decided to take him, together with his cousin Sasha, to Orkney one summer. We explored Skara Brae and Maeshowe, and were rowed in a little boat across to another island. There we hired a car from a farm. It wouldn't have passed any MOT test, and braking meant driving on to the rough verge, but as the car never left the island and there was hardly any other traffic, it didn't matter. The boys seemed to enjoy the whole experience, and the fact that James could read runes added to the interest.

I had a bad moment on the first evening. I returned to Kirkwall with two hungry boys, to find all the cafés were closed by 6 o'clock. I managed to find some food, possibly sandwiches from a pub, and made sure we were not caught out again.

Another unforeseen difficulty was the weather. We had flown from Aberdeen and enjoyed several superb sunny days. So sunny, in fact, that the islands were covered in mist and no planes could land. No planes arriving meant, of course, no planes for taking off, and so every morning I had to decide whether to take the ferry to Thurso and the train down to Edinburgh. Meanwhile, I knew that my mother was arriving in Edinburgh for a visit. After a few days of sun and mist, I opted for the ferry. We sailed past Hoy, stayed the night in Thurso and caught the train very early next morning. Meanwhile, in Edinburgh, the girls had done a splendid job of looking after my mother, the only time, I think, that she ever stayed with us.

Chapter 12 – Decisions and New Life

John was being engulfed by the Encounter Group Movement from America, with its philosophy of 'go with your feelings' – in other words, 'feel free to sleep around'. One Valentine's Day, he said he no longer loved me, so I needed to make some decisions. John was about to lose his job; the family needed looking after, together with, for some months of the year, John's parents. My mother-in-law Mary had had a bad stroke, and while they were with us they needed me to cook for them as well, which of course I was happy to do.

So, in the mid-seventies, I was in the humiliating position of having a husband who needed me as housekeeper, while he amused himself (discreetly) with other women. I gave myself two challenges. The first was to learn to swim, which I managed to accomplish in the local pool. The second was to teach in a comprehensive school, for which I needed training. I enrolled at Craiglockhart College for a year's post-graduate course. Craiglockhart had featured in WW1 as a hospital for soldiers suffering from extreme stress and was now a Roman Catholic training college for primary teachers. Luckily, they accepted me for training as a secondary maths teacher. The nuns were very friendly, despite my being an Anglican, but when I asked the Chaplain whether I could receive Communion at the end of year Mass, he literally slammed the door in my face.

I enjoyed my year though, except for being taken to experience an apparently 'good' maths lesson. I watched the faces of the girls 'switch off' as the woman teacher lashed the class with sarcasm. I was determined I did not want to teach like that.

Then I found myself in the deep end as a probationer teacher in a huge RC comprehensive school in the west of Edinburgh. Life was not easy; my head of department loathed me, and the headmaster was more or less mad. He made me sign a statement saying that there had been a riot in my class. I refused to use the strap, but that didn't stop the ex-sergeant major charging into my class, seizing a pupil, and administering the strap in the corridor. The result: "Sorry Miss, I can't write." My more relaxed style of teaching worked for me, and I hated the attitude of some teachers who treated pupils with scorn. I was given no help with a class who wanted to leave and had no interest in learning. It became apparent that if there was no stabbing or tumult, and no furniture was thrown out of the window, I was doing all right. I hope Scottish education for the less academic has progressed since then.

I made some good friends among the teachers, including Marianne, who taught secretarial skills. Her husband Francis had once been secretary to George Sitwell (father of Oswald, Sacheverell and Edith) and had helped an author with the writing of Sir George's biography. This author had offered Francis and Marianne the use of a villa just outside Florence for some weeks in the summer. Would I like to join them? It turned out to be a formative experience.

For technical reasons they were delayed, and I found myself alone in Florence for several days. I had to brace myself for marching into a café for pizza and breakfast coffee, and managed to cope with being chatted up in a park. I was near enough to visit Pisa, and was halfway up the Leaning Tower when a cheeky voice called out, "Hi, Miss!" St Augustine's had followed me to Italy.

With no guide book, I just wandered round Florence. I found myself in a quiet courtyard with Della Robbia medallions, and sat on a step absorbing its simple beauty. In a tiny museum near the Ponte Vecchio, Galileo's middle finger was preserved in some fluid. It was my first experience of being alone in a foreign country, and it seems there is something extra special in chance encounters and discoveries.

The key to the villa was 'under the third oleander from the left', and inside it was dark and cool. There were geckos climbing up and down the walls, and in the evening we watched fireflies dancing in the fields. One night I slept outside under the stars. The highlight for me was a visit to the castle where Francis had worked with Sir George. To his great delight, an aged servant was still there and remembered him. Marianne and I left them in animated conversation while we wandered along the crumbling terrace. I shall always be grateful to Marianne for that unexpected and delightful treat.

I found other friends in the 'alien's corner' in the staff room at St Augustine's. Brendon, who was Welsh and taught Latin and English, and Bernard MacLaverty from Ulster, whose first book of short stories was just being published. While I was there too, I had my first, and so far only, visit to prison. A colleague, seemingly friendly and a good teacher, had become embroiled with a couple in selling cannabis and had been sent to Saughton prison. The sound of keys turning in locks behind me was somewhat unnerving, but I was glad to have visited him. Then I realised that the police might be following up my contacts, so I had to ask James, then a teenager, if he had any cannabis around. He assured me that he hadn't.

With the marriage falling apart, John and I went to a counsellor. A wise man, who listened and said little. One afternoon at home, as I looked out of the window, I realised that I had to leave John. I also knew that telling him had to wait until the next counselling session. I was no match for John's manipulative skills. The counsellor just said, "My work is done," and then we had to start the grisly process of dividing up possessions and finding new places to live. Who gets the steak knives? The three-piece suite? The linen? The saucepans? The carpets? The pictures? Telling John's mother was particularly difficult. For Mary, John was her 'blue-eyed boy' who could do no wrong, and when she asked whose fault it was, Bompa and I just kept quiet.

It was a distressing time for all of us. John settled in a flat, and I bought a strange apartment, big enough for all the family, near the railway. It was somehow comforting to hear the trains rumbling past. I tried to alleviate some family misery with exciting holidays. One year, I took Sarah and Kate to Tangier. Crossing to Gibraltar, we were in a white fog with almost zero visibility and the fog horn sounding all the time. A frightening experience in such a crowded shipping lane. Another evening, Sarah and I were watching storks on a roof, when I realised we were being surrounded by young men. Sarah was twenty, blonde and attractive. It was the moment for me to adopt my 'Lady Bracknell' voice, "Time to go back, Sarah." We held our heads up and walked smartly back to the hotel. While the girls stayed by the pool in the hotel, I walked around Tangier, keeping my eyes lowered and my body well covered, which was natural for me anyway in the heat. One day, women from the Rif mountains had set up stalls. I wanted to buy a piece of cloth; the little squat woman spoke no French, and I had no idea of her language, but with mime and smiles we managed a satisfactory transaction. On our last day I bought a handbag, but only after the proper ritual of mint tea and amicable haggling. Another shopkeeper was not pleased when she had agreed (in French) a price for some dresses, but when I returned with the girls, she realised we were British. She should have quoted a higher price.

Another year I took three daughters to Venice, and lost them near San Georgio. I'd been watching the 'big cat' (a catamaran which went down to the Lido) further down the river, and when I turned round, they had disappeared. I returned to the hotel, comforting myself with the thought that at least there were three of them, and that Sarah was sensible. They duly turned up at the hotel an hour later, very happy. They'd been commenting on yachts moored on the quayside and some young men heard their voices and invited them on board. Some years later, Sarah chose Venice for her honeymoon.

After two operations on my legs for varicose veins, I needed time by myself and escaped for a few days to South Uist in the outer Hebrides. I climbed the highest hill, and sat on the dunes by the coast gazing out westwards towards the Atlantic. There I was pounced on by a Hebridean shepherd, murmuring what I took to be Gaelic endearments. He calmed down as I gently stroked his back, and then he departed in some embarrassment. I assumed he had recently lost his wife.

Meanwhile, life for me in Edinburgh was becoming increasingly depressing. I hated being on 'the fag end of a failed marriage', and clergy wives were avoiding me. It was time to go back to England. The question was, where should I go? I'd never had that question before. The home counties were out, partly because of the cost, but more because I did not want to be 'poor Jane' to my brothers. I had happy memories of Herefordshire, and spent a half term in Ledbury, to see what it felt like. Very beautiful, of course, but what on earth would I do there? My future was decided in the Christmas holidays with an advertisement for a house in Batheaston, near Bath. It was a large old house on the High Street with remnants of a stable, and a garden going down to the river path. There was plenty of room for all the family, and when the summer term was over, Tessa helped me with the move. I have been in the village ever since.

Batheaston

I had arrived still full of anger and resentment, and it was the house and garden that helped my rehabilitation. I removed every vestige of ground elder in the garden, and armed with an ice axe and a crowbar, dug out the Cotswold tiles that lined the garden paths. I found this furious activity somehow neutralised the anger. Many of the tiles could be used on the roof, as it turned out the house needed major renovation. One day, the builder told me it was about to fall down. "But," he added, "we have jacked it up." The work that followed somehow mirrored my own recovery, and, although money disappeared like water down the drain, I was being healed. One morning, I woke up and found that the anger and resentment had finally gone. I was free.

The children were moving between university, Edinburgh, Batheaston and travel. One daughter was in crisis in Hawaii; John agreed to fly out to help and I said I'd try to get a cheap flight. In those days the only way to get a cheap flight was through a 'bucket shop', a sort of semi-legal arrangement. With some trepidation, I climbed up to a seedy attic somewhere in a back street in the West End of London. The man agreed to the transaction, provided he accompanied me to the bank to get the money.

With Tessa at boarding school, I was alone for much of the time, writing dialogues and poetry and reassessing my life. I was quite overcome by the warm welcome from the congregation of St John the Baptist, and with my new friends I celebrated my fiftieth birthday in the big house. We rolled up the carpet and danced 'Sir Roger de Coverley' and 'Strip the Willow'. Of all my birthday parties, that was by far the most enjoyable, probably because I was free to do exactly what I wanted. Other major birthdays have been arranged to fit in with members of the family. As for my Christian faith, it had been blown apart, but thanks to the vicar, Paul Lucas, it was gradually being re-formed.

I joined an Ecumenical Order that gave me just what I needed; the chance to toss around radical ideas; ask awkward questions; study church history with experts, and in general explore faith without being labelled a heretic. A journey of faith is bound to be very individual, and I have been really fortunate in being able to continue the pilgrimage under several vicars and with fellow Christians, in an ecumenical context. It seems strange that, with each of us having a unique personality and life experience, some Christians should expect 'one size fits all' with regard to faith. I also think it's incredibly arrogant for any religion to proclaim that it has a monopoly of spiritual truth. Now I am enjoying stimulating ideas from Richard Rohr and Rupert Sheldrake.

I needed a job, but at the time teaching jobs were ring-fenced for locals, so I answered an advert for a scout for a publishing firm. I tripped along corridors of colleges and universities, armed with optimism and a briefcase, but the job turned out to be hopeless. The firm was Maxwell, and the name Pergamon was anathema to academics. I did meet Maxwell once. He sat at the head of the table at a meeting in Bath – a huge dominating presence with dark bushy eyebrows and piercing eyes. No wonder few people were able to stand up to him.

After various temporary and part-time teaching jobs, I worked as assistant to a dental technician. It was while driving back from Frome one summer afternoon, after delivering dentures to a surgery, that I witnessed a fatal car crash and learned some strange truths about memory. One was that I remembered everything in slow motion; the other was that, although the window was down, I had no memory of noise. I assume that, with so much visual stimulation, there was no room in the brain for registering noise. The police said afterwards that these phenomena were quite common.

Batheaston is a large, interesting, old village. The opening and closing of the gate onto Solsbury Hill is a remnant of the old Celtic year, and there are still Commoners who have ancient grazing rights. Among comparative newcomers were Elizabeth and Leslie Hilliard, retired doctors who lived next door to me in a beautiful Queen Anne house. They had no family and were using their wealth to encourage cultural restoration schemes in Bath. After restoring Beckford's Tower, they acquired a house in New King Street, supposedly once occupied by William Herschel. They asked me to be secretary to their newly formed Herschel Society. The plan was to restore the house and create a Herschel Museum. Committee meetings could be fraught, with Elizabeth gently calming Leslie down as he became impatient with the lack of support, but it was a joy to be working with Michael Tabb, James Elliott and Frank Brown, the advisors, respectively, in astronomy, historic renovation and music. Eventually, with the help of the Greenwich Maritime Museum, the project succeeded, and now the museum attracts visitors from all over the world.

Frank became a special friend, and through the university concerts that he organised, I was able to meet and talk with several classical musicians, and hear something of their ordinary lives. One evening, we helped carry a square piano out from Longleat where Melvyn Tan had been giving a charity concert. He told us what a difference it made to musicians having people in the audience who actually appreciated the music. Frank and I also had fun dressing up and dancing at various fêtes champêtres in and around Bath. For one of them, I cobbled together a mock-Georgian dress from bits of material left from Cousin Freda. It included a beautiful embroidered panel of ivory silk, probably from her Presentation dress. After much happy dancing, I realised the dress was beginning to come apart. Luckily it just held together until the end. Much as I loved Frank, I knew instinctively that marriage would be a disaster, but trying to explain this positively was difficult, and I know that, without wanting to, I managed to hurt him deeply. How does one cope with a deep friendship between a man and a woman, each unencumbered, when the expectations are different?

There were other dancing opportunities; one was Scottish country dancing, where we took turns in choosing and leading the weekly programme and ended the year with a ball in the Guildhall with a live band. The other was a Liturgical dance group. We danced in churches for special occasions, the highlight being the story of Philip and the Ethiopian eunuch which we performed in Wells Cathedral. I don't suppose the congregation enjoyed it much, but for me it was a truly moving experience. Then we were asked to do a peace dance outside Bath Abbey. How to dance peace? We sat thinking for a long time before realising that for peace to have meaning, we needed first to dance conflict, and then peace through reconciliation. The conflict (to music by Bartok) was exhausting, involving masks and vigorous movement, but we had learned something important about peace.

When money ran out, I moved to a cottage with plenty of period charm but some strange decoration. The main bedroom was entirely painted black, with spotlights trained on the bed. That, together with the darkroom downstairs, invited some interesting speculations! Stan Rhymes, the village furniture remover, was quite used to hauling furniture through an upstairs window where the cottage stairs made that necessary. He was helped by his brother Ken, a true eccentric, who was only too happy to stop and discuss anything and everything when you met him in the street. The village has become so sanitised and suburbanised now that much of its ancient character has been erased. Has the same happened to the inhabitants? Are there any happy eccentrics left, I wonder.

I was seriously worried when John wrote that he might apply for a job in Bristol. He was able to create a sort of charismatic aura around himself, and I needed to keep well away. Luckily, the job didn't materialise. Meanwhile, I was enjoying a vigorous social life. As well as my friendship with Frank, several widowers emerged from the shadows. All this sudden attention was almost intoxicating, and I was probably not paying enough attention to being a mother. Then a clearer future opened up when I fell in love with Bertram, and we married a few years later.

Chapter 13 – Second Marriage

Looking back, I can identify factors that helped make our marriage so happy. Apart from the love and respect we had for each other, we were not marrying out of need. We had each been managing on our own for some years; there was no question of domination either, and our finances were shared equally. When he first proposed, I said it was too soon after his wife had died, and that I still had family at home. His old-fashioned response was to go to Florence for some months, studying art history and Italian. We kept up regular correspondence and our friendship continued to flourish.

A friend of Bertram's had warned him, "She has four unmarried daughters," but of course I would never have expected him to pay for any weddings. When they did materialise, they were all very different. We had all-age dancing in Edinburgh, vegetarian cuisine at the Isle of Dogs Yacht Club (before Canary Wharf was built), and a ceremony on Raven's Ait, an island in the Thames near Hampton Court. This was especially exotic, as the bridegroom was ethnically Indian, and the mass of colourful saris, embroidered with gold and silver, made the British look positively drab. Finding a wedding dress for the bride had been somewhat challenging though, as she had only arrived back in Britain a short time before, and was breast-feeding her baby son.

James's wedding to Christina in Kavala, in northern Greece, was a totally new experience. It seemed as though the whole town had crowded into the church, and I had to fight my way to the front for the elaborate rituals. These were punctuated by glimpses of an orange T-shirt, as the photographer crept around making the video. Outside I had prepared a Greek phrase for the handshaking, but was often greeted in English, so in the end I just produced my best smile. Huge numbers sat down to the meal in the hotel, but when the band struck up, the men left their food to dance. Imagine that happening in England!

I knew little of Greek culture, but had asked James whether special gifts to the bride were expected from the bridegroom's family and it turned out that that was indeed the case. He took me took to the shop where Christina had already chosen appropriate jewellery. Luckily gold seemed far less expensive in Greece than in Britain, and I was relieved to have done the right thing. We also arrived very much in family mode, which I think pleased Christina's friends and family. Beside Eleanor, who was seven, and acted as flower girl, we had a four-year-old, two toddlers, a baby and a pregnant mother. The baby turned out to be the subject of several informal domestic rituals, in which she appeared completely unfazed and behaved impeccably.

Apart from everything else, Bertram proved a delightful travelling companion. We drove to Chinon, where Joan of Arc visited the Dauphin; to Vienna, finding houses connected with Brahms, Schubert and Beethoven; to Lisieux, to pay homage to St Theresa, and to Nantes where Bertram's ancestor had played the organ in the cathedral. As a driver, my most terrifying moment was in Switzerland, on a narrow road with a cliff on one side and a ravine on the other. Luckily nothing was coming towards us. Many of our visits to France coincided with Bastille Day, which was always fun; the mayor, bristling with medals, proudly leading the local band through the street. In a village by the Dordogne, we were invited to the street party supper, sitting on benches, followed by fireworks from the bridge. In Dinard, the fireworks were answered by those from St Malo across the river Rance.

Egypt just took my breath away. My sketchy grasp of history had to go back more than a thousand years. Did the Greeks get their inspiration for temples from Egypt? Our hotel was near enough for me to walk up to the Great Pyramid in the cool of the evening, when the crowds had gone. I was alone, apart from a man on a horse. I felt the truth of the saying 'All time is equidistant from eternity.' After Luxor and the Valley of the Kings, we sailed up river to Aswan. The water level at Lake Nasser had receded so far that the local guide told us, "If we have no rain in the next two years, Egypt dies."

The last few days were spent at the Red Sea, then only an embryo resort. There were as yet no hotels. We slept in little concrete huts, with larger huts as restaurants. Colourful fish were visible from the shore, and I regretted not having gone out in a glass-bottomed boat. Running barefoot along the sand, I did find bits of coral, at the same time suffering sunburn on the tops of my feet. I had been apprehensive of the heat, but, by covering up, found it easily bearable. Many of the British were badly sunburned.

As a Christian, Israel had extra relevance for me, but I was glad we had an Israeli, rather than a Christian, guide. On a grassy hill looking down to the Sea of Galilee, I was much happier standing quietly by a thorn tree, than singing hymns in the Chapel of the Beatitudes. Again, by the Garden Tomb, which seems the most likely place for the actual tomb, the beautiful silence was destroyed by the arrival of a group of hymn-singing Christians. I love singing hymns, but there are times when, for me, silence allows a deeper spiritual experience. We walked down from the Mount of Olives past Gethsemane and over the Kidron brook, and I picked up a piece of bark from a very old olive tree. Could it have been two thousand years old? Watching Orthodox Jews praying at the Western Wall, I wrote a prayer and pushed it into a crack.

A different memorable experience was the Dead Sea. I felt I had to bathe, but kept a tight grasp of the fence as I was terrified of 'turning turtle' with the extra buoyancy. It was spring, there had been snow that winter, and long dormant seeds were just starting to flower. Coachloads of Israelis were arriving to see the miracle of the desert blooming. We visited Masada, and I picked up tiny fragments of pottery as reminders of its tragic history. The airport was the only place in Israel where I felt threatened, and I'm glad we went in 1992 before the West Bank Barrier was created.

In the autumn of 1989, we experienced something of the Iron Curtain. As we sailed into the Baltic at Travemünde, people were bathing on the left bank while the right bank was covered in barbed wire, with a guard in a watch tower. A helicopter hovered above as we sailed east, with a Soviet warship shadowing us, and when we docked in Leningrad an armed guard sat at the foot of the gangplank. Fourteen years later, as we sailed into what was now St Petersburg, we were welcomed at the dockside by a band.

I was overwhelmed by the Mosque in Cordoba, as surely everyone must be, and with the Christian cathedral inside. Christians, Jews and Muslims, it seems, managed to live in Spain reasonably amicably until Ferdinand and Isabella started their vicious expulsions. I enjoyed Cadiz and Seville, but I found the performance of the white stallions disturbing. Is it right to force these magnificent horses to behave in unnatural ways for the amusement of people?

Bertram's age did provide some scary moments. One was in the Alhambra in Granada, when he was taken ill and the tour party had moved on to the next part of the palace. I gave him water and an aspirin, and tried to find help. I didn't speak Spanish and couldn't explain the problem, and it felt like hours before our leader appeared and helped Bertram back to the bus. I now keep an emergency aspirin in my handbag, in case of possible heart attacks.

Bertram and I shared a love of opera. At the Bristol Hippodrome we joined local enthusiastic followers of the Welsh National as it progressed into world status, nurturing many young singers on the way. Audiences at Bristol were true lovers of opera, although there were some productions we didn't like. The chorus in Fidelio dressed as terrorists (freedom fighters?) and a Carmen who couldn't dance, were received less enthusiastically. We had opera holidays in Wexford, Prague, Warsaw and Krakov, and an outdoor performance of Mozart's 'Seraglio' outside the Topkapi Palace in Istanbul, probably very near the old harem. By far the most memorable was Verona. I had been suffering from the heat during sight-seeing, and then in the evening, as we watched the sun go down behind the Arena wall opposite, I could start to enjoy myself. From high up on the stone seats we scrutinised the fashionable 'glitterati' in the centre, and watched the company gathering behind stage, preparing for the Grand March in Aida. No elephants, but a wonderful assortment of acrobats and tumblers. Apparently some famous singers, including Pavarotti, couldn't be heard properly in the Verona Amphitheatre, but there was no difficulty with Placido Domingo, who's long been one of my favourite opera singers. On the second evening, there was a frightening reminder of the Roman origins of the Amphitheatre, when someone tried to grab our tickets.

As Bertram got older, cruises became more appropriate and he coped with storms much better than I did. The worst storm was in the Bay of Biscay, after which some passengers left the ship at Lisbon and flew home. The crew left sandwiches on the floor of the cabin, and I found if I took pills, and kept horizontal, I could avoid seasickness. At one Sunday morning service we sang 'Eternal Father strong to save', with the piano firmly battened down. We once raced along the Mediterranean due to a medical emergency, and on another occasion made an unexpected visit to Stornoway owing to a storm on the way to Iceland. We encountered a family of orcas off Tobermory, and the captain allowed the ship to circle round so that we could see more of them. They appeared as interested in us as we were in them.

Fellow diners on cruises were usually pleasant enough, but two were memorable. One insisted that we sat in the same places at the table each night. If I hadn't been sorry for him I would have objected, but I realised later how lonely and isolated he was. The other was a loud-mouthed businessman for whom, it became clear, bribery was a necessary procedure. I was far too scared to challenge him. Our last cruise was at Christmas 2004, but only when we got home did we realise the full horror of the tsunami.

Bertram was very loyal to his friends, and must have felt some obligation to befriend Bunny, whom he'd known from childhood. Meeting someone with an attitude to truth only loosely connected to fact was a new experience for me, but I had to admire his brazenness when he took ten years off his age to get a job packaging shoes in Oxford Street. I was mystified as to why he had invited us to meet someone at lunch. Was he perhaps hoping to marry this German woman? I found her quite terrifying, and it seemed obvious that when she realised Bunny had no money, she would have nothing more to do with him. He seemed to live in a fantasy world.

The bungalow garden gave much scope for creativity. I encouraged self-seeding flowers like aquilegias and love-in-a-mist, at the same time running an all-out war with bindweed. Using Bertram's engineering expertise, we built a pergola which broke all pergola rules by going downhill and curving at the end. For me it gave coherence to the space and added to the interest of our guests at summer lunch parties.

One day, a strange wild woman harangued me from the garden gate. I discovered that she spent time concocting unusual herbal remedies and was to be treated kindly, at the same time avoiding her recommendations. In medieval times she would no doubt have been labelled a witch.

Another colourful character was Mrs Winchester, who lived in a cottage across the footpath from the back gate. Never one to miss a bargain, she would buy paperback books from our church fête, put them in her trolley, and sell them in Bath at a profit. She once 'escaped' from a local care home because "there was no-one to talk to." She was a good actress too. Normally a brisk walker, when she recognised me coming towards her on the pavement, she immediately turned into a poor old woman. When she died, it seemed as though a whole era had died with her.

Chapter 14 – USA and Other Experiences

When I saw in a magazine the photo of Crater Lake in Oregon, I knew I had to see it, and in 1993 the opportunity arrived. Rachel and Ravi, on a round the world adventure, asked me to join them in California. We drove north from San Francisco, and then up through the forest to the lake. Strong sunshine and midsummer snow intensified the whole experience, and a chipmunk joined us as we gazed out on the water. No wonder it was a secret, sacred place for the indigenous people.

We drove down the coast to California, past Coos Bay, where ghostly figures of brown pelicans flying north at dusk seemed like creatures of another world. Inland we explored the giants of the redwood forests, then drove further south to Monterey. A magic moment one evening was at the end of the pier at Pigeon Point. A sea otter was having its supper. After diving for fish, it lay on its back, fish between paws, munching. Seagulls hovered around waiting for scraps.

Of course, I fell in love with San Francisco and the Golden Gate Bridge, and I could even see the bridge from the window of my youth hostel dormitory. I was somewhat taken aback at the communal showers, my middle-aged body contrasting sadly with the lithe elegance of my fellow hostellers. On a happier note, Rachel and I found ourselves in Grace Cathedral. A blue and white circular labyrinth was laid out on the floor, and a young woman was playing a cello. We took off our shoes and joined the meditative walk.

Some years later I revisited the cathedral. The labyrinth had now been engraved in stone, but the magic was gone. Is it a mistake to revisit a place with special memories? Do different visions cause confusion? For me, the earlier memory is usually the stronger.

We stayed a few nights in the tented village of Yosemite. Everything had to be bear-proof, with strict instructions about food. Apparently a bear can smell food from half a mile away. Rachel and Ravi did some climbing, while I met a gorgeous, turquoise-coloured lizard on a rock. We stared at each other for several minutes.

Years later, I got to know other parts of California. Portola is in the northern hills, full of lakes and forests, where the snow can still be deep in midsummer. The railway snakes down the valley to Sacramento, a beautiful city, the capital of the state and home of the Railway Museum. Remnants of history were all around: the Gold Rush, and the trials and deaths of those crossing the Sierra Nevada, and the builders of the railway. I'd flown to Reno via Chicago. Looking down from the plane window, I could identify rivers and railroads, and then a bright, fuchsia-coloured blob appeared. After a few minutes, trying to visualise a map of the States, I realised it must have been the Salt Lake. The chemicals, from six miles up, had produced that stunning effect.

A few years later, I joined Tessa and the family again for a week in Yellowstone. I changed planes in Minneapolis, meeting the family at Bozeman, a tiny airport in the Rockies, where I was greeted with an open fire and carpet on the floor. Families from all over the States were meeting up in the warm, friendly atmosphere. I was relieved to have arrived at all, having flown through a thunderstorm, with lightning shooting past the plane (the next flight was cancelled).

It was the time when George W. Bush was trying for re-election, and I had to be careful in breakfast conversations in the hotel. One woman was quite openly relaying some of the iniquities of the regime, whilst on another morning I had to watch my words with a couple who I sensed were Republican. I found Yellowstone thrilling, and the children, although young, thoroughly enjoyed it all. The boys were delighted when my hat blew off and landed on the hot ground by Old Faithful, and so couldn't be retrieved.

We didn't encounter any bears, but managed to get close to bison and elk, and one evening spotted a coyote slinking into the wood at dusk. Laid-back motorcyclists rode jauntily by, their long hair trailing in the wind (helmets were not compulsory in Montana). We then drove south to Jackson, and I had my first sight of paragliders, running to the edge of the cliff before taking off. We crossed the Great Divide where it zigzags across Montana. More recently, I crossed it again in Colorado. Something about rivers starting so close but running in opposite directions intrigues me. Closer to home and on a smaller scale, we have the Tweed and the Clyde rising near each other, but flowing respectively east and west.

A year after Bertram died, and I had downsized to a flat, I decided to visit the States again, this time on a coast-to-coast holiday by rail. Near Ground Zero, St Paul's Church (where George Washington had worshipped) was especially moving as it was also where 9/11 rescuers rested between shifts.

There was a powerful atmosphere too in the Native American Museum at Washington DC, where three-dimensional displays led the imagination into mourning for a lost culture. In Chicago we were shown bullet holes from gang shootings but, as so often, it was a discovery I made by accident that was particularly memorable. Lining a tunnel was a set of huge tile pictures relating the dramas of Chicago's history, including, of course, the Great Fire.

I'd had a bad moment the previous evening, when the rest of the party had disappeared after the boat trip. I was cold and hungry, and the prospect of food seemed remote. I did find a bar eventually, but it taught me a lesson: now I choose holidays where the evening meal is easy to find.

In Denver, Colorado, my bathroom had a very long worktop. The hotel had been the headquarters of the Bunny Girls, and my bathroom had presumably been where they applied their make-up (and bunny attire?). I loved Denver, and made use of the free bus service that ran up and down the main street. On a coach tour into the Rockies, we were told at a 'photo-stop' that the road ahead would be closed for the winter (it was October 20th), but then a message came through that the pass was open, and we drove high into the mountains, passing a snowplough at the top.

In the Grand Canyon I decided to brave the Pink Jeep tour, where we were driven at alarming angles around the floor of the Canyon. In Los Angeles there was, for me, something disappointingly 'tacky' about the Hollywood area. The staircase leading up to the hall for the Oscars had a tired look, despite the glitzy edges to the risers. The whole place just breathed artificiality. The best part of LA was a night on the Queen Mary, and being invited to dinner at the Winston Churchill Restaurant. It was a very good dinner. Among many intriguing features of the ship was the pink-tinted mirrors in the main saloon. Many passengers used to get sea-sick, and their complexions looked less alarming in the tinted mirrors.

On the Amtrak double-decker trains, bunks were orientated along rather than across the carriage, and I could watch the moon and stars moving as the train turned. The tiny spiral staircase down to the bathroom had to be negotiated carefully, and I was glad to have the cabin to myself as sharing such a small space must have been difficult. We moved relatively slowly, and were amused when a voice warned us to take care as the train might reach 70 mph. Goods trains took precedence, and once we waited for 112 wagons to pass. When the holiday was over, Tessa collected me from San Francisco and I spent a week with the family in Davis. The railroad goes through the town, and from the house I could hear the haunting Amtrak hoot, bringing back memories of my epic journey.

When James was appointed Director of the British School in Athens, I was able to visit their beautiful house and garden, and to take advantage of Athens's new Metro, built for the 2004 Olympics. I spent a day wandering around the Greek and Roman agorae, every now and then looking up the hill to the Parthenon. I was there for the baptism of my youngest granddaughter who, at eighteen months, did not appreciate the litre of olive oil poured over her by the

Orthodox priest. Anglican baptisms seem very tame in comparison.

More recently, while in Crete, I had a near-death experience. Apparently, as my body was 'shutting down', I told the tour manager that I'd had a wonderful dream. Annoyingly, I can't remember it at all, but my interpretation is of some kind of message, 'Not yet Jane. More work to be done.' Now, like others who have had similar experiences, the fear of death has lost some of its hold. I had been saved by the cleaner. That morning, she had decided to start from the other end of the corridor, and so reached my room earlier. Was this really just a coincidence? I don't speak Greek, and she had no English, but on the last morning we said goodbye with a tearful hug and I was able to give her a small present. Back in the UK, my daughter remarked that I seemed to be in a euphoric state.

After the death of one of our churchwardens, I volunteered as emergency warden in St John's and remained in office for four years. A hectic time soon arrived when our vicar Alison left to try her vocation in a Benedictine monastery. Known as a 'vacancy' in a parish, the churchwardens are faced with many responsibilities, of which mine was finding a priest for each Sunday.

I arrived early in church one November morning after a deep snowstorm, and was mopping up a puddle when various messages arrived. First, the priest couldn't come because the road was blocked; secondly, Pam, who acts as sacristan, was snowed up in her farmhouse. What to do? We were saved by Bill, a retired priest who had come just to worship, and who cheerfully stepped into the breach. Sometimes, it seems, angels do arrive when needed.

Weddings and funerals can also bring anxieties. One bride was very late because the button hook for the dress was lost, another because the stretch limo was unable to make the sharp turn into Northend. At one winter funeral, I turned off the heating when it seemed near the end of the service, only to hear the minister talk for another twenty minutes. There were churchyard complications over burials of ashes, and I became confused with three widows with the same surname. Much as I enjoyed having influence in the life of the church, it was a relief to be free of the responsibility. How much, though, do I really want to be free from obligations? Not too much. I think it was Plato who implied that one needed the balance between too much and too little challenge in life.

It's been with members of the family that I've relished annual visits to North Cornwall over more than fourteen years. We fell in love with Port Gaverne; watched guillemots and razorbills, like miniature penguins, assembled on the cliff before flying south; picnicked on beaches; tackled various bits of the Coastal Path and on occasions watched filming of *Doc Martin*. One memorable year, about sixty basking sharks arrived in the bay.

Much as I love the sea, I am fully aware of its dangers. One summer, we had real anxieties when one of the family swam out on a fast-receding tide and disappeared round the corner of the cliff. All was well in the end, but I shall never forget agonising minutes and trying to decide whether to call the coastguard. On another occasion, near midnight, when Bertram needed medical help, I sat by the sea waiting for the ambulance and the only noise was water gently lapping on the stones.

For a long time, I'd been wanting to cruise down the Danube; that dream came true in 2015, starting at Budapest and visiting seven countries. I learned so much about both the history and the present situation of the Balkans. The word 'liberation' often meant nineteenth century liberation from the Turks, rather than a more recent liberation. Local guides in Croatia and Serbia were passionate about their countries, honest about present difficulties, and desperately keen that we should not write them off as failed states. One said, "We don't need money, we need good leaders." When we reached the mouth of the river, weather conditions allowed us to enter the Black Sea where we turned round, watched by white pelicans standing on the sandbank.

Two years later, sailing up the Elbe, the special highlight was Wittenberg and all things related to Luther. On the last day I had a truly anxious hour in Prague with a fellow passenger, trying to find our way back to the bus. After several wrong turns we found ourselves back in the main square, and I began to think we really might miss the bus altogether. It's still a very painful memory.

I think now it is time for me to explore more of Britain, even though I already live in beautiful surroundings. There's always something to look out for along the river or canal. I've watched a kingfisher repeatedly dive for fish, disappearing into the bank to feed the family. I've seen the water ripple and fizz with the hatching out of fish, and in the spring, families of ducks and goslings. A highlight last year was on the Isle of Arran, watching a seal engaging in yoga-like exercises on a rock.

Looking back, my life has been enhanced by much good fortune. Anxieties and heartbreaks, yes, but good health, supportive friends, and a wonderfully loving family. The future of the planet now lies in the hands of my grandchildren and their generation, and I pray that they may have the wisdom, generosity and determination to save the world. May their lives, too, be full of joy.

Cork
1916

Kieran McCarthy
& Suzanne Kirwan

Cork
1916

A Year Examined

The
History
Press
Ireland

Dedicated to our forebears who have
paved the roads we now travel upon

First published 2016

The History Press Ireland
50 City Quay
Dublin 2
Ireland
www.thehistorypress.ie

The History Press Ireland is a member of Publishing Ireland,
the Irish book publishers' association.

© Kieran McCarthy & Suzanne Kirwan, 2016

The right of Kieran McCarthy & Suzanne Kirwan to be identified as
the Authors of this work has been asserted in accordance with the
Copyright, Designs and Patents Act 1988.

British Library Cataloguing in Publication Data.
A catalogue record for this book is available from the British Library.

ISBN 978 1 84588 245 7

Typesetting and origination by The History Press
Printed and bound by TJ International Ltd, Padstow, Cornwall

Contents

ACKNOWLEDGMENTS

We would like thank Beth Amphlett at History Press Ireland for her advice, experience and vision to publish this book; we would also like to thank Tim Vaughan, editor of the *Irish Examiner* for his support with copyright and heading up a newspaper with linage of progressive journalism going back 175 years. We would also like to acknowledge the contribution of our friends, Mairéad Mooney, Seán Kelly, Cathal Ryder O'Donovan, Mags Horan Gould.

St Patrick's Street, *c.*1910.

INTRODUCTION: THE STORM OF EMPIRE

T he year 1916 is viewed as a seminal year in Irish history. The Easter Rising and subsequent historical reckonings are pitched as the baseline from which modern Irish society emerged – they are forever etched into the Irish historical consciousness by various sources – government, institutions and civil society. For a whole array of purposes, the events of that year have been constructed and re-constructed, imagined and re-imagined time and again since the foundation of the state.

For a century, the stories of the Easter Rising and the Irish Citizen Army have morphed into powerful national metaphors for Irish identity. The events are written and spoken about in almost mythic terms, defined and re-defined, distilled and re-distilled into key events and moments in the Easter period of 1916 and onwards into subsequent years – the Rising, the Volunteers, the reading of the proclamation, the Irish Citizen Army, the standing down of those ready to fight outside of Dublin, the role of the GPO and its shelling by British forces,

the surrender, the executed leaders, the questions of clemency, the internment camps, the beginning of the War of Independence, the quest for sovereignty and democracy, the role of objects of nostalgic currency such as participation medals, copies of the actual proclamation, the Citizen Army flag, letters and documentation. These and much more are all aspects stitched into a national history framework – a cultural consciousness – a continuous conversation about Irish heritage by successful Irish governments and by civil society on what the building blocks of a national nostalgic and a national collective memory should be and their meaning, relevancy, value and connection to today's world.

This book, made up of extracts from the *Cork Examiner*, shows that there were in fact multiple conversations to be heard during the year 1916, a kaleidoscope of ideas which provided the context and framework for revolution – everyday life being one; some led Cork citizens to connect with the Republican mantra at the time and others to just survive and struggle with

Cork Docks, *c.* 1910. (SOURCE: KIERAN MCCARTHY)

the bleakness of a national and local economy. Entering the *Cork Examiner* on 1 January and progressing page by page one discovers key nuggets about the nature of Cork society, the soul of Ireland's southern capital, the ongoing conversations about maintaining a contemporary status of being one of Ireland's distinguished port cities, and all the advantages and problems that run with that.

This book includes a cross section of the more important themes that emerged during the year and many of the articles we have chosen will resonate with the contemporary public and themes within the media today. The articles are reproduced verbatim and we have not edited the trains of thought within paragraphs. However, due to space constraints we have not published full editorials.

The *Cork Examiner* on 1 August 1916 celebrated its 75th anniversary and a proud tradition of 'influencing public opinion' and offering 'fairness', as they noted in their editorial on the day. As a newspaper it was an active driver in the control of media, place and even time. In 1916 and in general the *Cork Examiner*, which appeared six days a week, was structured into eight pages. There were two pages of advertisements, two pages of local and national news, two pages on the war and two pages on regional/southern Ireland news, from issues from Dungarvan to Cahersiveen.

Censorship was in operation and was defined by Westminster's Defence Against the Realm Act. Indeed, it is only when this Act is written about that the Volunteers in Cork under Tómás McCurtain are spoken about, the miscommunication in keeping Cork Volunteers in Cork during Easter Week 1916 and the scale of such structures such as the internment camps. The output of the newspaper is biased. However, it is very interesting to explore the knock-on effect of what became public news and what did not but lingered in personal archives in correspondence between volunteer leaders and soldiers. How does one interpret what was meant for the public realm or not? Whose story and history is it? Hence, it is difficult to realise how much was given by Westminster to the press to publish. Therefore questions need to be asked of the press coverage: what is real and what is not real, true, half true or false? Can news stories be taken at face value or not?

Throughout the year, you can sense the swirl of power – the grasp of political power influencing the media, the imperial structures such as Westminster showing a way and providing the role of a mother figure of sorts, the press from Westminster holding it all together – creating a vision of what it should be under Prime Minister Asquith. There was a continuous need to discuss why Ireland was important in the empire – on the front lines of the war and in economic output – and that the Irish citizen need not feel disconnected from the imperial society. There was the continuous pitch that Home Rule was on its way soon. But, even physically time was behind – twenty minutes behind Greenwich and it is a debate, which occurs several

Cork Harbour from Queenstown, present-day Cobh, c. 1910. (SOURCE: KIERAN MCCARTHY)

times throughout the year, until the twenty-five minutes is given over to Ireland in a Daylight Saving Act.

Throughout the year, pages and pages of writing and pictures are given over to the adventures and tragedies of the First World War. There are local Cork people shown in family photographs bound for the front line and provocative pictures of the front lines themselves, complete with descriptions of desolation and in-depth geographical detail of hills, valleys and rivers from France to Denmark. Views of the trenches, thousands of miles of scarred landscapes, blown up cities, collapsed road networks, burnt-out homes, death at every corner – such images echo throughout the newspaper of 1916 and beyond. The trenches are almost metaphors for the entrenched European society of the day – the Allies and enemy not backing down – who will conquer? 'Any day now it will end' – such remarks in editorials continuously work into the consciousness of the reader. Socially a European cultural identity infused society, which begs the question, whose culture was at risk? European? English? British and Irish? John Redmond's Home Rule Strategy versus Edward Carson's Unionist? The political chessboard is active throughout the year with different perspectives and holding onto power. Physically European culture grasped Cork Harbour and

the Irish Sea as they became part of the battlefields of the seas and the fight for the Atlantic and North Sea. The torpedoed *Lusitania* of 1915 and the scuttled ship the *Aud* of 1916 haunted such maritime spaces – the presence of the other, the unknown enemy, in a submarine waiting to take its chance and maim, sitting there on the ocean bed.

The daily published lists of deaths and the honours bestowed on participants glorify and construct a raison d'être for being on the front line. The naming of dead Corkmen and the families they left behind – the quests by the soul of city to be part of it – whether it was through the thousands of tons of Lambkins tobacco sent to the front line, to the picture shows of the war in the Palace Theatre and Cork Opera House – or even the regular flag days in support of the Red Cross and the Munster Fusiliers. Then there were the conversations throughout the year about attaining a munitions factory for Cork – the empty shells almost standing in as metaphors for the empty promises of waiting for it – to provide jobs for those who did not go to fight on the masculine territory of the front line. The role of equality amongst the sexes features prominently – the men who have gone off to fight in the war versus the women in Cork who have stayed to put weaponry together, fund raise, volunteer at the Red Cross, engage in the quest for women's votes, and in campaigning for women's places such as junior doctors in Cork hospitals – these are also discussion points as the year progresses.

Despite the rationing of food and materials, the pulses of society in Cork retained it as an ambitious place. By the early twentieth century, the population of the city was 75,000 – the middle-classes living in the expanding suburbs whilst the majority, the working classes, lived in slum conditions. Unemployment and emigration were high. Unemployment, requests for wage increases, union interventions, the role of employers and the needs of ratepayers reverberate in the pages throughout the year. The debates of the Cork Industrial Association pops up in discourse throughout the pages of the paper, their efforts culminating in the large-scale announcement of Ford Tractor and Car manufacturing coming to Cork in 1917. The Cork Harbour Board revelled in this announcement as well as plans for the physical rejuvenation of its quays. Another artery of the city was its train network travelling into County Cork. One can read about the benefits of such lines as the Cork Bandon and South Coast Railway, the Cork Muskerry Tram and the Cork Blackrock and Passage Railway Line connecting people, animals, fisheries and places from the coast and hinterland to the city and vice-verse – igniting the region and

St Patrick's Bridge, *c.* 1910. (SOURCE: KIERAN MCCARTHY)

View of Cork from the west, *c.* 1910. (SOURCE: KIERAN MCCARTHY)

city into one. The same direction was pushed by the Munster Agricultural Society – whose aims consistently led to discussions on the role of land, cattle, the prices of Ireland's traditions and industries – exports destinations, and ultimately the intertwinement into the British Empire.

The city's institutions such as its hospitals – Mercy Hospital, South and North Infirmary, and institutions such as the city and county gaols, the Magdalene Asylum, the Sailors' Home as well the city's workhouse or Cork Union record the need to address the needs of society and to provide more financial aid and food to citizens immersed in large-scale poverty.

The other pillars of Cork society were its educational ones – the core schools that appear are the North Monastery, the South Presentation Convent, Crawford Municipal Technical Institute and the Cork School of Commerce. All continue through the press to showcase the importance of education and life-long learning in escaping from poverty traps in the city's vast slum network, and to help the overall societal pull to a better life.

The role of the Catholic Church in society is ever felt – the refusals to leave cinemas open for business on a Sunday, the role of public professions of faith in galvanising public expressions of religion through events such as the confraternities and Corpus Christi, are written about in depth. The death of Bishop O'Callaghan ended another chapter in the city's religious life and opened a new one on the rise of Bishop Cohalan and his take on non-violence and faith-based community approaches.

The public representation by city councillors and Lord Mayor Butterfield on municipal issues from the provision of social housing to park provision is enormous – there is the role of escapism in the programmes of Cork Opera House, the Palace Theatre – and even in Cork Park Racecourse – as horses galloped across its mud-soaked landscape. GAA matches, athletics, handball, cricket are all recorded in depth in the Monday edition.

What we have attempted to create with this book is to construct a sounding board of sorts for all the voices and ideas about Cork and its role in the seminal year of 1916. There are voices on the role of the ambitious city in Ireland and further afield to questions of poverty that have never been completely solved or overly discussed. Many of the topics – housing, fair wage, political partnerships – still rage across our newspapers. There is much to learn from this time – not just on the political side but that life itself in any city keeps moving and that society needs to grow and evolve with it – and that even from a dark time in Ireland's past, there is much to learn about the diverse framework of historical events and how they shape ourselves and our future.

Kieran McCarthy and Suzanne Kirwan

JANUARY

1 January

A CORK KNIGHTHOOD

The Lord Mayor of Cork [Alderman Henry O'Shea], who has just received a knighthood, will have the hearty congratulations of his fellow-citizens on the honour that has been conferred upon him. During all the years that he has been in public life, Sir Henry O'Shea, as he now is, worked whole-heartedly for the welfare of his country first and next for the city where he is so deservedly esteemed by all classes. During the unusually extended period for which his fellow-members of the Corporation elected him to preside over their deliberations and represent the city on all official occasions, he always upheld the dignity of the ancient city of Cork, of which he is so proud. It will be recalled that notwithstanding the very many demands on his time, he never failed to represent the citizens at any of the great public demonstrations that were held in the cause of Home Rule. He had the honour of seconding the resolution proposed by Mr Redmond.

Adopting the Home Rule Bill, at a National Convention held in Dublin, he took a prominent part in the movement to have Queenstown continued as a port of call for American liners, and went, at considerable inconvenience, on more than one deputation to London, in connection with that question. He hospitably entertained the several distinguished persons who visited Cork during his term of office as Lord Mayor of his readiness to support any charitable or philanthropic movement in the city there is no need to refer, except to say that amongst his other qualities will account in no small measure for the pleasure with which the announcement of his knighthood will be received by the citizens of all classes.

THE NEW YEAR'S STORM

Some of the passengers who were on the train walked into the city from Victoria Cross, while others availed of the electric tram service. The tree in falling broke the telegraph and telephone wires, so that communication in that direction was interrupted. Some trees were blown down in the direction of Douglas, Blackrock and Ballintemple. The city tram service was interrupted for some time during the earlier part of the morning, but the breakdown was set right in a short time and the normal service resumed.

The trains on the various railway systems into Cork arrived in fairly good time, except the Rosslare express, which did not reach Cork until near 2 o'clock.

No definite information could be obtained as to the cause of the delay of the Rosslare train, which was due to reach Cork at 10.15, but it was stated that some trees had fallen across the line in the vicinity of Fermoy. Telephonic communication with the latter station was interrupted. When the train arrived it was ascertained that the delay was occasioned by the rough weather, which delayed the cross-channel steamer and that the train was delayed by trees blown across the line.

Cork Tram, *c.* 1910. (SOURCE: CORK CITY MUSEUM)

About 12 o'clock a portion of a house including the chimney stack fell across Dunbar Street, the slates falling into Margaret Street. No one was hurt by the accident but a number of people going to 12 o'clock mass at St. Finbarr's Parish Church, had narrow escapes from the falling debris. The police were promptly on the scene, and reported the matter to the City Engineer through the Fire Station, Sullivan's Quay. Mr Twomey, of the Engineers' office with a staff arrived at the place, and diverted the traffic from Dunbar Street through one of the thoroughfares connecting it with Mary Street.

Several hoardings in the city suffered from the effects of the storm. Crosses Street, near St. Finbarr's Protestant Cathedral was blown away. The large hoarding near the Coliseum Cinema Theatre was shaken somewhat, and it was thought advisable to divert pedestrian traffic from the adjacent footpath.

In the Barrack Street area a large number of slates and some eave shoots were blown off. During the afternoon the gale moderated very much, and at intervals the weather was practically calm. But the calm intervals were broken by strong gusts of wind. So far no serious accidents to persons have been reported.

During the afternoon some persons were treated at the North and South Infirmaries for slight injuries sustained from falling slates and mortar.

4 January

AN EXCELLENT PROGRAMME

It is a considerable time since such an all-round excellent programme was arranged as that presented to patrons of the Palace Theatre this week, and both performances drew unusually large audiences. This should continue during the week, for every turn in the bill is one of merit, and audiences are sure to be well pleased. Pride of position is given to Sonata, described as an actor – musician. He is an artist of great versatility, for not alone is a master of the piano, violin, concertina, and bagpipes, he is a very clever actor. His representations of the child musician, the Scottish Shepherd, the French light comedian, etc, are exceptionally good, and it was little wonder that his turn last evening was received with tremendous applause. The Decars and "Tomato" supply a comedy act which is nothing short of extraordinary. They are assisted by two geese and a donkey, all of which are trained to do tricks that are interesting and amusing to an unusual degree. Turns of this nature are not often brought to Cork and that under notice is one well worth seeing. Miss Bessie Slaughter is a singer whose beautiful contralto was heard to great effect in "The magic of your Voice", and "The Lost Chord". Both songs were rendered with a finish and charm which gained the artiste the hearty plaudits of the audience. Ex-Corporal Morris is a man who has seen active service, but was discharged owing to defective eyesight, and his versatility on the stage gains him a very cordial reception. He is a musician of merit, and is in addition a clever mimic. Dan Crew is a Scotch comedian, who renders a couple of songs very well, and he also was extended a cordial welcome.

5 January

AN INVALUABLE FEVER HOSPITAL

The monthly meeting of the Committee of the Cork Fever Hospital and House of recovery was held yesterday, Rev Father O'Regan in the chair. Mr Cody remarked upon the large amount of the debt and said that some effort should be made to wipe it off. The public bodies should be urged to contribute more generously. Mr John Scott said that the large increase in the debt was owing to the enormous amount of extra work done by the hospital within recent years. Dr Sutton said that during the year 1915 they had treated 500 patients in the hospital with great success, the mortality rate being exceedingly low.

M. Kinmonth agreed with Mr Cody's remarks, and said if the public knew such a large amount of good work was being done for the citizens, he felt sure they would contribute liberally towards keeping the hospital out of debt.

Mr Charles Daly said he had no idea until he became a member of the committee, of the large and invaluable work which the hospital was doing. Such a hospital was absolutely essential for a city like Cork, and he thought if a special appeal were made to be public, and these facts brought before them, that a generous response would be the result.

Sir John Scott said that it was intended to make a special appeal to the public for funds in consequence of the exceptionally heavy expenses which had to be met. He suggested that a small committee should be appointed to take this matter in hand.

FISHING MATTERS

A good many Cork families must have been disappointed yesterday at the almost total failure of their fish supply. This failure has occurred rather frequently of late, and while in a large measure it can be attributed to the severe and boisterous weather experienced, as well as to the naval restrictions on the hours and places for trawling; still it opens up a serious question for housekeepers this side of the globe. The fact is that our local supply of fish is dependent on more considerations than mere demand. The demand for fish in Cork at this period of the year is not above normal, but the supplies caught off our Southern coast are either expressed to England by train or carried there direct by the trawlers that catch them. As often as not our supplies are sent to us from English markets, so inadequate and irregular are our local methods and sources of supply. A golden harvest of the deep is allowed to go unreaped owing to the lack of local enterprise. We read in the Dublin market reports for Thursday that Ringsend, Howth and other vessels brought the metropolis its fish dinners for yesterday.

Yet in Cork, which is in close touch with the fishing stations, it was impossible to purchase fresh fish after noon yesterday. A properly controlled fish supply would prove a priceless boom to a city like Cork. The wonder is that local enterprise

Fish packing at Baltimore, County Cork, *c.* 1910. (SOURCE: CORK CITY MUSEUM)

has failed to realize the fortune that is going a begging by the total lack of proper fishing facilities. A plentiful supply of fish would be greatly appreciated by the working classes, who are at present deprived of their weekly fish dinner owing to the prohibitive prices charged.

12 January

A BRAVE CORK OFFICER

He was a cool lad, yes as cool as they are made. He cared nothing for personal risk. He was out to do his work – duty would be more a suitable word. He smoked his pipe just as I am doing now, and he rushed just as I rushed. He was no different from the rest of that mad, charging crowd of men; and yet that hardly seem correct. There appeared to be that indefinable something about him that attracted one. What it was I am unable to determine. Perhaps it was because he was the only one who smoked his pipe in that insane holocaust of men. We reached the German parapets together and lay alongside each other. Contrary to all expectations the enemy trenches were full and very little damage appeared to have been done by our artillery. This fact did not deter the spirit and daring of the cool lad. His age would be anywhere between 20 and 25, clean limbed and well built. Just one of those sturdy youngsters that one will occasionally meet within the course of a day's wandering.

To know him and see him under such exceptional circumstances was a gratification few would deny themselves, nay, it was more, it was to have lived. I watched with the utmost astonishment his demeanour during those trying moments. He was still smoking and calmly surveying the scene in front of him, just as you or I might do. He shifted his pipe and muttered something about the barbed wire not being effectively destroyed and of charging the second German line. Bullets were whipping around us at a most merciless fashion, while the incessant shrieking, ripping, tearing and exploding of shells caused a panacea of feeling that is indiscernible and through it all he was the same imperturbable youngster, his pipe was slackening, and he devoted a few moments of hard pulling to revive it. He amazed me and almost stupefied me with a visible display of coolness under such circumstances. Inwardly I felt pleased and, concluded that here was a leader. He was exhibiting a splendid spirit – that old, tenacious spirit which has conquered worlds and made empires. He now gripped his rifle, opened and closed the bolt a few times to ensure its smooth working.

A few pieces of grit or sand in the mechanism bothered him, and he essayed the time with patience to blow it out. Having done so, he loaded and got to business. The traverse on his left was filled with Germans who were still full of fight and pretty well protected from exploding fire. He shifted a few yards further down to where a better opportunity offered by a slight breach being made in the wires, and opening fire after shifting his pipe to the left side of his mouth, so as not to impend his aim. The lying position not proving satisfactory he exposed himself even more so the terrific hail of bullets that were spitting viciously around us by getting up to kneeling position. How he lived for the time he did in that storm of lead is a wonder. He died a painless death. I shall keep a hallowed spot for that youngster in my memory. He was Lieutenant Sealy King of 2nd batt. R.M. Fusiliers, killed on the German parapets at the action in front of the Rue de Bois on the 9th May, 1915. A cool lad and a brave man. Peace be his! "PATSY".

13 January

A SUNDAY OPENING QUESTION

At the Law and Finance Committee, yesterday (Councillor T C Butterfield presiding), the first business taken up were the applications of the Southern Coliseums, Ltd, and the Imperial Cinema Co, George's Street, to open their respective theatres on Sundays between the hours of 3pm and 5pm, and from 8.30pm to 10pm, or any hours that may be suggested.

In connection with the matter, Rev Jeremiah O'Regan appeared before the meeting to oppose the applications on behalf of the Lord Bishop of Cork Most Rev Dr O'Callaghan. He said, "I beg to inform you that his Lordship the Most Rev Dr O'Callaghan is utterly opposed to the granting of the two licenses for which application has been made. It is gravely apprehended that the granting of the two permissions sought would mean nothing less than the driving of the thin end of the wedge for similar applications from the other places of amusement in the city, which application you could not then consistently refuse.

The unhappy and much-to-be feared result of this would be that in a very short time these places would be in full swing on Sundays, the religious days and sacred character of the Sunday relegated to a place in past history in Cork, and the day might not be far distant when the atmosphere of our city would be permeated with the spirit of irreligion which has become the curse of so many of the great continental centres in recent years. But, someone may say, these entertainments are allowed in other places in the country; why not then in Cork? Well, the answer to that is our ecclesiastical authority's chief concern is the religious safeguarding of their own people, and they cannot

Bishop Dr Thomas Alphonsus O'Callaghan. (SOURCE: CORK CITY LIBRARY)

be taking the cure in the matter from what is being done in other places. Do you not think, in all considerations and common sense, that six days a week ought to be enough for the management of these places of amusement to devote to the filling of their coffers without trespassing on the sacred character of Sunday to overflow them?"

THE DOMAIN OF JOURNALISM

It is with sincere regret we chronicle the death of Mr M B O'Neill, J.P. The sad event occurred at his residence, 1, Western Terrace, Western Road, early yesterday; the deceased was a native of Listowel, being a member of a talented Kerry family, which gained considerable distinction in the teaching profession. He entered the domain of journalism, and for many years was a valued member of the literary staff of this journal up to his retirement some years ago. Mr O'Neill was a man whose geniality and good nature won him many close friends, and the warm affection of his colleagues in the Press, particularly the Cork Press, with which he was so honourably and long identified. He was a man of high literary ability and well qualified to attain success in his chosen profession. His activities as a pressman made him intimately acquainted with the prominent men of his time, and his reminiscences of the more stirring times in Ireland, particularly during the early days of the Land League, were matters of great interest to his younger colleagues.

EXPECTATIONS OF THE GAELIC LEAGUE

The annual meeting of the Cork Ard Coiste, or the Executive of the Gaelic League was held at the Grianan, Queen Street. Mr Saoirse Mac Niocaill, MA, Chairman, presiding.

The Chairman in reviewing the work done during the past year said shortly after the committee was formed it passed a resolution asking volunteers to use Irish, and he was glad to say that this had a very good effect, and that now headquarter orders were sent down to the Irish Volunteers in Irish and English, and there were a good many of the volunteers in different parts of the country who were drilled and commanded in Irish almost exclusively. Last year the St Patrick's Day procession was organised entirely by the Ard Coiste, and was a great success. They had asked Irish be used in the services at the churches on St Patrick's Day, and he was very glad to say this request was met with a very good response, but they could not regard things as completely satisfactory until they had Irish services in every church in Cork, Catholic and Protestant. With regard to the Irish language collection, he mentioned that the street collections were beyond expectation considering the times they were passing through. It was very hard on some of the members to give time to the collection, as they had to be out of the City during the week, and were not able to collect the whole City. The outlying districts were left to the branches to collect, but the work was not done. What impressed him very much was the readiness of the people of Cork to subscribe to the Gaelic League.

19 January

SAD PARTICULARS

A most shocking fatality occurred at the Glanmire terminus of the Great Southern and Western Railway about six o'clock yesterday. The particulars are extremely sad. William Bergin, living in the Lower Glanmire road, and in the employment of the company for over forty years, as a carpenter, was following his occupation in the repair of wagons when he met his death under circumstances which will be fully investigated at an inquest in the North Infirmary to-day.

Bergin was engaged settling the "buffer" of the wagon when the sad occurrence took place. These wagons were at a point called "the sick place" which is at the southern end of the station premises, near what is known as the "bank". The wagons, which were being repaired by the deceased, Charles McCarthy, his assistant, and Denis O'Connell, assistant vice-man, were up against the buffer stop. On the same line of the rail, but about two yards away there was a group of thirteen wagons, the last one of which, it is stated, had its repair completed. This group of wagons were required to make up a goods train, and for this purpose an engine in charge of Michael Foster, with Geoffrey Pyne as fireman was sent to "shunt" them into position.

There was one wagon already attached to the engine, which backed slowly down to have the thirteen wagons hitched on by Shunter Andrew Condon. The unfortunate deceased was engrossed in his work at the time, and took no notice on [sic] the shunting operations. The very slight impact necessary to put the engine and wagons in position for coupling sent the 13 wagon rolling back. Poor Bergin was fixing the 'Buffer', over which he was leaning, of the stationary wagons. The result was that he was almost immediately caught between the 'Buffers', and crushed to death. His comrade Denis O'Connell was working at the 'links' of the wagon and therefore escaped uninjured; while McCarthy was engaged within the wagon.

20 January

TRENCH NARRATIVES

My dear Boy, it was a beautiful morning when our party started out in the three motor cars for a visit to the actual front line trenches and some of the regiments holding them. At Plugstreet there are shallow excavations, with a built up parapet of sandbags, narrow and tortuous. Sandbags is misleading as the filling of stuff is greasy clay always exuding moisture, and caked with mud. The floor of the trench every little while you come on all sorts of quaint dug outs used for sleeping quarters for the men off duty, kitchens, telephone offices, stores for bombs, for grenades, for provisions, signalling apparatus, trench tools, etc. A detailed list of all the multifarious implements and contrivances that are thought to be necessary for the vanquishment of the Germans would be much too long even for your long winded father. We looked through trench periscopes and saw – a dead country. Nothing stirring, no vestige of life to be seen in the whole vista, and immediately in the foreground was a long, irregular mound or bank which we were told was the enemy's front trench. It was hard to realize it but curiously enough I felt it better to take our staff officer's word for it than to climb over our sandbag parapet and go see for myself. I thought most likely if there were Germans they would all be strangers, and you know I never did like strangers.

James G Crosbie, *Cork Examiner*, Representative

EGAN'S SILVER LINING

Much regret was felt in the city yesterday when it became known that in the earlier hours of the morning Mr Barry M Egan principal of the firm of William Egan and Sons had passed away at his residence, Carrig House, Tivoli. Born in Cork seventy-three years ago, Mr Egan came from a family that for generations had been connected with the trade and art of working the precious metals. At the early age of 12 years he entered upon his apprenticeship as a watchmaker, jeweller, and silversmith in his father's workshop. When in due course he had acquired the trade and incidentally it may be mentioned that to be a first class worker in silver is one of the most difficult of arts to acquire, he applied himself assiduously to extending the business. Even as a very young man he proved himself possessed of the line judgement and shrewdness in business, qualities which developed as the years advanced. He was a keen student of art, and was always anxious to obtain information on everything connected with the business to which he devoted himself. From his earliest years his great ambition was to revive the manufacture of silver plate for which Cork was so noted in the eighteenth century.

He threw himself heart and soul into what may have been regarded as a hopeless task. The silversmith's art had practically disappeared from Cork, and there were those who thought that in the course of time would disappear from Ireland altogether. Mr Egan, however firmly believed that Irish men were still capable of working in metal with the same skill as their forefathers, who wrought those many works of art which have been the admiration of the civilised world. And while so anxious to revive the art in Cork, he always maintained that it should remain characteristically Irish. With this view he made an extensive study of Celtic ornamentation, and it might be said that there were few better able to express an opinion as to its merits. His efforts in favour of local silver work were crowned with success, and finally the time came when it was possible for him to found the silver factory in Maylor Street. The first important order which he received for the new undertaking was the manufacture of the mace for University College Cork.

AN ACT OF CHARITY

At a meeting of the committee for the purpose of providing necessitous children with meals at school, Mr John Horgan T C, Chairman, presided. The Chairman said it was a source of great pleasure to know from all quarters that the arrangements made for the supply of the meals had given great satisfaction. The committee were very grateful to the managers of the schools and the teachers for the manner in which they took up the question and helped to make it the success it was, for were it not for the assistance given in perfecting the arrangements the project would not have been so successfully carried out as it had been. It is only due to them that the committee should express to them their thanks. He thought the time opportune to draw the attention of the Corporation and the public to the fact that the Act ceased to operate from May next.

A serious effort should be made to bring pressure on the Government through the members of Parliament to have the Act continued, but so amended as to give local authorities power to levy a rate of 1d in the £ on the rates. The halfpenny rate was insufficient to meet the demand, and the result was that to put the scheme into operation they had to depend on the charity of some citizens. That was unfair, because it meant that some people had to pay twice, while other people with a fair share of the world's wealth escaped their responsibilities. The Act was a great blessing to the poor children, and every effort should be strained to secure its operation for at least the winter months.

REPORTING AT THE MUNICIPAL SCHOOL OF COMMERCE

Mr A F Sharman Crawford, Chairman, presided at the monthly meeting of the Committee. The Principal submitted his report in the work of the session, 1914–15. The following are extracts: It is safe to assume that were it not for the war the steady, gradual, and rather remarkable developments which has attended our school since its opening would have been well maintained during the past session, when as the above return shows, we had 443 individual students, representing 1,358 effective subject entries compared with 498 individual students and 1,328 subject entries in the previous Session.

As will be seen from the accompanying returns, there was a decrease of 55 individual students as compared with the previous session representing a decrease of 170 in the subject entries. The average percentage of actual to possible attendances was 57 as compared with 60 in the previous session. This decrease was due to a number of our students having gone on active service, and to the general disturbing influence of the war. Considering the unusual circumstances, and the fact that the reduction in schools in other distracts has been considerable, it is satisfactory that the decrease in attendance is so small, the number of individual students last session showing an actual increase of 4 as compared with two years ago.

Cork School of Commerce, Jameson Row, South Mall, c. 1916. (SOURCE: CORK CITY LIBRARY)

A WHITEGATE BOY AT SEA

Freddie Hynes, a Whitegate boy, was but barely over seventeen years of age when he had crammed into his life enough incidents to satisfy anyone's appetite for adventure. He is a son of Mrs M E Hynes, Hill Road, Whitegate, and she certainly can take no small pride for the courage of her gallant boy.

On the 30th of March last year he wrote from H M S Triumph a letter which naively opens with the splendid condition of his health, and expecting that his family will be surprised on hearing the reason for his being on the ship named, he last having written from the Ocean. The latter was torpedoed in the Dardanelles.

He wrote:

We had been bombarding for several days, and got off very well, only receiving a few hits. They had three men killed an AB, a petty officer and an officer, whilst the injuries to the ship were negligible – a steam launch, a launch cutter and pinnace were smashed to pieces. They attacked a very strong – fortified place, but the Turks were very poor shots. On the 18th the whole fleet proceeded to attack the greatest forts and got on very well, silencing several of them. In the afternoon, one of the French ships, the Bouvet, struck a mine and sank in one minute and twenty nine seconds, only 25 men being saved, for the other ships could not go to the rescue or send out boats due to the heavy Turkish fire. It would have been very little use to get out a lot of boats, for they would only be a target for the Turks. About 3.30 the Irresistible got hit, it is believed by a torpedo, for her engine room was blown away. The Ocean went to her help, and tried to take her in tow, but she was too far gone, and we left her and resumed the battle. We were having great success until about 6.35 when we got hit. I suppose it was by a torpedo. Whatever it was, it lifted her clean out of the water. We were all at action stations. I was down below supplying ammunition to one of the 6 inch guns, and when the order came "on deck" I nipped up smartly. I had nothing on only a flannel and a duck pants. All other things were in my locker including £2 6s to bring me home to England to which place I expected we were soon going to refit. I left everything anyhow, and got on board one of the destroyers that came alongside.

HONEST QUALITY AT THE CORK CONSUMERS LEAGUE

M r E Sheehan, MA (chairman), presided. Referring to recent letters in the Cork press on food questions, he did not think there were general complaints as to the quality of bread, milk, and sugar locally; the general run of shopkeepers and farmers sold honest quality, but there were many complaints as to tea. People also sent complaints to him that certain bakers were discriminating between their customers and giving reduced prices and discount in addition to certain people. If the public wanted prices of necessaries reduced, they must take a much keener interest in the food question. However, it was some satisfaction to find that their efforts were appreciated by many, and an offer had come to them from a leading city band to assist them in every possible way, whether at public meetings or otherwise. He felt they must express their gratitude for that and it was an indication that their efforts were not entirely in vain.

FEBRUARY

WE WANT FOR OUR YOUTH

The time-honoured custom of the new Lord Mayor's visit to the North Monastery was observed with suitable ceremonial yesterday. The Right Hon. The Lord Mayor (Councillor T C Butterfield) was accompanied by the High Sheriff-elect, the Town Clerk (Mr F W McCarthy), and his secretary (Mr William Hegarty). The Civic Party arrived at 11 o'clock and the fact that all four past pupils of the schools lent a special interest to the occasion, and gave a stimulus to the warmth and enthusiasm of the reception.

The Rev Superior (Brother McNally) and his assistant, Brother B McMahon, received the distinguished party, and while passing through the various class rooms, the Lord Mayor pointed out to Brother McNally, the seat he once occupied as a young pupil in no11. The Intermediate Science, Technical and Metal Work Halls were then visited. These have ever been the wonder and admiration of the visitor. Here the bench, the chisel, the saw, the plane, the forge, the driving wheel, and the rare display of art, trade and engineering models and science apparatus show what rare facilities are afforded to train the hand as well as the mind of the youthful learner. "Tis this sort of thing," observed his lordship, "we want for our youth".

All the senior pupils were then assembled in one of the large halls, and Brother McNally formally addressed his lordship. He said: "In offering you our congratulations today, we are joined by 2,000 pupils from our schools at Our Lady's Mount, Sullivan's Quay and Blarney Street. It has been a time-honoured custom for the newly elected Lord Mayor and High Sheriff to pay a visit to all the public institutions of the city. We are proud of you as a successful professional man, as a true citizen, as a Catholic, and last, though not least, as a past pupil of these schools".

IN THE SPIRIT OF LABOUR

The sixth ordinary general meeting of the Cork Employers' Federation, Limited was held yesterday at three o'clock in the Boardroom, Commercial Buildings. Sir Alfred Dobbin, JP, Chairman presided. The chairman read the report of the Executive Council for the year 1914–15, as follows:

The trade of Cork and district is and has been, in a prosperous condition, undisturbed by labour trouble of any importance. It is pleasing to note that notwithstanding the terrible war, which is raging over the greater part of Europe, the trade of Ireland has been good during the past year. This prosperity is also reflected in the business life of Cork and district, and employment for the working population has been plentiful. The good feeling, which has existed between employers and their employees for a considerable time past continues.

This, we hope, as time goes on, will not only remain, but will steadily increase, and that both masters and men will realise to the fullest extent that their interests are identical, and that by their joint efforts, any little difference which arise from time to time may be adjusted in a friendly spirit, and that strikes from which we have been comparatively free for so long, may become a thing of the past. As you are all aware, the members of our federation, on the outbreak of war, gave every encouragement to their men to volunteer for service in the navy and army; the promise made to them to look after the financial interests of their dependents has been loyally carried out by us, and will be continued to the end, which we hope is not far distant, when the men return victorious, to be welcomed home, and reinstated in their former employments.

ONE OF CORK'S OWN

Cork Butter Market Trustees: Mr Daniel Horgan, JP, in the chair, R G Cox (secretary); The secretary's report was as follows:

The supplies last week, though small, compared favourably with the corresponding week last year, the quantity of fresh butter being somewhat in excess. Demand was still quiet, and though fresh butter took an upward turn on Friday, the advance was maintained. The weather, though mild, has been rather too moist, and road transit would be restricted in some districts. The 'Grocer' of last week reports as regards the London Market – Danish is 2s lower.

This market is in an unsettled state: still prices show no decided tendency. Recent fluctuations in value have disturbed conditions. It was at one time thought that the unexpected prohibition of French butter exports, at least for a time, would give the market a certain stimulus, and quotations were generally hoisted, but the resumption of the export of unsalted French butter gave the market a set-back, together with big arrivals from New Zealand. From the same source we learn that the Highland Laddie [ship] has arrived with 3,897 cases from Argentina, and from Australia the Mooltan [ship] with 6,602 boxes.

Cork Butter Market, c. 1910. (SOURCE: CORK CITY LIBRARY)

OBSERVATIONS ON
THE WORKING CLASS

On Tuesday, 1 February, the second of the Economic Conferences organised by Professor Smiddy and Mr Rahilly was held in the spacious Examination Hall of the University College Cork. Professor Smiddy, in introducing the lecturer, pointed out that the results, which would be put before his hearers, were not the product of theorising or speculation. Father McSweeney had made an extensive investigation into the lives, housing, incomes, and standards of living of over 1,010 wage-earning families in Cork. The results would, therefore, have a living interest for the workers of Cork, whom it behoved to consider what steps might be taken to improve the material conditions of the wage-earning classes below and on the margin of subsistence. Professor Smiddy stated also that the lecture delivered by him at the previous conference on "The Importance of Economic and Social Studies for the Working Classes" will be available in a few weeks in pamphlet form.

Father McSweeney, at the outset of his paper, deprecated mere hearsay evidence and vague statements concerning the poverty of a city. The most interesting class of families comprised 345 families whose total weekly income did not exceed 19s. The total earnings of these families, which included 1,832 individuals, was £243 17s 5d for food alone. Taking the prices and rates prevalent before the war, the support of these individuals in the workhouse would cost the rates £233 2s for food alone.

It is therefore obvious that there are hundreds of families subsisting in Cork at a rate, which is insufficient to provide an adequate subsistence. Father McSweeney did not confine himself to mere numerical and statistical results. He made his treatment vivid and impressive by reading many "human documents" – records of struggles, despair and want. Poverty is very complex and many-sided, and raises problems in every region of social activity. The lecturer dwelt on the bad housing conditions of the city and gave some startling results of his own observation. He dealt with the problem of elevating and educating the children, and on the deleterious effects of blind alley employments. He also referred to the question of drink and improvidence; he regarded much of the excessive drinking as the effect rather than the cause of poverty.

MATTERS OF A FAIR WAGE

Public Health Committee, Cork Corporation: Mr John Horgan (Vice-Chairman) presided. A deputation of the carriers in the domestic department appeared before the committee to request the Corporation to increase their pay from 8s to 10s a day for each man and horse.

Mr Coroner James J. McCabe, Solicitor who appeared for the carriers said he was instructed by them to state that 10s a day was the lowest figure they do the work at. Mr O'Riordan said: "Is that an ultimatum". Mr McCabe said that was rather a warlike way of putting it. He reminded them that when the tenders were opened the last time 9s was the lowest. His clients would work on for the rest of the week so as not to inconvenience the public, but if the Corporation did not pay them 10s a day they would discontinue work on Monday. The Chairman said that the majority of the committee recognised that the load system was a bad one. They would prefer that the horses and men worked a certain number of hours per day. Alderman Simcox asked what were they paid at present. Mr Galvin said 8s a day. The Chairman said that out of six tenders received only one offered to work at 8s a day, the remainder being 9s a day.

Alderman Simcox said it now cost 27s 6d a week to feed a horse, as oats and hay were now nearly double the price of that time last year. Alderman Kelleher said if they granted the demand of the men now it would come to another £500 a year. He suggested that a joint meeting be held of the Public Works and Public Health Committees to go into the whole question of cartage. Mr O'Connell moved and Alderman Simcox seconded an amendment that they increase the rate of pay to 9s a day; on a division they voted for the amendment – 4 to 3.

THE CALL OF DUTY

An all-khaki recruiting meeting was held at 2 o'clock yesterday evening in Patrick-Street, all the speakers at which were dressed in khaki. Colonel Barry, who presided, said that meeting was held for the purpose of giving their country friends, who may be in town an opportunity of attending. The first speaker would be well-known citizen Lieutenant O'Riordan, who had recently joined the colours to act as recruiting officer for the Mallow district. Lieutenant J F O'Riordan, solicitor, said it was a pleasure to him to come before them and ask them to do what he had done, namely, to don khaki uniform and become a soldier in the cause of liberty and patriotism and in the cause of Ireland.

While such a war as the present was in progress, every man must be prepared to make sacrifices to do his duty, when empires were trembling in the balance. By joining the army they would only be doing as their ancestors had done – fighting against tyranny and oppression. The Irish Brigade of old fought to uphold the flag of liberty, and today Ireland was united in the same common cause, which had a similar object in view. In Flanders or at the Dardanelles the men of Cork had done their duty. Some of them had gone down, but every man of them had fought in the cause of Ireland and of liberty. Now that they had something to fight for, with Home Rule on the Statute Book; every man who had any thought for the land they all loved should come at the call of duty and join the army.

14 February

CORK TO THE FRONT

The manhood of some districts of Cork City may be said to be at the front. The numbers that have gone from the vicinities of Barrack Street, Fair Lane, Blackpool, must make an extraordinary total. The best indication is to be got from the fact that all the members of some bands are now in some one of the services waging a relentless war on Prussian tyranny – a crushing force that seeks to destroy all systems that are not of its making. The Munsters, in common with the other Irish Regiments, are endeavouring with all their might to overthrow the destroyer of Louvain, and in the illustration we give today are many men of the Munsters – an unrivalled fighting regiment. At Mons, when absolute destruction threatened the Munsters, it is said that the Germans often heard the rallying cry, "Blackpool to the Front," and it meant a magic call to desperate men to dash to the support of those who were even harder pressed – it was the last call that many a Prussian heard.

CHARITY AND POW SUPPLIES

The charitable work performed by the various bodies constituted to provide food and clothing for prisoners of war has many times been deservedly credited by the unfortunate men who are interned in Germany and Turkey, with it being the only barrier between them and absolute destitution. It is true that in some camps the prisoners have not at times been too badly used, but it is safe to assume that cases of favourable or even fair treatment are unfortunately not the rule. All classes of Prisoners of War interned in Germany stand much in need of the help of their compatriots, and therefore the people of the South of Ireland who have friends or neighbours interned in that country; many feel certain that by contributing to one or other of the prisoners' aid societies they will be alleviating want and suffering. The Midleton committee of the RMF and Prisoner of War fund has performed excellent work since it came into existence on 10 October 1914. It has sent to the Prisoners of War in Germany, 162 parcels, each weighing 11lbs. To the 2nd RM Fusiliers, France, 100 parcels, and to the RM Fusiliers, Salonika, 50 parcels, and weekly 1,000 cigarettes to prisoners and parcels of bread, and 1,000 cigarettes to the RM Fusiliers at the Front, all of which are received. Miss Aishlin, Castleredmond, Midleton, and Miss Penrose Fitzgerald, Honorary Secretary the Grange, Midleton, are two assiduous workers, and they or any other members will gladly receive donations for the fund.

A LIFEBOAT TO THE LUSITANIA

The annual meeting of the Cork Branch of the National Lifeboat Institution was held on Monday at the City Hall. Mr Donegan read the annual report, which stated that the Cork collection for the past year showed a substantial increase, while the expenditure was considerably less. Their collection amounted to £200 as compared with £185 in 1914, £110 in 1913, and £105 in 1912, while the expenditure amounted to £15 18s 1d as against £33 8s 7d in the previous year. Having dealt with the work accomplished, the report went on to state that when on the 7th of May last, the *Lusitania* was sent to the bottom in the vicinity of the Old Head of Kinsale by the foulest act of cruel piracy ever committed, the Courtmacsherry lifeboat crew made a most gallant effort to save life. It would be remembered that there was no wind and they were in consequence unable to avail of their sails, and had to row a distance of 15 miles. It was no fault of theirs that when they arrived it was only to find a sea of dead. They made a noble effort, and stuck to it with dogged determination and no men could have done more. The Lifeboat Institution has realised the necessity for motor propelled boats and the *Lusitania* case affords one of the strongest arguments in favour of motor propulsion, but the cost of these boats was so great that it must be some considerable time before they can be universally adopted unless the funds of the Institution were augmented. He might mention that fearing that the *Transylvania* (homeward bound) would be similarly attacked and sunk by German submarines, and as the weather continued calm for some days after the sinking of the *Lusitania*, they sought a loan of the cork Fishery Conservators' 45 hp Kelvin launch, and took her round to Courtmacsherry, and remained in readiness to tow the lifeboat should the occasion arise. The *Transylvania*'s course was altered, and landed her passengers at Greenock. In war, as in peace, the lifeboat must always be ready for duty.

18 February

RAIL CONNECTIONS TO THE COUNTY

Cork Bandon and South Coast Railway: The 138th general meeting of the proprietors of this company was held today at noon in the Imperial Hotel, Cork. Mr Joseph Pike, Chairman, presided. The total number of passengers the company carried was 503,531, showing an increase of 31,000 and in money £2,037. In parcels and miscellaneous traffic there was the satisfactory increase of 18,885 tons, representing £1,588 in money. Of this increase 4,134 tons was in coal and coke owing to a greater quality having been sent over the railway from Cork instead of being shipped direct to the western ports by coasting vessels. This traffic would be capable of considerable development if modern loading appliances were erected on

Terminus of Cork, Bandon Railway, c.1910. (SOURCE: CORK CITY LIBRARY)

Victoria Quay. Lime, brick, stone and slate etc all showed decreases, building operations having been to a great extent suspended owing to the war, and to the quality of stone required for the streets of Cork having been reduced. In barytes traffic there was an increase of 2,639 tons, enhanced prices and the total cessation of the usual continental supply to the markets having led to an increased output from the mines at Clonakilty and Bantry. Imported grain showed an increase of nearly 19,000 tons. This increase was altogether in grain sent from Victoria Quay to the Great Southern and Western Railway system. The traffic had almost doubled in the past 12 months, and like coal, would be capable of great development if additional sidings were constructed

on Anderson's Quay and on the new timber wharf at Victoria Quay.

They carried 2,650 more cattle. In pigs there was an increase of 4,676, but though prices were good, the heavy cost of feeding stuffs was restricting the raising and fattening of these animals at present. The fish traffic from Skibbereen, Kinsale and Bantry was about normal, while from Baltimore there was forwarded 1,645 tons of fresh mackerel and herring, showing an increase of 850 tons over the previous year's consignment from that port, and making a record year. The completion of the new pier now being constructed by the Congested Districts Board and the Cork County Council, and to the cost of which the company were contributing should, with proper packing and loading facilities, make Baltimore a very important fishing station.

AN ITALIAN OPERA

On Saturday afternoon the Harrison Frowin Company presented Verdi's "La Traviata" to a house, which for a matinee was well filled, without being crowded. The outstanding feature of the performance was the successful rendition of the "Violetta" music by Miss Raymonde Amy, who threw much sympathy and delicacy into her solo singing, as well as in the duets with "Alfredo" and his father. She gained much deserved applause. Mr William Boland was a robust "Alfredo", and sang his part with ease. Mr Jay Ryan did all that was required of him as "George Germont". He was encored for "Heaven Calls Thee Home", and repeated it. The other parts were satisfactorily filled, and the artists were quite capable of doing more than was required of them. The staging was effective, especially in the first and third acts. Through the courtesy of the manager of the Opera House (Mr Frank Pitt) a number of wounded soldiers were accommodated with seats in the orchestra stalls.

MCSWINEY AND THE DEFENCE OF THE REALM

Terence J McSwiney BA, Victoria Road, was summoned by Mr C A Walsh, DL, for that on 2nd January, 1916, at Ballynoe, Co. Cork, he made statements likely to cause disaffection to the King, that is to say statements making reflections upon and likely to cause dissatisfaction with and hostility to his Majesty's Government – statements that defendant and those acting with him were in a position, fully armed and equipped, to defy his Majesty's Government, against the form of

Terence McSwiney. (SOURCE: CORK CITY COUNCIL)

statute 5 George V, and regulations in such a case made and provided. And that on the same date, at Ballynoe, the defendant attempted to cause disaffection amongst the civilian population of the United Kingdom; and further that on 13 January last, at Victoria, Cork, he, without lawful authority, had in his possession a certain cypher capable of conveying military or naval information. Dr HA Wynne, Crown Solicitor, appeared to prosecute.

Mr Healy, witness, addressed the Court, and said the defendant was a University graduate, and his degrees and diplomas were taken away by the police, who forgot to return them. He complained that the prosecution was not brought for a bone fida purpose, but was really a political case.

Why were the Ulster Volunteers not prosecuted for carrying arms, or why were the Cork Training Corps, with their barracks in the Mardyke, not prosecuted? The Irish Volunteers were formed three years ago, only after Sir E Carson's Volunteers were allowed to go through the country armed. The Irish Volunteers were formed for the purpose of defending the liberties of Ireland when Home Rule was in operation. They were the first armed Volunteers since the famous Volunteers of 1782 – or if they went back further, the Volunteers, who sailed from the Cove of Cork with Sarsfield after the treaty of Limerick. The Irish Volunteers were for Ireland first, foremost, and all the time.

24 February

THE IMPENDING PAPER FAMINE

Sir – The present time seems to afford a favourable opportunity of drawing public attention to a matter which possesses considerable importance not only for Cork, but for the whole South of Ireland. The present campaign for economy does not appear to include waste product, such as wood, paper, rags, etc. Of paper articles alone, there are tons being wasted in the city of Cork by individuals and more especially by institutions. In view of the approaching restriction of the paper supply, the question is likely to acquire considerable urgency. Already the orders for printing invoices and such like have nearly trebled in Cork, owing to the fear of an impending paper-famine.

The present paper crisis brings home to us the extraordinary fact at present there are in Ireland only two really important paper mills – at Ballyclare and at Saggart. In the forties there were 60 paper-mills in Ireland; and as late as the sixties, there were four or five mills in Cork: Alfred Greer and Co at Dripsey and Grenville, James Ryan's Gurth Paper Mills at Blarney, Allen's on the River Shournagh near Blarney, Phairs at Butlerstown, Glanmire. At the Cork Industrial Exhibition of 1883 Messrs Greer and Ryan both exhibited – but only wrapping paper.

Before the war about £40,000 worth of unprinted paper was annually imported into Ireland direct from abroad, besides about £90,000 worth of wood-pulp. Surely, it is possible to supply a portion not only of this but of the paper which we import from England. The raw materials for paper-making are plentiful; all we need is the pulp-mill.

To quote the words of an eminent authority, the late Dr W K Sullivan, President of Queen's College, Cork: "Cork and its neighbours possesses quite as many – perhaps in some respects more – advantages than several of the localities where paper-making flourishes, and it ought to be again, as it once was, a considerable centre of the paper trade" – yours etc, Alfred Rahilly, University College, Cork.

25 February

THE MILITARY CORDON OF CORK HARBOUR

Annual Meeting, Cork Blackrock and Passage Railway: Sir Stanley Harrington presided. For many years past they had been confronted with serious difficulties, which they might be able to surmount if they had larger resources at their back … The present position was due chiefly to three causes, viz., the closing of Crosshaven by the military authorities on the outbreak of the war; the increased cost of coal, labour, stores etc., and the erection of a new pier at Queenstown. The gross revenue showed an increase of £1,419, and had they been permitted by the military authorities to carry on the usual summer and excursion traffic to Crosshaven, they would have had large additional receipts.

As to the closing of Crosshaven, shortly after the commencement of hostilities, the military authorities prohibited civilians from approaching the coastline between Ringabella Creek and Crosshaven village, either by day or night. All the summer residents were ordered away, but as a matter of equity they were refunded a portion of the cost of their season tickets. No persons were allowed to enter the district without military permits. All excursion traffic by train and boat was prohibited, with the result that the Crosshaven traffic was practically killed. This state of affairs continued up to June 27th, 1915, when a slight modification of the regulations was made, exempting visitors from the necessity of permits, but no excursion traffic was permitted, and as a consequence hardly anyone visited Crosshaven.

From the first day of the war they had done everything in their power to assist the naval and military authorities. There was a great demand by both services, for the transport of stores to various camps within the Harbour and to Haulbowline. Finding it impossible to satisfy their requirements with the existing goods steamers, the directors purchased an additional vessel, the "*Taffy*", at great expense, and though able to carry all the naval and military stores offering, they were doing so without profit.

28 February

GOOD AND BAD ANGELS AT MAGDALEN ASYLUM

I n Cork Cathedral yesterday, after the first Gospel of the 12 o'clock Mass, Very Rev Father Matthew, OSFC, Holy Trinity, made an eloquent appeal for support for the St Mary Magdalen Asylum, Cork under the care of the Sisters of Charity. There are Magdalens in the

Magdalen Asylum, Cork, *c.*1910. (SOURCE: CORK CITY LIBRARY)

city of Cork today – women who traffic in vice and trade in sin. But they were to be more pitied than blamed. They had no home but the home of sin and shame. Wither are they to turn; where can they go? The good angel in the Magdalen Asylum called to them – was waiting to welcome them back – waiting to enfold them in the arms of mercy, to pity, and to pardon. In the Asylum, under the care of the Sisters of Charity, there are one hundred of these poor things who have been received to penitence. In the Asylum they received food and clothing. There they are instructed in useful purposes of life; and there by the teaching and example of the Sisters of Charity, they are led to higher and holier things. There they lead pure and holy lives; and some of those who were once the curse and scourge of the city are now its joy and pride. But where would they be were it not for this Magdalen Asylum?

29 February

PROSECUTION OF THOMAS KENT

Before Messrs R F Starkie, RM (in the chair), J Kelleher, Ald M J O'Riordan, TC; Jeremiah Lane, TC, and Sir Edward Fitzgerald, Thomas Kent, who resides at Coole, Cork, was summoned at the suit of District Inspector Walsh, under the Defence of the Realm Regulations, with having on the 2nd of January last made statements likely to prejudice recruiting in Ireland, with having on the same occasion attempted to cause disaffection amongst the civilian population, and with having on January 13th had in his possession a five chambered revolver, and 27 rounds of revolver ammunition, and 54 rounds of ball cartridge for carbine, without the written permission of either the competent naval or military authority. Dr H

Thomas Kent.
(SOURCE: NATIONAL LIBRARY OF IRELAND)

A Wynne, Crown Solicitor, appeared to prosecute, and Mr F J Healy, B L (instructed by Mr Maurice B O'Connor, solicitor.), defended.

MARCH

1 March

CONSUMERS OF THE CORK GAS COMPANY

The ninety-fourth general meeting of the Cork Gas Consumers Co was held yesterday at noon at the offices, 72 South Mall. Mr William B Harrington Chairman presided. They had a most anxious time during the past six months. When addressing them at the last meeting he had hoped they had seen the worst of their troubles, but unfortunately the reverse had been the case. Freights, coal and every item of expense in connection with the production of gas instead of lessening, had advanced still more. Then again, they were often not able to get the coal for which they had contracted, owing either to there being no ships available or to trouble in the mines, and they had the greatest difficulty at times in getting any coal at all, and they had to take whatever they could get at enormous cost. But, worse still these odd cargoes which they were compelled to take in order to keep going were unsuitable for their plant and caused in consequence no end of trouble at the works. The pipe, which conveyed the gas from the retorts, got so choked it was with the greatest difficulty the gas supply was kept up. Almost all gas companies in the United Kingdom had, he understood suffered, more or less from the same cause, and one gas company, he heard had to close down altogether. He was pleased to say, however, they had recently got in the right quality of coal, and he had every reason to believe the supply would continue to be normal.

In consequence of the increased expenses under every heading they had to reduce the dividend, and notwithstanding the advance of 6d per 1,000 to private consumers. They had also been compelled to increase the price the same amount to the corporation for the public lighting, and though it was with the greatest reluctance they advanced the price at all, they would really have been justified in putting on considerably more than 1s per 1,000 extra, instead they had to meet under every heading. To take one item alone, that of freights. Before the war the normal rate of our coal was 5s per ton, and one of the last freights they had to pay was 24s, nearly five times as much, or, in round numbers £1 per ton more. This difference in the cost of freight would mean on the amount of coal they used in the 12 months fully £25,000 in excess of what they were in the habit of paying. The shareholders would see then from that one item alone how terribly they were handicapped in their earning power, but, as he had already pointed out, they were also suffering from increases in costs of coal and all items of expenditure as to the future all depends of course on the expenses they would have to meet, and he regretted to say the tendency all round was still upwards.

7 March

A REJECTED BOOK ON IRISH AGRICULTURE

The object of this article is to bring before the public, in particular to the notice of the many public boards – county councils, rural district councils, municipal and urban bodies, and all those whom are committed to the care and direction of Irish public affairs – a grievous wrong that has been done to the people of a Board that has sole control of well over 50 per cent of the Irish youth: a wrong perpetrated not alone at the expense of the people of the rural districts, but which for years has vitally affected everyone in Ireland. At a time that was really not suitable for its use, a clever work on practical agriculture was taught in the National Schools. The time when it would have been of real worth was during recent years, but its highest, value would have been at the present hour, when from all directions is coming the urgent call for tillage, in particular the appeals addressed to the small holders and the agricultural labourers. Some years ago for no reason the Commissioners of Education withdrew the book. Had this strange decision never been arrived at, there would have been left the medium of splendid instructions to the children who to-day are men and women – thousands of them holders of labourers' cottage and plots, or farmers. The use of the book amongst city children was equally desirable, for throughout Ireland there is in most cases owing to want of even rudimentary knowledge a complete indifference to the splendid uses that could be made of the small gardens and plots attached to suburban and town dwellings.

INDUSTRY OUTLOOK

The thirteenth annual meeting of the Cork Industrial Development Association was held in the Council Chamber City Hall yesterday, at 3.30. The Lord Mayor (Councillor Butterfield) presided. The Secretary (Mr J L Fawsitt) read the annual report. Having dealt with the Association's activities in respect of such questions as proposed surtaxes on the product of Irish breweries and distilleries, War Office contracts for Irish firms, orders for munition supplies for local firms, and tourist development, the report referred to the bright future that appeared to be in store for the country until the war broke out. The report went on to state that the war, while it checked, to a large extent, emigration to the United States and the British colonies, has likewise, put a stop to our export trade in certain commodities to foreign countries; has greatly diminished our exports of other articles, and has seriously affected production at home, chiefly in the great linen and allied industries of the North, an in numerous smaller concerns all over the country.

One heartening feature of the situation is that the war has had the effect of not alone stopping the decline in tillage in the country, that had been progressing unchecked for the past half century, but has succeeded to a limited extent, no doubt, in quickening food raising in Ireland. Such prosperity as appears to exist to-day is more or less artificial and cannot be expected to contribute after the cessation of hostilities on the continent. The prosperity noticeable among our agricultural community is due to the fact that farmers are selling freely because of remunerative prices obtainable for their produce, but there seems to be no doubt that these fancy prices will decline materially when peace once more reigns in Europe.

IRISH WEEK

Dear Sir or Madam, – Next week, commencing with Monday, March 13th, and ending on the Saturday following, including March 17th, our National Festival, will be "Irish Week". The Council of the Cork Industrial Development Association make a special appeal to all classes in the community to make the coming week one from which some material advantage will result to our nation.

Irish manufacturers are asked to arrange for special exhibitions of their wares in the business establishments throughout the country.

Irish merchants and retailers are requested to make special displays of all Irish goods in their shop windows and on their premises.

Irish distributors and shop assistants are exhorted to bring Irish made fabrics specially under the notice of their customers; and

Irish consumers, that is the public generally, are expected to confine their purchases, as far as possible, to goods of Irish manufacture, asking for Irish articles and insisting upon being supplied only with Irish goods.

The general observance of this policy, on the part of our people next week, will mean that our professions of patriotism are real and sincere, and that we are prepared to give practical testimony to the love of country and race within us. It will mean, also, a great and much needed flip for Irish industries, will enable Irish producers to capture the Irish market for even that one week of the year, will encourage our manufacturers not only to maintain but to increase their output and the variety of goods they manufacture, will embolden our capitalists to sink additional money in Irish industrial enterprise, will help to find increased employment for Irish workers in Irish factories, will hearten Irish shopkeepers to stock and more largely distribute Irish goods; and lastly; will keep in circulation in Ireland the money we spend on Irish articles next week, and enrich our country to that extent.

J.L. Fawsitt, Secretary, Cork Industrial Development Association, 9 March 1916

12 March

ACTIVITIES AT VICTORIA HOSPITAL

Annual Meeting, Victoria Hospital; Right Rev, Dr Dowse presided at the annual meeting of the above, held on Saturday, and there was a good attendance of subscribers. The Honorary Secretary (Mr A W Dobbin) read the annual report, in the course of which it was stated that the times were so abnormal it was very difficult to survey the working of the hospital in comparison with any ordinary year. The council assisted by the ladies' committee endeavoured in every possible way to effect a combination of efficiency with economy, a difficult proposition in the case of a hospital, because it was continually faced with the fact that nothing but the best was good enough. There was an increase of £135 in provisions as compared with 1914, a decrease of £35 in fuel and light, a decrease of £53 in the medical and surgical department, due to ordering a good supply of medicines and appliances before the advance in prices. Donations and subscriptions showed an increase of £30 over last year. Patients' payments and probationers' fees also showed increases. On the other hand, there was a falling off of £74 in extern nursing, and a decrease of £50 in the free beds and cots. The last was a matter outside the power of the council, who at the same time hoped that they may be able to record an increase next year.

The hospital was under a deep debt of gratitude to Colonel and Mrs Longfield, Mallow, for their munificent gift of £1,000. That did not come into this year's accounts, but the council thought it well to refer to it in the report. It was a matter of regret that for a considerable time the wards equipped for the use of the naval and military authorities were allowed to be idle. However, on the last occasion when wounded soldiers came to Cork the accommodation offered was availed of to its fullest extent. Cordial thanks was tendered to the collectors for their untiring energy, and to Mr Guest Lane for the amount of time and trouble he had devoted to the legal side of the hospital's business. During the year they were deprived of the services of Dr C B Pearson who joined the RAMC [Royal Army Medical Corps]. Dr R C Cummins joined the medical staff as honorary anaesthetist.

13 March

PROPOSAL FOR A MUNITIONS FACTORY

At the Hotel Metropole on Friday, Mr J Redmond, MP, introduced a deputation of business men from the All-Ireland Munitions Conference to the Minister of Munitions (Mr Lloyd George). Mr Redmond said he had the honour to introduce an important deputation of business men from the various parts of Ireland, men representing large business interests and also representing all phases of political thought in that country. The deputation had come not to ask for a favour at all, but they had come to endeavour to help the Minister in the work in which he was engaged. They thought that Ireland had so far shown her anxiety to help as far as she could, but they also thought that with proper facilities given to her she could help very much more, and they had come to place their services entirely at the Minister's disposal, in order to carry out the object they had in common – that was to produce as much munitions of war as was possible. The first question was that of establishing a receiving depot in Ireland. A receiving depot had been established for the purpose of munitions pure and simple, but the committee desired that the receiving depot should be extended so as to cover not only strictly speaking munitions, but to cover all things required for the war, that was clothes, boots, spades, and all sorts of things that were required.

14 March

ILLUSIONS AT THE PALACE THEATRE

The great Fasola, Indian Fakir, tranformist and illusionist, has won the astonished admiration of peoples in all parts of the world. It is now many years since he was last seen in Cork; and in the interval his reputation has increased and his fame has grown so much, indeed, that even judicial ignorance of his name would not be claimed. Carlton used to declare: "I'm a marvel," and was entitled so to do. He was a conjuror. Fasola may with equal justice say: "I'm a marvel" – as an illusionist. He simply mystifies. The audience at the Palace last evening were too bewildered to give the conventional expression to their appreciation of his turn. But in this was the greatest tribute to the greatness of Fasola; and in view of the fact that his "disappearances" include a lady seated at a piano; and his "revelations" a lady in a case which was empty and into which nothing is put but apparently tea; the public can judge that Fasola positively flabbergasts his spectators. The act is one to see and wonder at; to think on it, or to speak of it, is to make the wonder grow. Mr Fred Maisson is a splendid entertainer, and his effort is a decided relaxation. He sings a couple of descriptive songs in a manner which is very effective. And his songs, "Two Little boys and the apples" and "Cohen Paid the Tram Fares" are good. His success is in the hearty laughter he creates.

ST VINCENT DE PAUL

The quarterly meeting of the members of the Society of St Vincent de Paul in Cork was held on Sunday. His Lordship the Most Rev Dr Cohalan, Assistant Bishop of Cork, presided. His Lordship, in the course of an interesting address to the members, mentioned that Father McSwiney, OP, who had undertaken to deliver an address on "Social Work", was prevented from doing so owing to a severe cold. His Lordship hoped that on some future occasion they would have the pleasure of listening to Father McSwiney, who had studied the social needs of the city of Cork very thoroughly, and was in a position to give them information which would prove of immense value to them in their work as members of that grand society. It was a good many years now since the foundations of the society were laid in Paris by Frederick Ozanam and his heroic band of fellow-workers. Social conditions had changed largely since then, and the society was obliged to keep in touch with the altered conditions of life. Having contrasted conditions in Paris and other cities with those now prevailing in Cork City, his lordship said they could all from their experience recognize that social conditions in Ireland had improved immensely since the early days of the society, but they were still face to face with a good deal of negligence in religious matters and with many cases of hardship and poverty due to unemployment and other causes. That threw a very great burden on their society, and it was necessary this year, as they were aware, to make an additional appeal for funds in order to continue their work amongst the deserving poor.

EXHIBITS OF CORK SILVER

Perhaps one of the most interesting exhibits of Irish manufacture is shown by William Egan and Sons, Ltd, 32, Patrick Street. It is a century since the old silver industry, for which Cork was famous, died out, and for over two generations the south of Ireland was dependent upon foreign importations for silver ware. Such articles as presentation pieces, household silver, Church plate, had to be imported from England or the Continent, in a few cases they were got from Dublin. It is somewhat illuminating to note that Messrs Egan and Sons' factory is the only one in Ireland, outside Dublin. Beyond a few small articles, such as medals, there is no silver made today in any town or city of Ireland with the exception of Dublin and Cork. What Cork can do – we can see in Messrs Egan and Sons' windows. Amongst other articles is the Crozier made last year for the Most Rev Dr Cohalan, Auxiliary Bishop of Cork; the very beautiful solid silver casket, which was recently made for his Honour Judge Bird, on his retirement from the judicial bench. The casket is very highly ornamented in the old Celtic style, the details of which are finished with the utmost care and delicacy, and in acknowledging receipt of the gift Mr Bird expressed his appreciation saying: "Exquisite taste is shown in the design, and the skill with which the work is carried out is very remarkable, and reflects great credit on the persons who were employed. All who have seen them here are delighted with them and are loud in their praises of their beauty". The casket is one of a number which Messrs Egan and Sons have made for various Lord Chancellors and Judges since the opening of their factory.

17 March

A SOLDIER'S BUFFET

There is always something wonderfully inspiriting about the send-off or the greeting that first and lasts awaits the traveller. When Lady Limerick inaugurated the first of the buffets for soldiers and sailors in Charing Cross station, she had no doubt in her mind, not only the momentary influence of the refreshments but the further effects of her venture. For it gives the man who is fighting for his country a steadier moral backbone when she finds that without need of words his right to all the comforts that men and women can give him is recognised and that he is ministered to without any of the patronage usually associated with charitable endeavours, and that the kindly word is spoken as a sweet to his cup of tea, to help him on his weary road. Down at the Glanmire station a buffet on the same lines as those instituted in all the railway stations in the United Kingdom is kept going by voluntary subscriptions and by voluntary aid. There is about an average of 75 a day who are served, though it may be stated that the figure sometimes reaches well over a hundred and fifty; it, of course, being dependent on the movements of troops. Of the soldiers, one and all remark the spirit of the movement. It is quite apparent that they look on the buffet almost instinctively as a place where besides refreshments they will be able to drop routine for a brief while and accept the kindly looks and mild chaff that is associated with groups of men unknown to each other, and the two or three who are behind the counter looking after their welfare for the moment, anxiously.

18 March

ST PATRICK'S DAY PARADE

The arrangements in connection with the procession were admirably carried out, and all the marshals and officials were at their posts in good time. The points at which the different groups were to assemble had been very carefully arranged, and the various units of the groups proceeded direct to the appointed places, and took up positions in the order of their arrival. The Presentation Brothers' school boys, with the Greenmount Industrial School Band, who were to head the procession, until it was joined by the Lord Mayor and Corporation, were allocated Great George's Street, but no sooner did they reach there than they proceeded along the route via South and North Main Street. The Presentation boys under their teachers carried a number of picturesque banners and bannerettes.

They were followed by the Blackpool National Band, who led the Christian Brothers' pupils. The latter formed a very big body of several hundred pupils, carrying numerous banners and bannerettes of blue and white. Second place was given to the Irish National Foresters, who marched with their handsome banner on a lorry, and with outriders in the picturesque Forester costume. After the Cork Foresters marched a body of the order from Shanbally. In this section was included the Brian Boru War Piper's Band. The members of the Cork Catholic Young Men's Society came next, and were succeeded by the Hibernian Boys' Brigade, with band. The members of the Ancient Order of Hibernians, Cork, numbering several hundreds, marched next in order, with their officers leading. Athletic Associations were well represented by members of the Cork County Board and University College Football Club. Temperance bodies including the St Finbarr's West Total Abstinence Association numbering several hundreds, with the Cork Workingmen's Drum and Fife Band.

SPORT AND COURSING

A highly successful coursing season wound up in Munster with Cork's meeting on March 1st, and St Patrick's Day meet at Enniscorthy performed a like office for Ireland generally. The 1915-16 Irish season must be put down as a record both as regards the number of meets and the quality of the sport provided. Old established venues continued their successful line, and the new enterprises were brimful of promise. Despite the abnormal times in which we live, public patronage of coursing shows no signs of waning, and the Park meetings of the South, in particular, attracted "gates" which must be highly encouraging to promoters, and suggestive of fresh endeavour and increased attractions when October comes round again.

The newly-formed Cork Committee, though encountered difficulties which would have damped the ardour of less genuine enthusiasts, brought their initial meeting to a successful issue. Their ground is a fine racing stretch, well situated, and can be considerably improved. The enclosure looked small to the visitor, but the run up was of more than average length, and has that welcome bit of "lift" in it to suit dogs and hares alike, But the area enclosed this year was hardly spacious enough to encourage game, to provide uniform and genuine coursing trials. The quality of the game, too, left something to be desired, for though the hares all ran straight, they were not uniformly stout. The peculiar slant in the lie of the racing pitch caused a wide difference of opinion in the case of at least one of the trials. The different positions of the spectators gave many of them a different perspective. Those of the audience, however, who were wise enough to look on, not from the proximity of the slipper's box, nor yet from the neighbourhood of the escape, but from the line where the greyhounds close with their game, must agree that the trials were in general highly satisfactorily, albeit if sometimes on the short side.

INTERVIEW WITH LADY SHACKLETON

The Press Association says – Sir Ernest Shackleton's family had heard no news of the explorer up to this afternoon. Dr Shackleton has hope Sir Ernest will be able to meet the situation with which he will be faced if he arrives at Ross Sea Base after having crossed the Polar Continent. "I see it stated," Dr Shackleton stated to an interviewer on Saturday, "that the disaster, which has overtaken the *Aurora* is the one thing, which might have been foreseen or provided against; but I very much doubt whether it was not among the possibilities my son had contemplated in his plans.

Although he will be bitterly disappointed to find the *Aurora* has drifted away, he will, I am sure, immediately set about making the best of the business, though there must be considerable anxiety among his relatives and friends here regarding the fate of him and his companions. Should they be able to reach the coast and make use of the stores and fuel the Scott Expedition left behind them, they will be able to carry on during the winter until help can reach them. That, at the earliest, will be at the end of the present year, or perhaps the beginning of next year, if the season happens to be a bad one".

CONCERNS OF THE BOARD OF GUARDIANS

An adjourned meeting of Cork Union was held at 12 o'clock noon yesterday. Mr Goggin proposed – That we the members of the Cork Board of Guardians emphatically protest against any further taxation being put on this, already overtaxed, country, as the present taxation is so outrageously excessive as to become an unbearable burden on 4,346,535 people, as the following figures prove up to the hilt:- In 1913-14 the true revenue in Ireland was £9,627,000; for the financial year now ending that has grown to "17,457,000, an increase of £7,830,000 with a still further prospect in the forthcoming budget to reach £22,000,000, surely a crushing tax for 4½ million of people. We respectfully ask all Irish members of Parliament to strenuously resist one penny further taxation especially as this country has been partly

Ordnance Survey map of Cork City showing Cork Workhouse, Douglas Road, *c.* 1910.
(SOURCE: CORK CITY LIBRARY)

boycotted by the Government in the manufacture of munitions, although we subscribed millions of money to the various war loans, and gave liberally the best and bravest of our sons, who have been amongst the most valiant in many a hard fought battle in defence of the Empire. That copies be sent to the Prime Minister, the Right Hon. David Lloyd George, Mr John E Redmond, the two City members and Sir Edward Carson.

30 March

DISPLAYS AT CORK SPRING SHOW

The members of the Munster Agricultural Society are to be congratulated on their enterprise and energy in carrying on their shows during these trying times, as the encouragement of all the industries that pertain to the land is of utmost importance. The more the farmer is encouraged to improve the breed of cattle, horses, pigs, and fowl, and to get the better for the country in general. Our great industry is agriculture, and every improvement in the methods of production is a sound, business-like policy. The competitions, which they promote undoubtedly tend to stimulate farmers to advance with the march of progress. They have not been slow to appreciate this, as is proved every succeeding year by the manner in which they support the shows with entries, and by the great interest they display in the exhibits. This has been particularly marked since the occupier became the owner of the land, for he realizes now that it is he who benefits by any and every improvement he can make in the methods of production. In other words, he is now working for himself, and he is most anxious in the majority of cases to do his utmost to get the very best results from his labour. This is an age of education – especially technical education – and technical education with regard to the land and its numerous industries is sought and eagerly learned by the rising generation. Old methods and prejudices are quickly discarded now, when it is proved in a practical way that those who continue to adopt them have but a very poor chance of holding their own in these days of keen competition.

Display at the grounds of the Munster Agricultural Society, 1929. (SOURCE: *CORK EXAMINER*)

APRIL

3 April

FOR KING AND COUNTRY

Royal Sailor's Home: Chairman Butterfield presided; Dr Lee submitted the annual report, in which it was stated that during the year the number of seamen who availed of the institution was 2,428, and is classified as follows – men of the Royal Navy, 1,395; men of the Royal Naval Reserves and merchant seamen of all nationalities, 1,035. One hundred and thirty seamen arrived at the Home destitute during the year, which was due to the piratical sinking of the merchant ships off the south and west coasts. Other crews from ships sunk off the coasts were, upon instruction from various Consuls, met at the station by the House Steward, who arranged for their transmission to their destination. The amount of money lodged with the House Steward during the year and forwarded by him to the wives and families of sailors, was £1,381 15s 0d.

Dr Lee, Honorary Physician, reports that some cases of illness were treated by him during the year. In submitting the annual report, the Committee once more wish to draw the attention of the public to the very grave condition of the finances of the Home. The year closed in 1914 with it in deficit of £63, and this year the balance against the Home is £97. This is almost entirely due to the reduction of the grant received annually from the Lords Commissioners of the Admiralty to £20 in 1914, and £20 in 1915. The Committee, with great regret, have to inform the public that unless the annual income can be increased by about £30 to £50, it will be found upon them to close the Home. To close the Home would be an injustice to these men, and to the men of the Royal Navy, who are daily risking their lives for the safety and comfort of the nation; but unless the small increase in income is forthcoming annually, the Committee will have no other alternative. The Lords Commissioners have been again and again appealed to during the year to increase the grant – but without any success. Therefore, the Committee hope that the matter will be seriously and sympathetically considered by the people of Cork, and that more subscribers may come forward to help in this necessary and useful work. All their efforts, however, have not availed them to decrease the steadily rising debt, which is causing them the gravest anxiety. The committee wish to express their thanks to Mr and Mrs Mullins for their management of the Home.

The past year necessitated great and unceasing efforts on their parts in arranging for the accommodation of shipwrecked and other crews at all hours of the day and night. The committee beg to thank the Lords Commissioners of the Admiralty for their lordships' kind annual grant to the funds of the Home, also for the regular supply of illustrated papers of the use of the boarders. They also thank the ladies and gentlemen who kindly sent papers and periodicals. They thank the Cork Steamship Companies for their kindness in the transmission of sailors and the railway companies for assisting Mr Mullins in forwarding crews to their homes. They thank Mr A R McMullen, agent Shipwrecked Mariners' Society, for his ever ready assistance to shipwrecked and destitute seamen, and also the officials of the Cork Post Office for their care in arranging the matters in connection with the conveyance of moneys to the families of sailors. The committee before closing their report would wish to express to the relatives of those officers and men of the navy and army and mercantile mariners who have fallen for their King and country in this disastrous war, their deepest sympathy.

5 April

A MEMORIAL TO THE CORK UNION

Cork Rate-Payer's Association meeting: Mr J C Rowe presided at a meeting held in the Marlboro Hall. Mr Dorgan said that since the last meeting he sent on to the Local Government Board the memorial promoted by the Association, asking the Board to appoint paid Guardians to administer the affairs of the Cork Union, in consequence of alleged dereliction of duty and extravagance. The memorial was signed by 150 of the largest ratepayers in the city, and some in the county. The total valuation was £33,306, and all told, those who signed the memorial represented between £40,000 and £50,000 out of the total city valuation of about £150,000. That was, considered very satisfactory. They got refusals from only a very small section of men, who were more or less connected with the Union, or possibly with persons who were contractors to the Union. It was not a healthy state of affairs that men – who should think it their duty to sign such a memorial, and should think it an honour to be asked to do so, would hold back at the present time. They had been commented upon at the Guardians and elsewhere for promoting such a memorial, and it had been described as an unpatriotic action. He held that it was the Guardians who were guilty of unpatriotic conduct by allowing the affairs of the Union to get into the state in which they were at present. In that year, when they were expecting Home Rule to be put into operation, the Guardians were guilty of a grave wrong to the country. Apart from considerations bearing on the war, it would be wrong at any time to allow the Union into its present state of administration, but at the present time it was a crime against the country.

The Chairman, as one who had been a strong Unionist, said he had, like many others, felt inclined to fall in with Home Rule on certain conditions. But if the way that the Cork Guardians manage things was anything like what would be done under Home Rule, he was afraid many of them would accept Home Rule with hesitation.

Mr Dorgan said he was never in any way was opposed to Home Rule, but he thought that under the existing condition of public administration it was incumbent on them to consider whether Home Rule would be a benefit to the country. He considered that their attitude was the real Nationalist one. They were looking for the efficient administration of public affairs. He proceeded to deal in detail with the increase in the expenditure of the Cork Union. In a few years the estimates had gone up by over £12,000. With regard to the Harbour Board, he thought the giving of a pension of £600 to any official at the present time was going somewhat far. Mr Donegan had rendered excellent service to the Board, but it was a question whether any official ought to get such a high pension when the revenue of the harbour was going down. His successor was appointed at £550, rising to £800, which was a very high figure, and besides, that the Board would pay the premium on his £3,000 bond.

9 April

SPORTING RIVALS, CORK VERSUS KERRY

The challenge-match between Cork (Macroom Selected) and the far-famed Kerry team was brought to an issue yesterday in Macroom. The weather was of an exceptionally favourable character, and the interest evoked by the meeting of the football rivals was demonstrated by an attendance of large dimensions. Challenge matches of contests which are not directly concerned with the championship series do not as a general rule appeal with considerable force to the Gaelic sport-loving public, but in open events in which Kerry footballers figure, matters are somewhat different, and one has not far to seek for a reason. Though Cork has often been knocked out by Kerry in the inter-county contests, yet there has always been the best of feeling towards the men from the Kingdom, who have done more than their "bit" to uphold the supremacy of Munster in the football world. The big crowd that patronised yesterday's match must then be regarded in the light of a well-merited compliment to the ex-All Ireland champions.

But compliments are all right in their way, and the question then arises: Was yesterday's match up to the expectations of the concourse? It certainly was. The team fielded by Macroom, assisted by the Nils and Collegians, put up a big fight against Kerry, whose fifteen was a strong, representative combination. The play provided a fast interesting game, in which there was some strenuous footballing, and the fact of the Cork team drawing against the visitors was perhaps the best tribute that could be paid to the display made by Cork. The match was started auspiciously by the respected pastor of the parish, the Very Rev Canon John O'Riordan, who threw in the ball amidst no little excitement and enthusiasm. It was an interesting exposition of the football code, and the result – 1 goal 3 points each – was a happy termination.

10 April

RUNNING THE GAUNTLET AT DARDANELLES

Private Michael Kiely of the 1st Battalion Munster Fusiliers, and of 63 Barrack Street, Cork. He may well be described as one of the lucky ones, for he was all through the Dardanelles campaign, from the opening to the evacuation, and he remains one of six of his battalion who escaped death, wounds, or even sickness – a remarkable record in itself when all the circumstances are borne in mind. He was on the River Clyde when she was run ashore in the Dardanelles landing operations in April, 1915, and spent two hours in the water, during which he and his comrades were heavily shelled by the Turks, many of course suffering death in the unequal struggle. He has now been at home on a week's leave from France, and on his return he carries with him the best wishes of his many friends for the some measure of good luck that attended him in the Dardanelles. He is only 24, but it can truly be said that he has seen and experienced more than has been the lot or perhaps the desire of many of his age.

13 April

A MOVING SPECTACLE AT AGHADA

It was only the burial of a simple sailor – that's all. And it was the strains of the "Dead March in Saul" that drew silent admiration for an Irish hero. Leading Seaman W Barry was being buried in his native village of Aghada, where he had first seen the light, where he had learned to play as a child, and where he first learned the "R's". It was all so simple, but, nevertheless, profoundly impressive. I listened intently and watched with interest the proceedings which attracted the attention and fervent respect of the quiet, unobtrusive populace of Aghada. The muffled roll of the drums and the measured tread of the burial party found a connotation in the sacredness of the proceedings. Everywhere was harmonic silence and respectful attention. The day was hot, but not unduly so. Spring was once more in evidence, and producing an abundance in new lease of life. The birds chirped and sang, men spoke in a respectfully quiet undertone that marred not the sanctity of the incidents, and the sun shone most gloriously. It was a happy day – it was also a sad day. Another was burying her son – she also burying a hero; one who gave his life for his country at his country's call.

The quiet, silent and respectful attitude of my comrades added a splendour to the occasion, which can only be described as reverential. A military funeral is an impressive sight. The solemnity of the proceedings are each a grandeur in themselves. I watched that silent mote of humanity pay its last respects to an Irish sailor, who had come home to be buried, and as silent and respectful did I form one of such that moved slowly along to the little cemetery – the last resting ground of him who had so nobly and generously rendered his last account to his country with his life. Birth and death are acknowledged. To die is only to be placed on another trial for life. No more will be asked. The only breakage of that splendid silence was a heart-broken sob from somewhere near the grave. There was grief and sadness, and there was also the proud knowledge that he had done his duty like a simple Irish sailor. He had given his youthful and vigorous manhood to the protection of its liberties and the sacredness of its shores. I listened to the recital of the Burial Service, and I knew that the words found a responsive echo in our hearts, and I listened to the silent rumbling of the coffin as it was gradually lowered into the grave, and I knelt with my comrades to silently mutter a simple prayer for repose.

As I have said, it was only the burial of a simple sailor, accorded full military honours. Such incidents must not, during this terrible crisis, be allowed to pass. There is a moral here worthy of note and attention. This young lad – he was only 24 – heard his country's call and answered it. He saw his duty and went forth with the men of the Empire to protect its honour. There was no deviation from the true principles which animated him, even though that principle eventually led to the simple graveyard at Aghada. There was glorification in such action and the Empire – aye – Christianity – honour and applaud such gallant heroes. He did not wait for the coming of the invader and despoiler, but took his place in the ranks of the men of the Nation. May he rest in peace. I further watched and listened to the almost silent command which brought forth three volleys from the firing party, and I was struck by the singularity by which they were interposed by the roll of the drums. It was all so fascinating and alluring. The culminating point of attractive and sympathetic forces was reached when the buglers sounded the "Last Post", and the firing party at the "present". The loftiest point in our emotions had been reached, and we felt that we were doing what common justice and humanity demanded of us – military honours to a member of the senior service. I left the precincts of the graveyard and pondered on the thousands of other Irishmen who had so proudly given their all for love of dear old Ireland and the sacredness of their faith.

"PATSY."

17 April

A SHELL FACTORY DECISION

The announcement made officially to-day that a national shell factory is about to be established in Cork, and additional orders given for other munitions work, will be read with interest by the citizens. It now lies with the Cork people to facilitate the local committee in providing suitable premises for the new factory. An extensive shed or ground floor, well lighted, about 200 feet long and 100 feet wide, is required at once by the committee, for the purpose of equipping it for shell-making. It ought not to be difficult to procure premises answering to these requirements in Cork. Owners or others interested in such premises are urged to communicate without delay this morning with the local committee in order that the important work of shell-making may be commenced at the earliest possible moment. Today a representative of the Minister of Munitions will arrive in Cork with the object of inspecting available premises, so it will be seen that the Ministry of Munitions is thoroughly in earnest interested in extending the work of shell-making to Cork City. The decision to provide additional munition work for this city has been made at a most appropriate time. Employment has not been too good of late, and many hands will eagerly avail of the opportunity now offered to obtain a livelihood. It will be seen that Mr Lloyd George's promise, when addressing the recent deportation from Ireland, to take the claims of Cork into consideration, has been faithfully kept, and it only remains now for the citizens to co-operate in every reasonable way in facilitating the execution of the official orders.

22 April

ART SALE OF CORK'S PAST

The catalogue of the fine collection made during the lifetime of the late Mr Augustine Roche has now been issued, and is well worthy of perusal by all lovers of the antique. The auction sale which has been announced for some time in our columns is fixed to start on Monday week, 1st prox., and will continue for five days, when over 1,100 lots will be realised absolutely without reserve, by order of the executors. The opening day will be devoted to the disposal of the collection of old Irish glass and the valuable old china. The glass embraces many fine specimens from the early Cork factories, whose wares have become so justly celebrated, including jugs, decanters, salad bowls, pickle jars, dishes, candelabra, wines, rummers, etc. The china is both varied and attractive, including a good collection of old Oriental in plates, dishes, mugs, bowls, etc. Old English potteries are strongly represented in Chelsea, Worcester, Derby, Rockingham,

Minton, and Wedgewood, together with many fine examples of old Continental factories. Some carvings in ivory and wood, and a few bronzed, go to make up the first day's sale.

The three following days will be taken up with the dispersal of the extensive and valuable collection of old Irish and English silver plate. It may be mentioned that this portion of the sale comprises about 700 lots, including in all over 6,000ozs. The plate is mostly early Georgian, with some pieces of Queen Anne, and embraces as fine a collection as has been offered in Ireland for many years. There are no less than 70 salvers, 140 salt cellars, 170 cream owers, 60 sugar basins, a grand collection of old two-handled loving-cups, sauce boats, old chalices and patens, tea and coffee pots, jugs, porringers, tankards, candlesticks, casters, mustard pots, tea caddies, cruets, baskets, centre pieces, taper holders, and a multitude of various other items. The concluding day will be occupied with the oil paintings, water colour engravings, prints, mirrors, and the collection of antique furniture. The entire business is in the hands of the well-known local auctioneers, Messrs Marsh and Sons, and Mr James J McCabe, solicitor, Cork, is acting for the executors. Special preparations are being made to put the vast collection on view for next Thursday.

25 April

CORK PARK RACES

It was certainly very unfortunate for the large number of holiday makers who patronised the Cork Park Meeting yesterday that the weather was so unfavourable. Had the conditions been fine instead of wet, the proceedings would have had at least been one element of enjoyment. What with the rain, mud and pools of water, the defeat of five favourites, and the generally tame sport, there was only the good music supplied by a military band to relieve the otherwise depressing surroundings for the majority of visitors. Since last year a new iron paling, ten feet high and two hundred and fifty yards long has been erected around the cheap enclosures. Mr Walter Russell, the clerk of the course; Mr William Green, the secretary, and the other officials performed their duties satisfactorily. As usual the catering in the hands of Thompson and Sons was admirable and the race cards were a credit to the work of Guy and Co, Ltd.

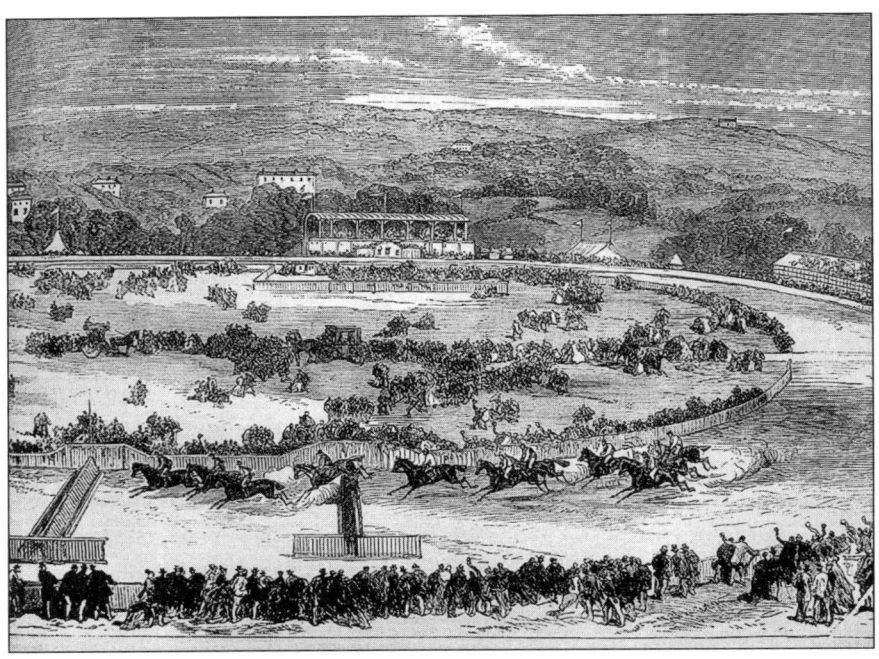

Illustration of Cork Park Races, 1870. (SOURCE: *ILLUSTRATED LONDON NEWS*)

Racing opened with a popular local victory in the Cork Hurdle, Crown Solicitor, the property of the well-known contractor, Mr J O'Callaghan, making all the running in the hands of C Aylin, and winning easily. The favourite was Mr Formby's Philander, the mount of Mr W J Parkinson, but though he ran well, he failed to stay, and was beaten into third place by Blackthorn, who should win a race before long.

Eight runners turned out for the Douglas Plate, a mile and a half handicap hurdle race, and four of them were well backed. The best support was for Raw Material, owned, like the first winner, by Mr J O'Callaghan, but after running prominently for nearly six furlongs, the horse dropped right out of the fighting line. Then Loch Stack, All-for-Ireland and Supremacy fought out a great finish, in which Supremacy just beat All-for-Ireland, with Loch Stack very close up third. Thus, Captain Holroyd Smith owned the winner, and his wife the third. Both horses were equally well backed, but had All-for-Ireland scored, it would have been a great turn up for the books, as he was a 20 to 1 chance. With a more powerful jockey he would certainly have just about won.

SIR ROGER CASEMENT AND THE LANDING OF ARMS

Press Bureau, 10.25 p.m. The Secretary of the Admiralty announces – During the period between pm April 20th and pm April 21st an attempt to land arms and ammunition in Ireland was made by a vessel under the guise of a neutral merchant ship, but in reality a German auxiliary, in conjunction with a German submarine. The auxiliary sunk and a number of prisoners were made, among whom was Sir Roger Casement.

The Press Association adds – Sir Roger Casement was in the British Consular service for 18 years, and was appointed British Commissioner to investigate the methods of the rubber collection and treatment of the primitive Indian tribes in the region known as Putumayo, on the Upper Amazon, a region dominated by the Peruvian Amazon Company. The publication of his report in July, 1912, which revealed the systemic perpetration of appalling atrocities committed by the Peruvian agents of the company occasioned profound indignation throughout the civilised world. He relinquished the Consul-Generalship at Rio de Janeiro in 1913, and afterward took an active part in the Home Rule controversy in Ireland on behalf of the Nationalist cause. Shortly after the outbreak of the war he was in America, and gave voice to pro-German views. He subsequently went to Germany, and was reported to have been received by high State officials in Berlin, who welcomed him for his anti-British sentiments. Reports from British prisoners of war incarcerated in Germany have made grave accusations against Sir Roger Casement of attempting to induce Irish soldiers in the prisoners' camps to renounce their allegiance to the British cause.

A SITUATION IN HAND, DUBLIN SHELLED

It was officially announced that Liberty Hall, the Sinn Fein headquarters, has been shelled by a gunboat in the Liffey, and the building occupied by troops. Reinforcements, including 10,000 troops from England with artillery, etc., have landed in Dublin. The situation is well in hand. It is declared that reports from the provinces indicate normal conditions prevail. The situation in Dublin has improved and adequate forces are at the disposal of the military authorities to cope with the situation. It is officially stated that German warships appeared off Lowestoft yesterday. They were chased by British light cruisers. Four people on shore were killed. Three British ships were hit. None sank. In a delayed message, sent from London on Tuesday, but received by us at 3 o'clock this morning, it is stated that in the House of Commons on Tuesday, Mr Birrell reported grave disturbances on Monday in Dublin, the Post Office being forcibly taken possession of. Soldiers arrived and the situation was well in hand. Up to seven o'clock last Monday night the rioters possessed four or five parts of the city.

29 April

DISTURBANCES AND MARTIAL LAW

The General Officer Commanding at Queenstown informs us it is not considered that there is any reason to fear any disturbance whatever in Cork, or that it will be necessary to impose any restrictions upon the citizens. In the secret session of Parliament, the Premier made it clear that the extension of the Military Service Act does not apply to Ireland. Last night the military authorities announced that the situation generally in the South of Ireland command is good. Reports received to-day from the garrisons at Galway, Cork, Wexford, Tralee, Limerick, Clonmel, Waterford, and other stations in the South of Ireland state that these towns are now, and have been up to the present, perfectly quiet. Reinforcements from England have arrived. In the South Irish command, adequate precautions have been taken to deal with any disturbances that may arise. Martial law has been proclaimed for all Ireland, the account says. It is hoped that the public will assist by implicitly obeying any orders given by the military or constabulary authorities, as otherwise it may be necessary to issue drastic regulation affecting the public generally.

It is also stated that all orders affecting the public issued by the G O C for the South of Ireland will be posted at the police barracks and Post Offices. Some delayed news from London throws some light on the situation in Dublin. The facts were mainly contained in a speech by Lord Lansdowne in the House of Lords, who said that there was a half-hearted attack on Dublin Castle, which was not pressed through. They occupied St Stephen's Green, they held up troops on their way from the barracks, and fired on them from the windows of houses on the route. The City Hall, the Post Office, the Four Courts, Westland-row Railway Station, and Broadstone Station were occupied by Sinn Féiners, and telegraphic communication was at first completely interrupted.

On Tuesday morning they were reported to be still in occupation of the buildings he named, and of houses in St. Stephen's Green, in Sackville street, and along the quays. By the evening the military had succeeded in protecting the line from Kingsbridge via Trinity College, to Custom House and the North Wall.

The casualties so far reported are: Soldiers, 15 killed, 21 wounded; policemen, 2 killed; loyal volunteers, 2 killed, 6 wounded. The insurgents, Lord Lansdowne said, have suffered a number of casualties. Eleven of the rebels were killed in the recapture of St. Stephen's Green. Large rein-forcements of troops have reached Dublin from England, the Curragh, and Belfast. There has been a small riot in Ardee, in County Louth, and "a rather more serious one" at Swords and Lusk (in Dublin County, to the north of Dublin).

30 April

THE SURRENDER BY PEARSE

On Saturday night we were officially informed that the following document has been signed by the leader of the Volunteers. It runs:

In order to prevent the further slaughter of unarmed people and in the hope of saving the lives of our followers, now surrounded and hopelessly outnumbered, the members of the Provisional Government present at Headquarters have agreed to an unconditional sur-render, and the commanders of all units of the Republican Forces will order their followers to lay down their arms.

Signed P H Pearse, dated 29th day of April, 1916.

MAY

2 May

PLEAS FOR THE MERCY HOSPITAL

The annual charity sermon in aid of the Mercy Hospital was preached by the Rev M Kiely CC, in SS Peter and Paul's Church yesterday after the First Gospel of the last mass in the presence of a large congregation. Taking as his text the words: "Behold he whom thou lovest is sick", from the Gospel of St John, the rev preacher said:- My brethren, I stand here to-day to make an appeal on behalf of the Mercy Hospital. The cause is such a good one, the Mercy Hospital does such charitable work, that the only fear I have is that I shall not do it justice. If indeed, I drive home these facts I shall rest content; for I am of opinion that if you understand what this appeal means you who are always charitable cannot fail to respond and give in generous measure. I shall, therefore, endeavour to place certain plain facts before you, and then in the light of these facts make my appeal. Understand then at the outset that in asking you to contribute towards the funds of the Mercy Hospital your money is not to be expended on the fabric of the hospital, nor is it meant to be a donation to the good sisters who are in charge of it and nurse the sick there. The money spent in building is obtained otherwise. For example, the new wing for children was provided by the generosity of a few benefactors; and the Sisters look for no other emolument than the reward of lives spent for God and the poor. What your money is required for is simply this, to enable the hospital to receive and give free treatment, whether medical or surgical, to those who are unable to pay for it. The Mercy Hospital has a long and honourable record.

THE REBELLION OF DUBLIN

The accounts from Dublin now to hand prove beyond doubt that the deaths and destruction caused by the mad orgy of disorder that raged in that city since Easter far exceed any guess that was made while communication with that unhappy city was cut off from the rest of the country. Our capital today resembles the pictures we see of some of the Belgian cities, and the great bulk of the population did as little to bring about the situation as the people of that much-tried country. The humiliating and torturing truth remains that all this devastation was caused by men professing to be Irishmen and acting in the name of Ireland. From the document that is published as having been posted up to proclaim the inauguration of the Irish Republic we get an insight into the men who were behind the "rebellion". They have no representative weight whatsoever. The majority have been for some years back closely connected with the Syndicalist movement which chose, some years ago, Dublin as the ground to try on their experimental programme, though its tenets were not as widely held there as they were in many other labour centres. They, however made trial of strength with capital in Dublin.

COMMANDANT PEARSE SHOT DEAD

Patrick H Pearse, Commandant General of the Army of the Irish Republic, and President of the Provisional Government, was 36 years old. A member of the Irish Bar, and the Headmaster of St Enda's School for Boys at Rathfarnham, Co. Dublin. He was born in Dublin, but was of English descent. After sentence of court-martial he was shot.

BURYING THE DEAD

Although no official figures have been issued by the authorities, it is known that the number of deaths of civilians caused in the recent revolt is considerable. Already no fewer than 160 have been accounted for, but the list which has been compiled is by no means complete, as many dead bodies were not recognised in any of the places open to public inspection. The 160 bodies mentioned are made up of 112 male, 20 females, and 28 unidentified. During the past few days many bodies have been buried in the Glasnevin cemetery, no fewer than 60 being interred there during yesterday. In Mount Jerome yesterday there were also buried 25 civilians, 2 officers, 3 privates and a member of the Veterans Corps. The body of The O'Rahally has been given a temporary resting place at Glasnevin.

Certificates of death from shot wounds have been issued in respect of 150 cases. Owing to the shortage of labour the bodies have in many cases been interred coffinless, in their clothes, in sheets and in blankets. Pathetic scenes are to be hourly witnessed at the several burying grounds. At Mount Jerome, the interments have been carried out at times under a crossfire from the soldiers at Portobello barracks and the rebels upon Rialto bridge, but no casualties have occurred during the performance of the gruesome task. Funeral processions are to be constantly seen in the streets, some of the hearses carrying more than one body. In some cases the bodies are conveyed to the cemetery in motor lorries flying the Red Cross, and assistance in this respect has also been given by several other organisations.

CALAMITOUS WRONG DOINGS

The Dublin disturbances still absorb the mind of Ireland. The dreadful occurrences in the capital, at a moment when war in all countries is the order of the day, are lost in the terrible aftermath that has involved the shootings and the sentencing of prisoners. While these have been imposed on a great number, no inkling has been given to the public of the degree of guilt of the parties involved, nor have the charges against them been indicated in the slightest manner. The bald announcement is merely put forward, leaving the imagination and many-tongued rumour to formulate the accusations against the unhappy men who have been condemned to death in the devastated city of Dublin. Everything now is quiet throughout the country, and the stillness of death apparently hangs over our much-tried capital. Is it not time, therefore, that the putting into effect of the extreme penalty should cease, and that some effort was made in the future that the accused should be tried under circumstances which would provide that some idea of the accusations and the gravity of charges of those involved should be judged by the public? It is very widely believed that on a very small circle indeed the responsibility for this terrible occurrence rests.

The story goes that a very large proportion of the men who took part in the fighting against the troops were not cognisant that they would be called on at any time to take the offensive against armed and disciplined forces; that through no deep-laid designs on their part did they find themselves confronting the forces of the crown, and the fact that they were connected with these mad happenings was rather the outcome of a sudden impulse than the result of a widespread plot. Under the circumstances we think it would have a very reassuring effect, especially now that everything is quiet, if an authoritative statement was made that further punishment would only be imposed after a public trial. The men, too, arrested throughout the country, who in the vast majority of cases must be innocent of evil design, should be brought speedily before a tribunal open to the public if a shadow of the case against them can be made, or liberated if, as must be the fact in a great many instances, no charge can be laid at their doors.

11 May

CONDEMNATION BY CORK HARBOUR BOARD

Meeting of Cork Harbour Board: Mr D J Lucy presided. The chairman said that last week the board passed a resolution denouncing the late rising in Dublin. Since then very tragic things had occurred in connection with it. No less than 13 men had been executed, and some thousands had been arrested. He now said, that as a sequel to their first resolution, and in keeping with their duty, they should yield to the side of clemency and Christian charity, and ask the Government to cease any further executions as sufficient had been done to expiate the offences of these foolish leaders in Dublin. The universal cry at the present, not only in Ireland, but in England, was that there should be an immediate cessation of the death penalty. He pointed out that such a course would not alone affect any bitterness that may remain, but may be entailed in the future. It would be in the interests of England to stop them for she had to look to the feelings of their kith and kin fighting England's battle on the fields of France and elsewhere, and also the feelings of an important section of the population in America, who were watching these events. He proposed that the board send a message to Mr Asquith asking him to use his clemency, and to stop any further executions as sufficient has been done to atone for what had occurred.

CORK'S CONDEMNATION

The Assistant Bishop of Cork, the Lord Mayor of Cork, the City High Sheriff, and Messrs John J. Horgan, solicitor; George Crosbie, BL; James J McCabe, LLD, members of UIL, Cork City Executive, sent on Tuesday to his excellency the Lord Lieutenant, Mr Asquith, the Prime Minister, and Mr John E Redmond, MP, a telegram which declared that, voicing the opinion of the great majority of the citizens of Cork, they protested most strongly against any further shootings as the result of court-martial trials, and against indiscriminate arrests throughout the country. Such shootings and arrests are having a most injurious effect on the feelings of the Irish people, and if persisted in may be extremely prejudicial to the peace and future harmony of Ireland, and seriously imperil the future friendly relations between Ireland and England.

The Irish Party passed resolutions calling for the stopping of executions and the withdrawal of martial law. The party also issues a powerful appeal to the Nation, putting before the country the choice between futile revolution and the constitutional movement, which had achieved such splendid results. In the House of Lords yesterday, Lord Crewe announced the resignation of Lord Wimborne, Lord Lieutenant of Ireland.

JOURNEYS TO MACROOM, CORK ANGLER'S ASSOCIATION

The second trout fishing competition for the season was held yesterday at Macroom, and it was mainly restricted to members who had not been prize winners in previous competitions. Strong inducements were held out to Waltonians to put forth their best endeavours, no fewer than nine prizes being presented. For premier honours in the open event the Association awarded a money prize of 15s; the second prize was supplied by Mr L O'Connor, and the third by Mr Tim McCarthy; Mrs O'Grady, Patrick Street presented the fourth: Mr G O'Connell the fifth, and the sixth, a special prize, was given by the Secretary of the Association, Mr R Manning for the largest trout. The programme also included a handicap contest for which the Association gave prizes of 15s, 10s and 5s.

A large number of aspirants journeyed by the 9.15 morning train to the scene of operations, plentifully equipped with quite a bewildering variety of lures in the form of artificial flies and other recognised ingenious devices for the capture of the wary trout. The novices, of whom there was a creditable muster, displayed a commendable zeal in their efforts to distinguish themselves and in not a few instances they quite exhausted the patience of the veterans with a multiplicity of interrogatories which might be advantageous to them in the course of the day's fishing. The counsel of the past masters in the piscatorial art was willingly extended to the tyros, who thereupon altered and changed their casts of flies with a degree of industry almost limitless. Thus was the journey to Macroom accomplished and it might be added that the train had no sooner entered the station when the competitors were on the road bound for the different fishing centres, full of hope and confidence.

A NEW TOY FACTORY

We are aware that our readers are thoroughly interested in the start of any branch of trade of which the working would entail the employment in Cork of those who have been hard hit by the war. A Committee has been formed to start a toy factory in Cork, their objects being (1) To start a new industry; (2) to give employment; (3) to help to exclude German trade when the war is over. The bulk of the toys supplied to the children of either the Old or New World come from Germany or Austria. From these countries, according to the latest pre-war annual returns, the United Kingdom imported toys to the value of £1,251.900; India, Australia, South Africa and Canada toys value for close on £300,000. The export of toys to France from Germany and Austria was £330,000 and to the United States £1,492,400. Some countries, whilst admitting goods such as raw material, machinery, and other materials essential to the manufacture of the finished article, excluded such imports as toys, amongst these countries being Japan, Switzerland, and Holland. When the war broke out these countries were in the position of being able to extend their trade, in particular the first named country, for the industry was already with them. The toy industry of Japan is now a great source of wealth. Ireland imports a large quantity of toys, the returns showing that a sum of over £20,000 is about the annual expenditure on toys produced outside our country.

Toy factories started in Ireland, even prior to the break with Germany, have done well. Where these toys have been on exhibition they have been much admired. A toy factory that was started in Dublin has been most successful. The promoters of the Cork industry received a most cheerful and encouraging report from the Secretary of the Dublin Toy Factory, who wrote: "We are very pleased to give you any information that may be helpful as we are very anxious to introduce toy-making into Ireland on a large scale. We have an enormous demand for our toys." Mr Riordan, Secretary of the IDA, who has given much careful study to the scope for new industries wrote: "Toy-making as an industry has good prospects in Ireland. Where they have been started already the factories are getting more orders than they can cope with". An influential committee is connected with the Cork Toy Factory, the Secretaries being Miss Rose Lynch and Miss Mamie Harrington. Before placing the project before the public this committee has done excellent organising work, having carefully examined the local demand for toys, which it is believed will in itself tax the output of the factory. Both the wholesale and retail Cork houses have promised not only to buy the Cork-made goods, but to create a market for such articles in England through the medium of the firms with whom they have business relations in the matter of toys.

The Department in Dublin has also been approached and has given towards the start of the Cork factory a grant sufficient to pay for a fully qualified teacher. The promoters find that the capital required for a satisfactory beginning would be about £850, a sum similar to that on which a factory on the East Coast of England made a start and now employs fifty persons, six sewing machines being in use. There is no doubt of the room in Cork for such a factory, and there is also the certainty that the toys made there should not alone be good and cheap, but many should in a measure be of a distinct type to those of other countries especially where ornamentation or costume would permit of original treatment.

16 May

MUSICAL TREAT AT FR MATHEW HALL

It is indeed but seldom that the citizens of Cork are afforded such an opportunity to share the joys of a real musical treat such as that as is being given this week at the Father Mathew Hall, Queen Street, where the oratorio and sacred drama of St Francis is being produced. The drama is written by Rev Mother M. Gertrude, the distinguished author of "Nemesius" and many other beautiful works. Professor J C Shanahan has put the libretto to music and to embellish the undertaking has appropriately introduced some of the fine choral compositions of Handel, Colburn, Gounod, Mendelssohn, Sullivan, and Wallace. He has enlisted to his support as principles the most popular and highly favoured of the male soloists in the city, and a choir of over 100. In addition to this the orchestra is led by Miss Eva Ryan so that there can be no doubt of the efficiency of the company under Professor Shanahan's direction to give a finished performance. However, this ready talent does not give a reason to deduct any praise from the merit of the work. Rather is it a source of gratification that such talent was available in the

city to portray all the appeal, edifica-
tion, sympathy, and exquisite beauty
of the work of Mother M. Gertrude.

In which is unfolded with a charm-
ing power the fascinating life story of
St Francis of Assisi.

18 May

PLACARD AT THE FRONT

Private Dave Mahony, Macroom, now attached to the Signal Corps of the Munsters, which form part of the Irish Brigade, arrived home on leave from the trenches on Tuesday morning last. Of the fighting generally, he says it is of the tricky kind, confined almost entirely to explosives. There is no open fighting, and that does not at all suit the men of the Munsters, who often long for an open hand-to-hand fight with the Germans. Gas is the one death–dealing element they dread most. Just about Easter, after abandoning their gas attacks for a period of six months, the Germans reverted to this cruel method of warfare. The result of the attack was most disastrous; "It seems to me," says O'Mahony, "that the Dublins and Inniskillings must have been caught unawares, because rats and mice, which are very prevalent, were to be seen turned up-side down, some of them quivering in their death agony.

When the wind is from a certain point all the men don their masks, and at first warning they pull them over their faces to keep out the deadly fumes. We heard of the Dublin affair just about this time, and it was a great shock to the boys. Things were unpleasant enough after the casualties we had experienced, still they made the best of it, and joked a good deal about it, saying there was no danger of great trouble as all the fighting men were out in France. One of those days the Germans put out two boards on their parapet. One bore the news of General Townshend's capture at Kut, with "30,000 men". Another had this query: 'Irishmen, why will you fight for England while they are shooting your wives and sisters in Dublin'. Captain Larry Roche made up his mind that the 'G' Company should bring in these boards. He sent out some of his men, but the danger was too great, and they had to abandon their task. Still there were men amongst the Munsters brave enough to take any risk, and who did the trick too. Lieutenant Biggane of Cork City and Corporal Kemp wrapped themselves in sheets of suitable hue, and crawling over the intervening space, with death hanging over them, they reached the enemy parapet and bore away, one each, the annoying placards.

MR ASQUITH COMES TO CORK

No little interest was felt amongst all classes in the city yesterday when it became generally known that the Prime Minister intended to pay a visit to Cork prior to his return to Parliament. It was taken for granted in coming here it was his object to interview leading citizens and to ascertain at first hand for himself the exact position of affairs in the city and county. A good deal of reticence was displayed by those who ought to know as to Mr Asquith's movements, and when he would arrive in Cork, as well as the place at which he would receive those whom he desired to see. It was not stated whether he would arrive by train or motor, and many who thought he would travel by train went to the Glanmire terminus to await the arrival of the 2.20 train from Dublin. But it was apparent to anyone having a little experience of the arrangements made by railway companies and the authorities, when less notable persons than the Prime Minister travel by rail, that it was very unlikely he would arrive by that train.

Not for the past few weeks was access to the platform so easy, and except for the number of persons congregated on the road outside as well as inside the precincts of the station, was there anything to indicate the happenings of any unusual event. But the general public did not quite realise this. The train steamed in exactly to scheduled time, but the Prime Minister was not in it. A number of cross Channel journalists who have been following Mr Asquith during his visit to Ireland alighted and it was ascertained that he was travelling down by motor. The hour of his arrival was not known for certain. He had, it was found, left Dublin somewhere about ten o'clock in the morning, and a motor-car might take five hours or more to negotiate the upwards of 160 miles. Putting two and two together, the journalists concluded that the distinguished visitor would reach Cork between three and four o'clock in the afternoon. Those who were to receive him professed not to know exactly when he would reach the city. It was found out, however, that he intended to conduct his interviews at the Municipal Buildings. The general public were not aware of this beyond what they could surmise from seeing a number of police in the vicinity of the Buildings. Consequently, nothing in the nature of a crowd collected.

A SAVING IN DAYLIGHT

Yesterday morning citizens woke up to find the new Daylight Saving scheme in full operation. All official clocks, at post offices and elsewhere were duly put forward as required by the new Act. Practically all other clocks showing time to the public on the streets of Cork were similarly advanced during the night. The innovation was not attended by any undue confusion or complications, and people seemed to accept it as a matter of course. There were, no doubt, those who thought the morning looked unusually early at 8 o'clock, while some found it easier to attend mass celebrated nominally an hour later than was their norm. But they all had the promise of an extra hour's daylight – that is those who get up according to the clock at their usual hour of rising. The new time applied to the railways, and taken all round they – as the chief businesses to which the Act applied yesterday – adapted themselves to the new conditions. It was to be noticed, however, that some of the trains did not arrive quite up to the minute, but this could not be wondered at, as two factors contribute to the punctuality or non-punctuality of trains on the smaller railway systems. While the railway officials do their best to start trains according to the timetable, they cannot well leave behind the passenger who is seen rushing into the station at the last moment. These little delays, when accumulated over a line of ten or twelve stations, aggregate something considerable when the train arrives at its destination. There was, perhaps, some excuse for the late passenger yesterday, and he must have asserted himself in at least too few instances.

In the city churches, Masses were celebrated according to the official time. An exception was, however, made at St Finbarr's West, on account of the number of country residents belonging to the parish, some of whom might have missed Mass if the new time was adopted. Next Sunday the Masses will be celebrated there according to the official clock time. The licensed trade was affected by having to close an hour earlier in the evening than usual, but as against this, opened an hour earlier. Taken as a whole, the scheme does not appear to have materially inconvenienced anyone and if it has the various beneficial effects which the promoters claim for it, few will be found to grumble.

RESOLVING DISTURBANCES IN CORK

The following is the text of Mr Tennant's reply in the House of Commons to-day as to the negotiations in Cork during the recent disturbances. Mr Tennent said it is not the case that Captain Dickie invited the leaders of the Irish Volunteers in Cork to meet him at the house of the Bishop of Cork, and he did not hold a conference with the volunteers. There were however, negotiations between Captain Dickie and the Assistant Bishop of Cork and the Lord Mayor, as a result of which a settlement was proposed as follows: If the Irish Volunteers handed in their arms to the Bishop and the Lord Mayor before midnight on April 30th and assisted the authorities to maintain order, the General Officer commanding was prepared to ensure no prosecution for offences other than acts of overt rebellion or traitorous correspondence with the enemy. Those who for a valid reason could not return their arms by the 30th April might be permitted to do so by May 1st, provided the bulk of the arms had been returned on 30th April. The Lord Mayor and the Bishop were to ensure that all arms were collected and placed in safety, and to give their personal assurance that this had been done.

On May 1st the Lord Mayor informed the military authorities in writing that the Volunteers had refused to hand over their arms to the Bishop and himself. He was immediately informed that any guarantee given to the Bishop and the Lord Mayor by the General Officer commanding on the condition that arms were handed in by midnight of 30th April was cancelled in view of the statement. Some arms were handed in to the Lord Mayor about midnight of 1st and 2nd May, but as I have stated no agreement was in operation. The Lord Mayor on May 2nd informed Captain Dickie that he could not guarantee the safety of the arms handed in, and they were accordingly moved for safe custody on 3rd May. I may add that no complaint has been received from the Lord Mayor as to any threat to try him by court martial. At their own request the leaders of the Cork City Volunteers were permitted on 29th April to visit the country districts to endeavour to prevent disturbances by country branches or their organisation, and Captain Dickie visited the Volunteer Hall on that date to arrange the details of this matter after the general negotiations with regard to it had been concluded.

As regards the arrests, it is the case that some arrests took place on 2nd May in accordance with instructions from the Headquarters of the Irish command. Similar arrests were made in other counties, but as no agreement was in existence no violation of agreement took place in respect of those arrests. I am informed that these arrested were released the same day in consequence of an appeal made by the Bishop of Cork. Two leading members of the Cork City Volunteers have since been arrested by the constabulary, and their cases are being investigated. As regards the general question raised in the last part of question 60, I can of course say nothing. My honorable friend will, I think, see that there was no breach of agreement on the part of any of those concerned, but that, on the contrary, the various parties involved acted for the best under very difficult circumstances.

24 May

INSIGHTS BY THE LORD MAYOR

Dear Sir – With reference to Mr Tennant's reply to a question in the House of Commons on Friday night and reported in your paper re negotiations between the military authorities and the Assistant Bishop of Cork and myself for the delivery of arms by the Volunteers, there are a few inaccuracies which I would like to correct; (1) As regards the statement that arms were to be delivered to me at midnight on Sunday, 30th April. That was the hour suggested by Captain Dickie; but I said that Sunday would not be a suitable day, whereon Captain Dickie remarked that "the Bishop will give you a dispensation". I again protested, and it was then and there agreed that 12 o'clock on Monday, May 1st, would suit all concerned.

Lord Mayor of Cork, Cllr Thomas C. Butterfield, 1916. (SOURCE: *CORK EXAMINER*)

Subsequently matters again came to a deadlock in consequence of an article which appeared in the "Constitution," stating: "We have been officially informed that the Cork Sinn Féiners have handed up their rifles to the police"; this appeared to be a breach of confidence on the part of the military, as one of the conditions agreed on was that no reference was to be made by the newspapers to disarmament. Fresh negotiations had to be entered into with the result that 12 o'clock midnight on Monday May 1st was again decided on as the hour for handing up to me the rifles in the possession of the Volunteers. (2) Mr Tennant also says: "The Lord Mayor on May the 2nd informed Captain Dickie that he could not give a guarantee for the safety of the arms". There is no truth in that statement. What occurred is as follows: At 12 o'clock on May 2nd Captain Dickie called on me and said: "Have I your assurance that so many rifles are in your possession". I answered, "You need not take my word: come and see for yourself", and accordingly led him to the room in which the rifles were stored. He then said: "Are they safe here". I replied, "I am sure they are". He added, "Let's have a look around"; we then proceeded to the upper part of the house, and after he had explored it he remarked, "It seems safe from the back, but there is danger from the skylight"; I replied, "If there was never a skylight there, and people wanted to, they could smash the roof"; nothing more was said on the matter and he left me under the impression that he was satisfied. Never at any time did I express or imply that I was afraid of a raid on my place by the Volunteers for the purpose of regaining possession of the arms, and I am still of opinion that none would have taken place - Yours faithfully, T C Butterfield, Lord Mayor.

25 May

UPDATE ON MUNITIONS FACTORY

General satisfaction will be felt in Cork with the statement made by the Lord Mayor at yesterday's meeting of the Corporation Law and Finance Committee as to the result of the negotiations that have taken place with the Munitions Department regarding the establishment of a new factory in the city. Following on Captain Downie's visit on Tuesday a formal offer has come from the authorities to take over the Bazaar Market at a rent of £200 per annum for the duration of the war. As things stood this institution yielded little or no net revenue to the Corporation for several years past, and it had been proposed prior to Captain Downie's first visit to Cork to arrange for the letting of a portion of the premises. That several offers would be obtained for it is certain, because the site is a really valuable one. The only difficulty that had presented itself at the time was how to arrange the present stall-holders. That trouble has been got over; the stallholders go to St Peter's Market, which has vacant space ample for their requirements. The ratepayers will gain to the extent of £200 per annum, but the material benefit to the city will be much greater than that.

CORK'S NEW YEAST FERMENTATION PLANT

We have great pleasure in placing before our readers the singular merits that are attached to a new Cork industry, and the important result that will rapidly accrue to the people of the South of Ireland through the continuation of its deserved success. This splendid enterprise is the Cork Yeast Company, and in its formation, equipment in the matter of machinery, system of working, and aims to produce the very best article, neither money nor energy has been spared. The factory is situated on the Watercourse Road, and until fifty years ago the premises were Hewitt's Distillery, which for over a hundred years was famous for its whiskey, but on the amalgamation of that concern with the other distilleries it ceased to exist as a distillery. The buildings cover a great area, and being of special strength in structure, having cast granaries, malting floors, and departments suitable for the reception of capacious tuns, vats, etc., but few alterations would ordinarily have been required to make the place suitable for its present uses; but as it was determined to make of the factory the best lighted, ventilated, and suitable group of buildings possible, important structural alterations were made at a big cost. Many floors were re-laid with substances that either assisted or suited the various temperatures that would be in use in the rooms, the flooring material ranging from Trinidad asphalt to the smoothest cement.

OPERA HOUSE WAR PICTURES

Last night the management of the Opera House provided an instructive entertainment in the term of a series of excellent cinema war records, which were shown to two "houses". Photos of a number of celebrities identified with the Allies cause, were very popular. These were followed by several very clever cartoons illustrating the artist's conception of things, and the pointed humour of some of them evoked considerable appreciation. Exciting scenes on the streets of Johannesburg, South Africa, proved of interest to many. Coming somewhere nearer home, British and French battleships were shown in action off the Turkish coast. Smaller craft are seen doing scouting duty. A French airman is decorated on board a battleship for some daring feats. Somewhere in France or Flanders is the next scene of operations. Neuve Chapelle and other villagers are shown after the German bombardment. The desolation of the landscape is effectively pictured. Nothing but ruins where once stood churches, schools, public buildings, or industrial establishments. A melancholy commentary on the whole thing is the graveyard, where lie hundreds and hundreds of soldiers who have fallen. From ruined villages

Cork Athenaeum, *c.* 1910. (SOURCE: CORK CITY LIBRARY)

one is taken to the British trenches, where all the phases of modern warfare is vividly photographed. A big gun is shown in action against a German blockhouse, which is blown into atoms. A battery of 18-pounders is shown in action.

Trench life is seen as it actually is, and some human touches are included in the picture. The Grenadier Guards march past to the firing line. A Welsh battalion is also shown. Both were applauded; but greatest interest centred round the Irish regiments. The Royal Irish, the Munsters, and the Connaughts were shown going to Mass at the front, and then marching off into action. These particular films are very well photographed, and probably many southern people will recognise friends. Captain William Redmond, MP, was recognised leading his company to the trenches, and he received hearty applause. The work of the RAMC can be followed from the time a wounded soldier receives first aid treatment in the firing line until he sails for home. A word of all-round praise is due to the camera operators, who made the records, for they secured fine pictures under exceptionally unfavourable circumstances of difficulty and danger. Some of the pictures were taken within 150 yards of the enemy's front trenches. The War pictures will be shown twice nightly during the week. There will be a matinee on Saturday at 2.30 pm.

JUNE

1 June

MUNITIONS FACTORY
AT ST PETER'S MARKET

Preparatory to the establishment of the Government Munitions Factory in Cork, provision has to be made for the accommodation of those tenants of St Peter's Market who will be disturbed, and this work, which is in the hands of the Corporation, is at present being carried out. There are in all some 78 tenants to be provided for, and as the accommodation available in the northern avenue of the Bazaar Market only measures 133 feet by 42 feet, with a wing 40 feet by 20 feet, about seventeen tenants, who would otherwise be without room, will have to be accommodated in a new annexe, which will be built in Portney's Lane, adjoining, on the site of some old houses recently thrown down. An amount of work has to be done, and this includes not only the draining of the northern avenue of the Bazaar Market, the concreting of a large portion of the floor of same, the removal of the gear at present in St. Peter's Market, but the entire building except for the back and gable walls in the annexe in Portney's lane. So that with the greatest expedition possible, some time may elapse before St Peter's Market can be handed over to the Government authorities.

Former building of munitions factory at St Peter's Market; today the building is occupied by the Bodega Bar and Restaurant.. (PICTURE: KIERAN MCCARTHY)

LAMBKINS TOBACCO TO THE FRONT

This is a figure to appal the Anti-Tobacco League, but whether the weed be noxious and harmful, as they claim or fragrant and soothing, the boys in the trenches must have their smoke, for the latter is their ardent belief. They require the very best tobacco, and therefore it is a gratifying thing to know that, among the brands of repute chosen to supply tobacco to the troops, Lambkin's of Cork figure well in the list. They have got their third order, and it is as usual being most carefully carried out. The picture shows a weekly consignment, part of an order of 20,000lbs for 320,000 men, so that each will receive an ounce of tobacco. The mixture is made up of two of the best American leaves and a special growth, the result being a smoke that is full flavoured and cool. The making up, packing etc., is mostly carried out, and gives a good deal of employment in their factory, as well as a fillip to the Cork box industry.

A BLANKET AND A PAWN BROKER

Mr Starkie pointed out that pawnbrokers were not allowed to accept articles in pawn from persons under fourteen years of age. Mr Fitzgerald said he was afraid some pawnbrokers made few inquiries in that respect. William Watkins, an assistant at Mr Henderson's pawn-office, 19 Shandon Street, gave evidence as to the pawning of the blanket by Kate Sullivan. He was too busy at the time to ask the girl any questions. He knew her face, but could not remember if he questioned her about her age. He knew there was a limit of age as regards persons from whom pawnbrokers should accept articles.

Mr Starkie – Did you think this girl was under fourteen years of age? I thought she would be about that. It is pretty hard to tell sometimes. Don't you think you might have asked her? I had a right to ask her. I admit that.

Constable Sullivan stated that when arrested the accused admitted the charge. Accused said that she pawned the blanket in order to buy milk for her child. The magistrates decided to allow the accused out under the Probation of Offenders Act.

NEWS FROM THE NORTH SEA

The anxiety that was manifested all day Saturday by the relatives of Corkmen serving in the various units of the British Navy understood to be on duty in the North Sea area was continued yesterday, and there were many inquiries as to the arrival of the casualty lists. The more definite news available this morning will at least allay the suspense of many persons who did not know whether the vessels on which their relatives served were in action or not. The vessels whose fate was uncertain are now accounted for, and it is announced that the three destroyers – *Nomad*, *Nestor* and *Shark* – have been sunk. Information from West Cork goes to show that the engagement has caused much suspense in many a home, especially in and around Kinsale, from which district alone several hundred are serving in the Royal Navy, a considerable proportion of them being in the Grand Fleet. Crosshaven, Ringaskiddy and Aghada are also represented. At the same time, so far as inquiries go to show, there is reason to hope that the actual number of casualties from Cork will not be exceptionally heavy. The full official casualty lists may require some days to complete, and meanwhile everyone will hope that of the great numbers of Corkmen serving in the Navy, those who have fallen victims will not be as many as was feared when the news first came to hand.

A BLEEDING COUNTRY

The news of the deportation from Dublin within the last few days of one hundred prisoners to Wakefield, Wandsworth, and Knutsford Detention Barracks can scarcely be expected to help in bringing about a détente, or to cause satisfaction amongst the people of this country. The continued existence of martial law in Ireland enables the military to act with absolute authority in such matters, but the various speeches of the Premier led to the belief that a more generous course of action would be pursued in connection with the persons under arrest. While it is true that Mr Asquith did not definitely commit himself to a promise that the Dublin prisoners or the prisoners detained in England would be forthwith released, still he conveyed that the Government was desirous of dealing in a humane and generous spirit with such prisoners, subject to certain exceptions. Replying to Mr Dillon, the Premier last week stated that the principle he would follow would be to treat with the utmost leniency and release as speedily as possible all persons except those who were concerned directly or indirectly with the rising and the preparations for it, and he also made an exception in the case of persons whose return to Ireland would be a source of danger to the peace of the country. It might be suggested that the deportation of another batch of one hundred prisoners does not indicate that the plan of leniency laid down by the Premier finds an echo in the action of the military authorities, unless of course it be the case that the latest batch of deportees comes under the heading of the exceptions which the Premier was careful to define.

However that may be, the broad fact remains that the continuation of martial law for all Ireland and the sending of large numbers of Irishmen to English Detention Barracks, now that the country has resumed its normal conditions, are not regarded by thoughtful people as wise or tactful proceedings, which can produce the result that all who are interested in Ireland's welfare would desire.

The announcement of the release of another batch of 200 prisoners, which also was made by the military headquarters within the past few days, is satisfactory as far as it goes, but the general opinion, which it may be said is growing more emphatic, is that this plan of release by instalments does not go far enough, and is not at all as effective, and cannot produce such beneficial results, both for Ireland and Great Britain, as if the Government had taken its courage in both hands and ordered a general amnesty. The latest list included several southern names, but it is a well-known fact that many Munster men are still incarcerated who took no active part in the recent disturbances, and their families, who have been left unprovided for, are naturally restless and discontented at the delay. It seems almost superfluous to state that this prolonging of the mental strain, under which numbers of Irish families are suffering, is not conducive to the promotion of a peaceful and friendly spirit, and one is forced to the conclusion that the authorities have learned little from the lessons of the past, and fail to appreciate the Irish temperament, which invariably responds to kindly and generous treatment, and is much more easily influenced by sympathy than by severity.

The magnificent part that Ireland has played and is still playing in the war stands to her credit, though it may be noted that this official boycott of the achievements of Irish troops in France and in Gallipoli, which necessitated a protest from the Irish leader before tardy justice was done, did not tend to inspire the people with admiration for the even-handed justice of official methods, or increase their appreciation for military red-tape. Some amends might even now be made if the Government, instead of standing on the strict letter of the law in the case of deported Irish prisoners, or instead of continuing to deport groups of accused or suspected persons to England, indicated its willingness to adopt a merciful course and promptly restored the remaining prisoners to their families. The task that Mr Lloyd George has undertaken, and to which ministers of different parties have given their blessing, could not fail to be simplified and expedited if the Government gave an immediate proof of their sympathy with Ireland, a country that is still bleeding and one which needs all the kindness and consideration that can be given to her.

8 June

THE MANSION HOUSE FUND

The decision of the Lord Mayor of Cork to confine the Flag Day collection in Cork to the purpose of helping the Mansion House Fund which is intended for the relief of the persons thrown out of employment in Dublin through fire, will unquestionably commend itself to the citizens. The problem that has to be faced is the alleviation of temporary distress, and that is a matter of extreme urgency which calls for immediate attention. There can be no second opinion that much suffering is being patiently endured in the metropolis, and any prompt method of mitigating it will appeal strongly to the Cork public. It should be clearly understood that the Flag Day collection is intended for the alleviation of temporary distress, and that the money obtained will be distributed amongst all the people who have suffered through lack of employment, and that no particular class will receive preferential treatment. The provisions for the families of deported persons will, as far as prisoners are concerned, be a tax on Ireland for years, and will require separate and special consideration and organisation, which it is safe to assume, will be readily and generously accorded by the whole country.

9 June

EPIDEMICS AND MORTALITY

Cork Fever Hospital: The annual report submitted by the Honorary Secretary stated – On the 1st January there were 65 patients under treatment, and 435 were admitted during the year, making a total number of 500 patients treated, as compared with 404 during the year 1914. Of the patients treated 432 were discharged cured, and 37 remained in the hospital on 31st December. There were 31 deaths during the year and of these it is with regret to be noted that many of them were brought to the hospital for treatment when they were beyond recovery. Deducting these cases, the mortality shows a very low rate, namely 4.8 per cent, which must be considered satisfactory. The medical staff and committee have frequently urged upon the citizens the great importance of prompt isolation and hospital treatment for cases of infectious diseases. Prompt isolation is one of the most important safeguards against the spread of an epidemic, and it is the duty of everyone to encourage prompt isolation, having due regard to the health of the citizens. The majority of the cases treated came from thickly populated districts, and needless to say, the means are not at hand in the humble abodes of the working classes for the necessary treatment of serious diseases. The Committee, therefore, earnestly hope that their fellow citizens will bear in mind the value of this hospital, not only as a curative establishment, but as a great means of preventing the spread of dangerous diseases in our midst. Of the cases treated 167 came from the north side of the city, and 165 from the south side, 42 from the centre of the city, and 61 from the county and rural districts.

13 June

CATHOLIC MISSIONS IN CHINA

China offers a vast field for the propagation of the Catholic faith, and those at home enjoying the great blessing of being within the fold of the True Church can do a great deal to help in the conversion of the Chinese pagans to Christianity. Reports from priests in missionary work in China show the need for help at home. Father W

O'Brien, CC, Crosshaven, Co Cork, has taken a great interest in this missionary work, and he will receive subscriptions towards the fund necessary to endow hospital beds and Catholic schools in China. It may also be mentioned that the good Sisters of the Presentation Convent, Crosshaven, are getting up a grand drawing of prizes, the proceeds to be devoted to the worthy object of helping the Chinese mission.

16 June

DEATH OF MRS GEORGE BOOLE

The death of Mrs George Boole [Mary Everest] in London at the age of 84, removes another link in the chain connecting the present of University College Cork with the past of the old Queen's College. Perhaps one of the most illustrious names associated with the college since its foundation was that of the late George Boole, who for a number of years occupied a Professorial Chair, and gave his unrivalled powers as a mathematician to the teaching of mathematics in its University. Some of his greatest productions were written whilst he held that Chair. His widow, who has just died, was likewise a talented writer and psychologist, and it is a remarkable fact that her genius has descended to her daughters, who, by the way, were all born in Cork. It is noteworthy that the late Professor Boole's grandson has obtained the two highest prizes in mathematics at Cambridge University, and has recently been made Professor of Meteorology by the Government.

18 June

VIRTUES OF GLORY, DEATH OF A BISHOP

Born in the South Parish, Cork, in 1839, at the age of eighteen years, the late Bishop O'Callaghan entered the Novitiate of the Dominicans at Tallaght, and elevated to the priesthood in 1864. He spent six years after that teaching in the convent at Tallaght, and then returned to Cork; and before his appointment as Prior of San Clemente he was in the house of the Order at Claddagh, Galway, and St Catherine's,

Newry, returning to his native city to the exalted office of Co-adjutor-Bishop to Most Rev Dr Delaney in 1884. On that occasion he was received with enthusiasm by the people of this ancient diocese, and has truly lived in their hearts through all the years of his episcopacy, for as Lord Bishop of Cork he displayed characteristic virtues of humility, devotion, and self-abnegation, as well as of firmness in every righteous cause, which made him the beloved of his brethren in religion and the esteemed and revered friend of those beneath his sway. But those virtues are so glorious that the light to the public on the efforts directed, and work dictated by the holy and eminent churchman who possessed them is dimmed, if not altogether obscured.

The way of his lordship, Most Rev Dr O'Callaghan, was not in the attraction of notice. He was meek and humble, but keen and appreciative, well understanding the manners and ways of men, and sensitive to the needs of the present and the exigencies of the future. He was first an apostle and then an administrator. His primary efforts were directed to give honour to God, and to give the people the facility to give that honour, and the means to keep strong in their faith, and the harbour to withstand the wiles and temptations of the world. His secondary labours were shaped in securing that his people would have the media to be instructed, taught and equipped to stride honourably through this vale of tears. Hence to-day throughout the diocese of Cork, by his wide guidance, under providence, stately churches rise their defiant spires, convents give their refuge, and monasteries and schools the advantage of secondary and primary education under the best and brightest conditions. In this happy state is discernible the influence and encouragement of our late revered Bishop. His interest in public matters was not less keen if not so active. As a young missionary he had seen much of his native Ireland, and the harrowing chapters enacted in his early days could not but have left their impression on his noble mind. He had witnessed the duress and hardships inflicted on the people too often not to have his sympathies stirred to their ardent support. As Bishop, therefore, he added to the strength of the Irish Hierarchy in demanding the rights of the people and in supporting the Irish representatives in the battle on their behalf. Too well aware also of the ill of dissension, and the tragedy of disunity in the country, his influence and assistance were cheerfully given to exhort the people to unite in their actions and policies, and to learn of the evil of discord in national demands.

AGHADA, HAMLET OR VILLAGE

Sir, - I wonder if you could afford me space in your widely-read paper to draw the attention of your numerous readers to Mr MacDonagh's book "The Irish at the Front"? I am not desirous of seeking a cheap advertisement for the publication; it does not require it. But on page 146, recounting how Corporal Wm Cosgrave, 1st Royal Munster Fusiliers, won the Victoria Cross in Gallipoli, the writer says "he (Cosgrave) was invalided home to Aghada, a little fishing hamlet in County Cork". As a native of Aghada, I take exception to its being reduced to a hamlet, and in any future editions – and there should be many – I would respectfully suggest to Mr MacDonagh that the word "village" be substituted. We have always been taught and have looked upon Aghada as a village. A battleship could be manned – in every unit from a skipper downward – from "Trapeen".

Aghada, in addition to being a village, is also a parish, and a fairly large one at that. In almost any ship in the British Navy you will find someone hailing from there, and I think I can fairly say that each and every one is proud of his connection with the service. I have not yet seen the casualty lists of the North Sea battle, but I shudder at the thought of the amount of mourning that the loss of these ships will bring to Aghada. No, Aghada is not "a little fishing hamlet" by any means. Many years ago it was a prosperous seaside resort, and if its population to-day is reduced to that of

Aghada, County Cork, *c.* 1910. (SOURCE: CORK CITY MUSEUM)

a hamlet the fault is not a native one; it can be traced to the same source as that sad and unfortunate occurrence in the splendid capital of Ireland several months ago; and when the key once more turns in the rusty lock of that building in College Green the men of Aghada, numbers of whom have placed themselves on the top rung of the ladder of their professions, often against unfair odds and without any occult aid, will watch with delight the return of their native village to its former prosperity, and will assist in utilising the natural resources of the district in the manner which Almighty God ordained that they should be used.

I trust that, should Mr MacDonagh see this letter, he will read it in the friendly spirit in which it is written. I am confident that he will forgive me when I tell him that I am very jealous of the status of my native village, which I believe every Aghada man cherishes with as equally an affectionate remembrance as I do.

Sam Passey
HMS St George, 6th June, 1916.

24 June

POLITICAL TANTRUMS

A meeting called by poster "to protest against the dismemberment of Ireland" by Messrs O'Brien and Healy, MPs, was held in the City Hall last night. A considerable section of those present displayed green, white and gold favours, and before the starting of the meeting, sang several national songs, and cheered with enthusiasm for an Irish Republic, Bishop O'Dwyer and Mr Ginnell, MP. Before the arrival of Messrs O'Brien and Healy many ladies with Mrs O'Brien occupied seats on the platform. Mr O'Brien entered as the audience were singing "God save Ireland". When it was finished large cheers broke out, and this Mr O'Brien took as a welcome and a glad reception. He posed and bowed repeatedly to the crowd, but was not long left in doubt as to the mistake he at first made. When Mr Hosford rose to propose a chairman there were hisses throughout the Hall, and he had to desist, and simply formally moved Ald. Forde to the chair. The latter had to hurry his introduction of Mr O'Brien for the hisses, interspersed with singing, were persistent and angry. Mr O'Brien was equally unwelcome and his oft repeated entreaties to interrupters were so unavailing that he became visibly excited and angered. Mr Tadhg Barry appealed for order, but with no good result, and finally Mr O'Brien had to finish up his speech abruptly. Mr Healy was not listened to at all, and only after an appeal by Mr Dermot O'Brien was there a lull in which a resolution was read by Ald Forde for submission to the meeting. This proposition was not heard, and Mr D. McDonnell, LL.D., formally seconded it. It was then declared carried, while some persons in the platform were in fisticuffs. The Chairman called for "cheers for O'Brien," but the groans were so insistent and imperative that Mr O'Brien realised the farce of offering thanks and left the platform. Mr Healy was jostled by some men who jumped on the platform. The crowd then took possession and had an impromptu meeting of their own. Before and throughout the meeting leaflets were scattered about the Hall.

27 June

LOCAL INDUSTRIES, LOCAL JOBS

Cork Technical Committee: Mr A F Sharman Crawford, JP (Vice-chairman), presided. Mr Curtis said that what he meant to convey in his remarks at the last meeting was that men out of their time in trade who came to the institute for study should be employed by the Ministry of Munitions as instructors. He did not mean to convey that boys and apprentices should be put into those positions. He was of the opinion that the preference in such work should be given to the men to whom he referred, and that strangers should not be imported and given such work.

Mr Ellis said that a discussion took place at another body, and a wrong construction was put on Mr Curtis' remarks at the last meeting. Mr Curtis referred to students and not University students. Some of their students were journey-men out of their time, and others were on the point of finishing their time, and those were the students whom Mr Curtis spoke about. They were the members of the building trades. Some of them looked for such work, but they were told that they were men of military age, and he (Mr Ellis) did not think it was fair that such a thing should have been said to the men.

Mr Coughlan stated that what Mr Curtis stated at the last meeting was that he trusted when the Munitions Factory was started that the claims of the artisans and skilled workers who attended their schools should be considered, as they were quite competent of taking charge of anything.

Mr Dennehy said that the engineers and other trades had relaxed their rules in connection with munition work, and there was a tendency by some people to abuse that relaxation. There was no objection to students from the institute going to the factory and taking off their coats and working like ordinary workingmen, but there would be every objection to making fancy jobs for anyone from the institution. If the Ministry of Munitions required skilled men, and that the men should be supplied locally, the local men unemployed should have first claim on employment. It would not do to have parties in charge who were untrained and not experienced beyond having a theoretical experience, and if the students went to the factory they should go as workmen.

Mr Curtis – It was to stop the importation of strangers that I spoke. The Chairman mentioned that some of the girls engaged at the munition work were being sent to Dublin to be trained, and he suggested that they should offer the Ministry of Munitions to start classes in the institute to train these girls. This suggestion was agreed to.

29 June

IRISH LANGUAGE OPPORTUNITIES

At the last meeting of the Ard Choisde of the Cork Gaelic League, Mr T O'Tuama presiding, a report was received regarding the examinations for scholarships offered by the Ard Choisde. The Honorary Secretary (Liam de Roiste) stated that seven schools had entered students for the scholarships. In two cases the classes were not considered satisfactory as a whole, though there were excellent individual students in each class. In the other cases the classes having been found satisfactory, the students were allowed compete for the scholarships. The examiners, Rev Dr Daly, P O'Domhnaill, Seán Tóibín, and Liam de Róiste found the standard attained by the competitors high. The examination was chiefly oral as the scholarships were intended to encourage the speaking of Irish by school pupils. Forty-two students were examined and judged by these; oral Irish is evidently well taught in the schools represented. The Examiner's Report continued: It is to be regretted that there are a number of schools, primary and secondary in Cork City, that did not avail of the opportunity given by the Ard Choisde to allow promising students of Irish to acquire a sound knowledge of the spoken language in an Irish-speaking district.

CASEMENT'S SENTENCE OF DEATH

Sir Roger Casement was today found guilty of high treason and sentenced to death. There was tense silence when each of the three judges assumed a black cap, and one of the most collected persons in court was the prisoner himself. It was nearly three o'clock when the jury retired. In a few moments they sent out for the 'original' code, and for a copy of the indictment. These were supplied to them, but the Lord Chief Justice refused to send them a copy of the evidence, which they also asked for. At this time the court was crowded, barristers in wigs and gowns standing all over the floor of the court, the public, including many ladies in the smartest of summer attire, being packed in the galleries. Casement had disappeared from the dock. Then followed the long wait of close upon an hour.

The Judges left the bench, and subdued conversation was general.

At ten minutes to four the Judges returned. The jury soon followed, and Casement again entered the dock. The names of the jury having been called over, they were asked if they were agreed upon their verdict. The foreman said they found the prisoner guilty. Casement was asked by the Crown if he had anything to say why sentence of death should not pass upon him according to law. All eyes were on the prisoner, but he remained perfectly calm, and read a long statement, which he prepared twenty days ago, the main gist of which was that he objected to the jurisdiction of the court. He was then sentenced to death in the usual form, and after waiting a moment or two and smiling at friends in court, he went below.

JULY

SEDITION AND UTTERANCES

The findings of the Commissioners, Lord Hardinge of Penshurst, the Hon. Sir Montague Shearman one of his Majesty's Judges of the High Court and Sir Mac Kenzie Dalzell Chalmers, the Royal Commissioners appointed to inquire into the circumstances of the recent rebellion in Ireland have issued their report, and it was presented today to both Houses of Parliament. But the general conclusion that we draw from the evidence before us is that the main cause of the rebellion appears to be that lawlessness was allowed to grow up unchecked, and that Ireland for several years had been administered on the principle that it was safer and more expedient to leave the law in abeyance if collision with any faction of the Irish people could thereby be avoided. Such a policy is the negation that cardinal rule of government which demands that the enforcement of the law and the preservation of order should always be independent of political expediency. We consider that the incorporation of large quantities of arms into Ireland after the lapse of the Arms Act, and the toleration of drilling by large bodies of men, first in Ulster and then in other districts of Ireland created conditions which rendered possible the recent troubles in Dublin and elsewhere.

It appears to us that reluctance was shown by the Irish Government to repress by prosecution written and spoken seditious utterances and to suppress the drilling and manoeuvring of armed forces known to be under the control of men who were openly declaring their hostility to your Majesty's Government, and their readiness to welcome and assist your majesty's enemies. This reluctance was largely prompted by the pressure brought to bear by the Parliamentary representatives of the Irish people, and in Ireland itself there developed a widespread belief that no repressive measures would be undertaken by the Government against sedition. This led to a rapid increase of preparations for insurrection, and was the immediate cause of the recent outbreak. We are of the opinion that the commencement of the present war all seditions, utterances and publications should have been firmly suppressed at the outset, and if juries or magistrates were found unwilling to enforce this policy further powers should have been involved under the existing Acts for the defence of the realm.

5 July

A SHOW OF ENCOURAGEMENT, CORK SUMMER SHOW

The members of the Munster Agricultural Society opened their annual Summer Show yesterday under most encouraging conditions. Since its inception many years ago, the Society has accomplished a large amount of useful work in the interests of the agricultural community, and it is indeed very gratifying to find that its sphere of usefulness continues. No doubt many obstacles and difficulties had to be overcome in the past by the members of the Society who worked in the most untiring fashion and a few years ago the institution became not alone one of the most important in the country, but also one of the most successful. The Society has entered on what promised to be a very prosperous

Display at Cork Summer Show, c. 1929. (SOURCE: *CORK EXAMINER*)

career when the war broke out, and its circumstances placed another difficulty in the way of the institution. It was feared that the fixtures conducted at different periods of each year would have to be abandoned, but with the enterprise which has always characterised their work, the members of the Society decided in the interests of the agricultural community, and with the object of advancing their pursuits, to continue the shows.

Of course, it was only natural with the shortage of all classes of stock in the country, that entries should have ruled small at the fixtures brought to issue since the outbreak of the war. A similar report has to be made in respect of the Show that was opened yesterday at the picturesquely situated and well laid out grounds in Ballintemple. Notwithstanding the circumstances to which attention has been drawn, the society has however achieved the object that it had in view when it was decided to continue the

shows – to advance and promote the interests of the agricultural community. The members of the Society deserve to be heartily congratulated upon that fact. The Show was opened under most glorious weather conditions, and with a continuance of sunshine on the concluding day the results should prove eminently satisfactory from every point of view.

Striking evidence of the popularity of the Society and its work was forthcoming in the manner in which the proceedings were supported. Throughout the day the attendance assumed very large dimensions, and the visitors thoroughly enjoyed themselves. Though there were dominations in the number of entries in the equine section as compared with previous years, the animals on view attracted considerable attention. It was an excellent exhibition, and good quality was displayed in every class, with the result that competition all round was very keen.

7 July

ATTENDANCE AT CORK CITY LIBRARY

The circulation of books and attendances: It is significant that the diminished book circulation is in these classes of literature that are mainly used by the male sex, which are the most directly affected in their occupations and leisure by the war, while the principle increases are in those classes fiction and juvenile – that are mostly used by women and children, who are the least affected thereby. There is, however, every indication that the decline in issues has reached the lowest ebb, as the circulation of books from the Lending Library [Carnegie Library, Anglesea Street] during the second half of the year showed an increase of 1,812, against a decrease of 1,385 in the first half, when compared with the respective periods for 1914–1915.

The newsroom attendance totalled 181,255 a decrease of 24,594. This is the lowest recorded attendance since the year 1895, and may be accounted for as one of the results of the war. Cork is a large military centre, and has contributed in proportion to population to military requirements, as well as, in a lesser degree, to naval demands; with the result that the male members of the community must have diminished, and their places in commercial life have been filled from the ranks of those who were more or less previously unemployed. It is, therefore, reasonable to assume that, with a diminished male population – who are practically the only frequenters in the Newsroom – and less leisure for those who are at home, the attendance in the institution of this kind must necessarily also diminish. That such assumption is justified is borne out by the fact that the week day attendances show a considerable decline, while Sunday and holiday attendances have remained normal.

THE BEST WHEELMEN

Not in the history of Cork sports meetings have so many entries been received and so much interest excited as in connection with this evening's re-union on the Mardyke under the auspices of the National Cycle Club; the Four Mile Cycle Championship of Munster. With 17 entries and the mile cycle handicap with 21 entries, events are looked forward to with increasing interest. The best wheelmen in our southern province have entered for them, and the sport exhibited will be close and keen. The 220 yards, 880 yards (scratch), (14 entries; the high jump, and one mile cycle (confined for the Lord Mayor's Cup are among the other events – altogether 12 in number – which will evoke a big need of popular appreciation and excite public interest to an unusual degree. Not the least attractive feature will be the boys' relay race between teams representing the leading city schools, while an open handicap event for junior boys will also figure in the programme.

In order to cater for all tastes the committee are this year putting on a dance programme, in which to special music by the band a half a dozen dances will be listed immediately the athletic portion has concluded.

Where there are about 160 to 170 entrants it needs scarcely be mentioned that punctuality must be observed by competitors. They must answer the call stewards immediately their respective events are announced, otherwise they will not be permitted to engage in the competitions. The competitors in the confined events must be on their marks at 7p.m. sharp. These precautions are absolutely essential to the successful carrying out of an unusual lengthy programme, which will necessitate something like 22 starts. Matchless scenery and beautiful music contributed by the Cork Workingmen's Band will lighten and brighten the experience of the thousands of visitors to the Mardyke Grounds. The Lady Mayoress will present the prizes at the conclusion of the sports.

13 July

POOR CHILDREN'S EXCURSIONS DAY

A meeting of the Poor Children's Excursion Committee was held yesterday, in the Council Chamber, Municipal Buildings. The Lord Mayor presided; H. Dawson, who acted as hon. Secretary in the absence of Mr J Hackett. Mr Dawson announced that the railway company had written to say that they would be able to provide the trains for the excursion on Wednesday, July 26th, on the same terms as last year. He further stated that the collection so far had realised £80, but they required £200 more.

The Lord Mayor said that he hoped the citizens would respond as generously as in the past to their appeal for funds. Anyone who had ever seen the joy and genuine pleasure which the excursion gave to the thousands of little children could scarcely help subscribing. Most of the people in the city whom he would expect to contribute, spent a good deal during the summer months on many excursions to the seaside or other places. If all these deprived themselves of just one of the pleasure trips, and gave the money they would spend on it to the Poor Children's Excursion, they would be doing a real good deed.

DUTIES AT CORK UNION

Mr Michael McCarthy presided. State of the house – In house last year 1,524; present 1,444; difference 80 less. In hospital last year, 932; present 861; difference, 71 less. In house last week, 1,435; present, 1,444; difference, 9 more. In hospital last week, 858; present, 861: difference, 3 more. Deaths during week ended 8th July 1916 – 3.

From Dr Cummins, Dr Giusani, Dr Morrissey, Dr J T O Conner, and Master Mr James Barry, the following report was received – In reply to the following recommendation of the visiting committee forwarded to us, viz "that the ward masters and ward mistresses at present performing day duty be transferred to night duty under the supervision of the assistant matron, and that this recommendation be submitted to the medical staff and master with the view of disposing of deputy labour, so that patients will receive proper attention at the hands of experienced officials at night".

We beg to state that it would be impossible for ward masters and ward mistresses at present performing day duty to be transferred to night duty as they have important work connected with the working of the hospitals. We suggest that a paid wards-maid be appointed for night work in the boy's hospital. We further suggest that the night nurses be transferred around various hospitals each month. We consider that it would be extremely advisable that a superintendent night nurse be appointed to visit the various hospitals during the night and report to the medical staff as to the care taken of the patients. For this appointment, the only suitable person would be a nun. We further consider that the nurses, when requiring permission to go off duty, should obtain written permission of the medical officer of her division and this permission should be forwarded to the Master of the workhouse.

THE 38 FROM FRONGOCH

Thirty-eight out of the several hundred prisoners ordered to be released from Frongoch internment camp arrived in the city yesterday. They were mostly from the county, the greater number of them belonging to Macroom and the neighbouring districts. They left for their respective homes in the afternoon.

During the evening others were arriving by the train getting into Cork at 8.35, and a number of sympathisers, headed by a couple of pipers playing national airs went to the Glanmire Station to meet them. One released Cork city man did travel by the train, and was welcomed by those assembled to meet him. The party then proceeded to the National Monument on the Grand Parade. It seemed as if they were about to hold a meeting, but whether this was so or not the police interfered and prevented any such taking place if intended. The party scattered into groups and disappeared in the side streets, and the crowd mostly composed of young people and women also dispersed. This crowd was largely attracted by curiosity, and took no part in the proceedings beyond watching the movement of those concerned in them. No damage of any kind was done last night, but on Thursday night a pane of glass was broken in the recruiting offices in Patrick Street.

MARKETING OF HAY

We are officially requested to state that in reference to the enquiries of farmers as to the procedure in the marketing of hay to the War Department it should be clearly understood that purchases cannot be completed nor advances made until the hay is safely ricked and protected. A consideration of the circumstances will show the necessity for this decision. Until the hay has been a sufficient time in rick, so as to be thoroughly dry and free from moisture it cannot be baled or pressed. The quantity of hay to be handled is great, and delivery cannot be taken in a short time. The hay should therefore be protected against damage by weather. Farmers will serve their own interest by ricking and protecting their hay as it is only on secure stacks that advances can be made, and the price will be according to quality. When safely stacked, applications to have the hay inspected and a purchase note passed should be made to the local purchasing officer.

HIGH SCALES OF RESULTS, CORK SCHOOL OF MUSIC

In the course of her report on the Summer Examinations held last month, the examiner, Miss Amie W Patterson, Mus, Doc, BA, NUI states that the examinations were attended by a large if not larger number of candidates than last year, and that the results have been of a slightly satisfactory character. All round, the students who presented themselves for examination gave proof that they have been carefully prepared; the fact that the test pieces were chosen with great care and courses adapted to particular cases showed that interest had been taken individually in each pupil by the respective professors. Of very special significance was the work if the various ensemble classes. First, my impression of last year in regard to the different grades in Pianoforte playing – i.e that the Professor of Piano (Dr W H Hannaford) and his accomplished Assistant Teachers (Miss Ida Swaffield, ARCM, and Anna O'Donoghue, LRAM) had been indefatigable in laying a sound foundation of good technique on the lines of scale, arpeggio, and sturdy playing – was wholly confirmed after a repeated survey of the methods followed throughout these grades.

In the violin classes again the thorough care and devotion which had been expended upon all pupils by their talented professor, Signor F Grossi, was clearly evident, whilst that capable instructor's accurate diagnosis of individual capacities was well demonstrated by the distinctive work of the two candidates recommended for the violin diploma (Miss Doris Foley and Mr Denis Noonan), who showed in their separate performances, how minutely they had severally benefited by instruction received in accordance with their own artistic tendencies. Coming to the organ students, I was delighted to find a very even development of technique and manipulation displayed by performers in all grades. This department is attended with much still, sympathy and thoroughness by the professor in charge (Mr Theo Gmur) features of his pupils playing being their steady and even pedalling, their general knowledge of the balance and resources of their instrument. It was also gratifying to find two lady pupils presenting themselves for examination in violoncello playing, both in their respective grades, doing much credit to their instructor (Mr E Rawhson).

Coming to the very important department of vocal production it is encouraging to notice that the number of pupils who are going through a regular course of voice-training in the Cork Municipal School of Music is largely on the increase, close upon fifty students entering for this examination alone. This, in itself, speaks for the popularity and success of the professor (Mr Wilberforce Franklin) as a teacher of singing. Of his excellent and comprehensive methods has been made in previous reports. Suffice it to say that in addition, nothing struck me more forcibly this time that the ease with which all the vocal students, even in the elementary grade, controlled the breath – a true index to the excellent foundation system upon which they are drilled.

20 July

THE SOUL OF A NATION

It was just an incident – an incident in the life of a nation. It was not an ordinary everyday occurrence, and yet it was. There was something indefinable about it, and yet there was something which we all knew and understood. We realised the moment, the moment of psychological adulations and euphemistic eulogies. I was present. There were others also. We laughed and talked, and said goodbye, etc., and so forth, just as you might do. One felt – well, that's the subject. We felt that we were taking part in the great drama of life, or, to be more precise, in one great scene. The day was one which might be termed "cool". The sun, which but a short time before displayed the intensity of summer, and here now it was hidden from view as it would deny itself from the ephemeralistic qualities of the moment. There was life and gaiety in the suburbs of the blue harbour. The sparse firs, with their gaunt like limbs of branches interspersed here and there with silver beeches, looked on the proceedings as rather droll – a sort of a Micauber expression. Gaiety without frivolity and yet again – oh well, I pass on. There was gladness and humour in the situation, and there was spontaneity of enthusiasm. There was that vigour of life which we all know so well in these trying times. Sadness was not an absent element, and away above it all there was that prosaic feeling, that humdrum existence with bores one. The landing stage was not in its gayest mood for the occasion. I don't know why. In its absence enthusiasm gripped us and kept us enthralled until the occasion became a blur – a sort of haze on the distant horizon – a horizon which was made too prosaic by the smoke of progress.

We quit the scene, and felt all the better for it. There was that unbounded enthusiasm, that solidarity of purpose which culminated in one great aim, which spelt the protection of our grand old country. Here now as I write on the evening of the day I can fancy it all again. Amid the light heartedness of the situation, which perhaps spelt many farewells forever, there was in the flux of the whole proceeding that soul moving lilt of a hearty cheer which iridised from the wells of strong hearts. There was more than all that. There was a spontaneous exuberance which gripped us all. I don't know why it moved me. I have seen similar enactments in this terrible crisis and in doing so I have seen the heart to old Ireland laid bare to the world. There was only one thought, "my country, right or wrong my county".

And so the scene enacted before me worked itself into my brain in conjunction with an indelibility of harmony. I felt pleased. I felt glad. Equally so did my comrades, who replied to the farewell cheer from their gate like perches on the stages. They, too, were a merry bunch. They were patiently awaiting their time when they equally so would be in a position to give a hearty cheer as they went to take their place in the ranks of the men of the world –the place of the man who counts. The band played "Old Acquaintance" – it was hardly appropriate. The boat drew from the pier, and from the depths of our souls we wished them good luck and safe return, combined with a cheer which drew admiration from Old Sol, who had now condescended to grace the proceedings by a shaft of his many beams. Even the old firs looked their best and the silver beeches put an added air of importance which fair strangled me. The birds warbled their lyrics, and the direful surge of the incoming tide was an added attraction in the culmination of an incident in the life of a nation. I don't mean the Alpha or Omega. Oh, no. I mean its very existence and our Ireland's existence as a nation in the great empire. This is simply the departure of a draft for France, and the incident took place at Aghada. It was the soul of a nation.

"Patsy"

THE NECESSITY OF TOY-MAKING

The Lady Mayoress (Mrs T C Butterfield) presided over the monthly Ladies' Committee meeting of the Cork Industrial Development Association. The General Secretary (Mr J L Fawsitt also was in attendance). The Secretary mentioned that a new toy industry had been started in the city recently and in connection therewith read the following interesting account of a visit to the new factory recently paid by the energetic Honorary Secretary Mr M A Ryan; "On a recent occasion I paid a visit to the newly established 'Cork Toy Factory', pleasantly situated on the river Lee. The premises in which the industry is carried on at No. 8 Camden Quay, formerly one of the fine old dwelling houses in this sunny district, are about the most suitable of all buildings for the purpose – the many spacious rooms lend themselves without further alteration to department work such as a toy industry necessitates. At present orders for dolls are too numerous that the factory has not been able to devote much attention to general toys, but with a staff of nearly 30 girls kept busy in the various branches of doll-making the work turned out is most creditable, and personally having had some experience of German, English, American, and latterly Irish made dolls, it is not flattery to say that those being made at Cork Toy Factory are equal to all others and superior to some.

The public spirited ladies who instituted the project are fortunate in having the practical assistance of a lady with original ideas. One of the foremost lines in which the factory specialises is the "water doll", one which the child can bring into its bath or the open sea, without injury to the doll. This is made in boy and girl patterns and garbed in bathing costume to suit. The boy "water doll" is selling more freely than the girl type.

A GOLDEN TICKET

The arrival of the Lord Mayor [at the Model School] was the signal for a rousing cheer, but to get the children into the order of single file to pass on the gate at which the tickets were handed out by Alderman Meade, assisted by Mr Hackett, Honorary Secretary, and Mr Lyons seemed a disheartened task. However, his Lordship full of energy and activity, and his well-directed efforts and commands willingly followed by Messrs Colburn Fawsitt, J O'Leary, Higgins, Lyons, J J Sexton. D Horgan, ex-Ald; H Dawson, C McCarthy and Mullins, SAA, and firemen and police soon had the children ready to be marshalled by Mrs Corcoran, Mrs Marsh and Miss Fitzgerald. Things then proceeded admirably, and at one o'clock close on 5,000 boys and girls had been given their tickets. It was a glad reward to the exertions of his Lordship and the committee to see the happiness beaming in the children's faces as they clutched the tickets, and it will be a sincere gratification to the generous contributors to the excursion fund that not one child was left without one.

Therefore, today favoured by gloriously fine warm weather, these thousands of poor children will have a royal day at Youghal by the sea. The trains run as follows:- 8.50am, 9am, 9.20am, and 9.45am. In these four special trains there will be plenty of room for all, and the children are asked to be quiet, and to take their time in getting into the station and the train. If good order is kept, there will be no delay in taking all away, but if there is any crushing or rushing accidents may be occasioned, but those who do rush and crush in for their place will be ordered out and left behind. The children, then, should walk quietly and orderly along the platform and into the train. It is regrettable that five children were injured at the distribution of tickets yesterday. They were taken to the South Infirmary, where four had to be detained. Their names are – Thomas

Youghal beach, *c.* 1910. (SOURCE: CORK CITY LIBRARY)

Callaghan, Shandon street; Bridget Malloy, Monks' School Lane; Eily Whelan and Victor Hurley, both of St Vincent's Place. They were badly bruised from the crushing, and are suffering from shock.

28 July

CORK ASSIZES

At 11 o'clock yesterday morning the Commission of Assize for the County Cork was opened in the County Courthouse by Mr Commissioner Matteson, KC, First Sergeant at Law. His Lordship addressing the Grand Jury, said there were eleven cases, involving twelve bills, to be considered by them. They were all cases of a more or less serious kind, but he was glad to say that one and all they were what may be called self-contained cases, of the ordinary kind such as are incidental to every large community. None of the cases, so far as he could see, had anything to do with ill feeling, religious party or otherwise, and did not indicate any general disturbance of the peace of the county. There was one murder case in which a servant boy was charged with murdering his mother. The evidence was altogether circumstantial. No one appeared to have witnessed the murder, but the case was strengthened by the suspicious conduct of the accused before his arrest. When investigated by the petty jury it may be found that the case was one of manslaughter, but the Grand Jury had nothing to say to that.

Their duty was to say if there was a prima facie case to go with the petty jury, and he thought they would have no difficulty in doing that. There was a manslaughter case of a rather sad character to be tried. A boy or young man of 18 or 19 indulged in a senseless and dangerous form of horseplay – throwing stones from behind a fence at persons. One of the stones struck a little boy of ten on the head and he died from the effects in a couple of days.

There was a bigamy case in which a soldier was charged with having contracted a marriage with a woman in the county, he being already married and his first wife living at the time. There were two bills against the one person for cattle stealing, a very common crime in former times but which now was not very common. There was one case of concealment of birth, and a case of assault on a little girl of ten years – a kind of offence which he was glad to say was very rare in that county and indeed in the South of Ireland. All the other cases were assaults, all rather serious. These would cause the Grand Jury

Cork City and County Courthouse, c. 1910. (SOURCE: CORK CITY LIBRARY)

no difficulty. All the cases were of the kind which one might reasonably be expected in a large community. He was glad to say that the reports supplied to him did not indicate any disturbances of the peace in the county. As a matter of fact the number of specially reported cases was lower than the number of the corresponding period last year. He was glad to notice that there was a falling off in the number of convictions for drunkenness and consequently of the cases of assault which arose out of drink.

AUGUST

1 August

JUSTICE FOR IRELAND

We have been subjected as might be expected at all times, to much criticism. Of late years it has taken the fork of pelting us with opprobrious names and insinuations that we were "purchased" for considerations that could be reduced to pounds, shillings and pence. On very rare occasions indeed, have we taken the trouble to contradict these slanders, relying on the good sense of our countrymen to treat with contempt these wild and untruthful assertions. We think the course we followed was wise, for not even the people who made them with so much venom for one moment believed themselves there was any foundation for these charges. Today, as at all times during the career of this paper it is under obligations to no party or to no men. We are as little committed to Mr Redmond as we are to Mr O'Brien or to the British Government and if we support the Irish Party with whatever weight we can command, it is purely because we are convinced that through the course it has taken lies the only safe and reliable path consistent with the honour and with the prosperity of Ireland. We are not and have never sought to be an official organ of the present or of any Party, but we freely acknowledge that at the hands of the present Irish party we have never sought but courtesy and goodwill. This, on the seventy-fifth birthday of the "Examiner".

Some were respected and widely known by their countrymen; others were only recognised and beloved by the narrow circle amongst whom they laboured. They left to us who continue their work a legacy that cannot be measured by mere money, but which, for all that, we regard as precious; to honestly and steadfastly strive for the independence and prosperity of our land, to obtain what is best summed up in the hackneyed but homely phrase that even irony cannot kill – Justice for Ireland.

THE LOOMS OF INDUSTRY

When Belgium was invaded by the German Army one of the best and most prolific flax markets in connection with the Irish Linen industry ceased to exist. This was a serious blow to one of our greatest and most flourishing trades. However, the enterprising men at the head of the business were determined to do all in their power to minimise, as far as possible, the injury that almost threatened to stop the looms in the numerous factories. Such a stoppage would have been more or less a disaster. It would have at once thrown out of employment thousands upon thousands of men and women for whom it would have been practically impossible to find work in other directions. Their lot would indeed have been pitiable, and their idleness would not only have meant ruin for themselves, but would have meant almost bankruptcy for the many towns which depend for prosperity on the money that they earn. Apart from this there was the possibility that if such an industry had to be shut down for any considerable time it might not have been revived with success for very many years. Thus, those who control it as soon as they realised the seriousness of the situation, at once devised a scheme for tiding over the difficulties with which they were faced. Part of this scheme was the revival of flax growing in the South of Ireland, and for this purpose the Fibrine Corporation assured the co-operation of a number of farmers in Munster. The Corporation supplied the seed and guaranteed to take the crop at £15 per acre with a 30s bonus if the crop was good. Under these conditions, about 250 acres were cultivated in the province. The Messrs Desmond, of Pembroke St, Cork who have a splendid farm at Ballycurreen, not very far from the city, not only planted 3½ acres but undertook all the work in connection with caring and distributing of the seed to the farmers free of cost. Yesterday the Messrs Desmond started the gathering in of the crop, and for this purpose employed sixteen bands – men, women and boys. It is a very simple and easy kind of labour. Instead of being cut, as is the ease with other standing crops, it is pulled out by the roots. Extremely little force is required, as the roots are very lightly held, and they come away perfectly clean, unlike weeds, which can at once be distinguished by the earth on the roots.

WAR IS HELL, YEAR 3 OF WAR

Today the war enters on its third year, and the end is not yet in sight. Two years ago the prevailing belief was that the Central Empires could not for long resist such a powerful combination as France, Russia, and Great Britain, but expert opinion which was better acquainted with the resources and preparations of Germany inclined to the view that the struggles would be a prolonged one, while the late Lord Kitchener based his calculations on a three years' conflict. Except possibly as to the protracted nature of the struggles, expert opinion founded on former wars has, in the main, been hopelessly wrong, and most accepted anti-war theories have been as ruthlessly shattered as German high explosives and heavy artillery have shattered the fortresses of France which were supposed to be impregnable. After the German troops had ravaged Belgium, invaded France, and almost reached Paris in their first onslaught, many theories had to be revised, and it must be admitted that the success of enemy methods necessitated their adoption by Allies, whose unpreparedness at the commencement supplies possibly the strongest proof that the history of the present times will offer to future generations as to where the responsibility must be laid for the drenching of Europe with blood. The struggle continues with growing fury, every devilish device that science could bring to the aid of the combatants has been adopted, and on land, on sea, and in the air the horrible machinery which carries destruction, death and desolation in its train is being utilised with a prodigality which more than justifies General Sherman's aphorism "War is Hell".

THE WHEEL OF HOME RULE

The sensible resolutions passed by the Cork Hibernians at their meeting yesterday ought to form a suitable headline for other bodies in the country. While condemning the action of the Cabinet in reference to the Lloyd George proposals the members pledge their loyal support to Mr Redmond and his colleagues, who have shown by their political sagacity and faithful tenacity to Home Rule that in the recent crisis, as always, "the interest of the nation can best be served at their hands". Contempt is expressed at the mischievous attempts made in a section of the Press to stir up hostility to the Irish Party, a contempt which, it may be said, will develop as time advances, for time, as in other cases, will prove the greater vindicator of Mr Redmond and his colleagues in this much debated question of an emergency settlement. The Hibernians declare themselves prepared to support any movements inaugurated by Mr Redmond for the purpose of securing during the recess, an expression of opinion from all that is best and patriotic in the country.

Anxious for the peace and future happiness of their country, the Hibernians also make the reasonable suggestion that an auspicious beginning will be made by the new Irish Executive if clemency be extended to those young Irishmen who are at present incarcerated for political offences committed in Ireland. It is to be hoped that this chivalrous request in favour of a body of young Irishmen, whose political views are widely divergent from those of the men who make it will not fall on deaf ears. The country is anxious to get away from the haunting memories of a tragic and unhappy week, and to prepare itself for the introduction of a Home Rule scheme which, if properly worked, will not only tend towards the tranquillity and prosperity of Ireland, but will succeed in establishing a lasting bond of unity between us and the other countries included in the British Empire.

9 August

DROWNING FATALITY AT CROSSHAVEN

At Church Bay, Crosshaven, yesterday morning a sad bathing fatality occurred. The circumstances surrounding it are poignant. Richard Williams, a boy aged about 13 years, second son of Mr Richard Williams, manager of Messrs Bakers and Co, French Church Street, Cork, was spending his vacation at Crosshaven. It was his custom to take a morning bath, and yesterday morning accompanied by his sister and Miss O'Leary, in whose house he was resident, and who was acting as maid to both children he went to take his usual bath. He jumped off from a springboard, and no sooner had he dipped in the sea when he was in difficulties. The sister who is aged about fifteen years together with the maid, realising the situation immediately attempted to effect his rescue; their efforts were unsuccessful. The attempt exhausted them, and they were removed from the water in direful plight. There were no persons about at the time of the occurrence, and before anybody appeared on the scene the little fellow was swept away by the receding tide and drowned. Later attracted by the cries of those who were with the boy a Catholic clergyman hurried to the spot and dived several times to recover the body.

10 August

THE POWER OF THE SOVEREIGN

The weekly meeting of the Commissioners was held yesterday in the Boardroom Custom House. The minutes of the Dredge and Work Committee were read by Alderman Kelleher. Alderman Kelleher in accordance with notice moved – "That the labourers employed by the board be granted an increase of 2s a week". He pointed out that the purchasing power of a sovereign now was only equal to 12s a couple of years ago, and said the present condition of affairs made it compulsory on the Board to grant this increase.

The Chairman asked Alderman Kelleher to adjourn the matter until the annual revision in January. He reminded him that it was only last May the men got an advance of a shilling. The expenditure of the Board at present was at high water mark, and their revenue was declining. To increase this expenditure at present would be suicidal. The proposed increase would cost them £600 a year. It was no pleasure to him to speak in this manner, but he felt bound in the interest of the Board to utter this warning note.

Alderman Kelleher contended that they were in a position to pay this advance, but the Chairman asserted they were not. The High Sheriff seconded the motion, and dissented from the Chairman's remarks. He said whenever it was proposed to increase the salary of highly paid officials there was sudden silence – not a murmur was heard – and the applications were generally granted, but when the working man came to ask for anything it was an entirely different story. The Board had plenty finances behind it, and could well afford this advance.

13 August

AN EXHIBITION OF HURLING

Two matches in connection with the above competition were decided at the Cork Athletic Grounds yesterday in the presence of a fairly large gathering. Father O'Leary's Total Abstinence Hall defeated Passage in the senior division, and the second string of the former team played a drawn game with Brian Boru in the junior department. A good exhibition of the code was given in each contest, and the play proved most enjoyable.

The opening stages of the game were in favour of Brian Boru, and after some determined attacks they placed a goal and a point to their credit. Total Abstinence Hall then assumed the aggressive, and registered three goals in quick succession. Play of an even character followed but towards the close of the period Brian Boru added a point to their score. Early in the second period Brian Boru took the lead by recording two goals. As the result of useful play they afterwards secured two more major scores, but Total Abstinence Hall succeeded in registering two goals and two points, and the game was left drawn on the score.

14 August

THE CONSERVATION OF FISH STOCKS

Mr E W Barnes presided. The Department forwarded a copy of a bye-law they had made prohibiting to have in possession in that part of the No. 5 or Cork district, which comprised the whole of the sea along the coast between Ballycotton on the east, and Barry's Head; any salmon or trout which had been illegally killed by means of dynamite or other explosive, and each and every person offending against that bye-law would, for each offence, forfeit and pay a sum of £5.

Mr Futter (Inspector) reported that since the last meeting one of their bailiffs, named Michael Finningan, Lissarda, was shot at three times by poachers while in the act of taking a net out of the River Lee. At the time the net contained three salmon. The bailiff's wounds consisted of shot, and he was removed to the South Infirmary, and detained for treatment, but he had since returned home. Two men named Kyrl Ford and John Murphy were prosecuted at Blarney for having in their possession on the banks of the river Lee a gaff. The case was dismissed. John Quirke and Thomas Cremin, fishermen, Blackrock, were prosecuted for using a net during the weekly close season for salmon and trout off Blackrock Castle. The case was dismissed but an appeal has been lodged by order of the Department.

17 August

REPORT FROM THE DISTRICT LUNATIC ASYLUM

The monthly meeting of the Committee of the Management of the Cork District Lunatic Asylum was held at the Boardroom at the Institution yesterday. Mr William Desmond, T C, (vice chairman) presided. Dr M Twomey, visiting physician, Youghal Asylum reported about that institution as follows – there are four patients confined to bed on the male side of the house, and four on the female side owing to debility and other causes. There has been no case of seclusion, restraint, injury or violence. The food supplies have been regularly examined and found up to standard requirements. There has been no case of zymotic disease, and the general health of the institution is excellent. This was considered satisfactory.

Former site of District Lunatic Asylum, today. (PICTURE: KIERAN MCCARTHY)

The Resident Medical Superintendent (Dr J J Fitzgerald) reported as follows – Since the last meeting 19 patients have been admitted, 6 have been discharged and 7 patients died. We have in residence 869 males and 1,002 females. In Youghal there are 401 patients. We have under care 2,202 patients. A male patient effected his escape. He probably either joined the army or employment with some farmer. The general health and conditions of the Asylum continue satisfactory. Three of our female staff are resigning.

21 August

FIGHTING TUBERCULOSIS

The outlines of a scheme under the tuberculosis (Ireland) Acts, for the prevention, detection and treatment of tuberculosis in this county of Cork, were submitted to the County Insurance Committee at their last meeting, by Dr Kearney. It would appear to be necessary that any scheme which may be brought into operation should provide for:- (1) the appointment of a Tuberculosis Officer at £400 a year, and, owing to the size of the county, of an Assistant Tuberculosis Officer at £300, with allowances for travelling expenses in each case. (2) the establishment of (a) branch dispensaries in the principal towns throughout the county, and (b) a central dispensary. (3) the appointment of, at least, one whole time nurse and the employment of a part-time nurse in connection with each dispensary, where the services of such a nurse can be secured. (4) beds in a sanatorium (5) Facilities for hospital treatment of surgical cases of tuberculosis. (6) the treatment, so far as possible, of advanced cases. (7) the payment of fees to doctors in connection with the treatment in their own homes ("Domiciliary treatment") of those patients who are unable to attend at a dispensary.

22 August

DEATH BY SCALDING

Mr Coroner McCabe, solicitor, and a jury held an inquest yesterday at the North Infirmary on the body of Margaret O'Connor, aged one year and five months and residing at 60 Cornmarket Street, who died in the above institution on Sunday morning. Mrs O'Connor, mother of the deceased, said she made tea for the breakfast on Sunday morning, and the little child toddled over to the table and put her hand on the saucer and upset the cup of tea which had no milk in it at the time. Witness took up the deceased and changed her clothes and immediately brought her to the North Infirmary. Dr Higgins stated that he examined the deceased and found the child was badly scalded on the left arm and also the abdomen. Witness said the death was caused by shock as a result of the scalding. The jury returned a verdict in accordance with the medical testimony.

23 August

THE PLAY OF PRESS CENSORSHIP

In the House of Commons yesterday, Mr T P O'Connor asked the Chief Secretary for Ireland whether it was a factor that a warning has been issued to the editors of all Irish papers on the subject of Press criticism of the Government and its administration in Ireland, and whether he was acquainted with the terms of the warning before it was issued.

Mr Duke said a notice was recently issued warning editors in Ireland against publications which were likely to cause dissatisfaction. The Press censorship was at present the Department of Military Administration, and the terms of the warning were settled by the censor. He was aware that the warning would probably be issued, but not if its terms.

Mr Scanlan – Have newspapers editors been warned not to criticise the Government in Ireland?

Mr Lynch – what we want to know is who is governing Ireland, and whether we can rely upon the assurances of the Prime Minister that General Maxwell has no power of interference with the civil side of the Government of Ireland?

Mr Duke replied that he was informed when in Dublin last week that by reason of certain incidents it might be necessary that a warning should be issued. The warning was directed at the publication of matter which offended against the terms of the Defence of the Realm Act (cries of "oh" ah Good old Days")

Mr Scanlan – May I ask if the right honourable gentleman can point to a single provision in the Defence of the Realm regulations which prevent newspaper editors from criticising the Government or any department of the Government?

Mr Duke – I have not the Defence of the Realm Regulations before me, but that there are provisions in them which prohibit the publication of matters tending to excite disaffection in the contrary. I am perfectly sure of that.

24 August

THE CAUSE OF MRS ALBERT ST JOHN MURPHY

A Cork lady who has had a long and eventful experience of hospital work at the front is making every possible effort within her power to raise a fund locally, which will be applied solely to the purchase of ambulance outfits for the 16th (Irish) Division. Soon after the outbreak of the war Mrs Albert St John Murphy left Cork for France and with the assistance of another lady established an hospital near to the firing line as they were permitted to do. They spent and are still expending considerable sums in the maintenance of certain departments or in supplementing the money allocated by the State, for they discovered that many things were required. That only taking an active part in the matronship could suggest, and that private persons therefore could buy. For instance, large quantities of particular drugs were needed. The large centres or distributing areas had been swept clean, and they were not to be had there, but Mrs Murphy knew that the demand had not reached Cork, and here the drugs were purchased with private money. In her hospital was a most polyglot collection, ranging from Spahis to Munster Fusiliers, all getting equal care and still of a most competent surgical staff and the ministrations of a nursing staff superintended by Mrs Murphy or her co-worker.

27 August

SESSIONS AT THE IRISH COLLEGE

T he sessions held this year at the College have been most successful, in particular that concluded last month, which it is considered established a record both in numbers attending and earnestness in their studentship. The movement has attracted now to its fold very many. University people all of whom having come to Ballingeary as disciples go forth later as ardent apostles, each one doing its best to gain more converts. The propaganda work that is now being done by clergymen, brothers or religious orders, and other persons of similar education and refinement is not alone filling the classrooms of Ballingeary but those of all other Irish Colleges.

The College of Ballingeary possesses a charm that is without equal. It is established in the centre of glorious scenery, looking over lovely valleys and on to beautiful hills, whilst it is but within a very short cycle ride or a pleasant easy walk of Gougane Barra, Keimaneigh, and other delightful places. The head of the chain of the picturesque lakes of Inchigeela is not fifty yards distant.

28 August

INCIDENT ON THE QUAY

At the South Infirmary at 3 o'clock on Saturday, Mr Coroner McCabe, LLB, solicitor, and a jury, of which Mr E J Fitzgerald was foreman, inquired into the circumstances of the death of Daniel Coughlan, a dock labourer, 6, Mannix's Lane, aged 35 years, who died in the Infirmary on Friday from injuries he received in an accident during the unloading of the collier of Elsena at Albert Quay.

Mr E L Alhausen, H M Inspector of Factories and Mr W J McNally, Organising Secretary, National Union of Dock Labourers and Riverside Workers, attended.

Mr W F O'Connor, solicitor,

Albert Quay, c. 1910. (SOURCE: CORK CITY MUSEUM)

appeared on behalf of the injured men; Mr J Cottrell Solicitor. (Messrs J and J Bennett) appeared for the master and the owners of the ship; and Mr B C Galvin, solicitor (for Mr A Julian, solicitor) represented the Cork Gas Consumers Co for which the Elsena was unloading at the time of the accident. He was accompanied by Mr J O'Mahoney, secretary of the company. Head Constable Mc Guinness, Acting Sergeant Hayes, and Constable Stephens represented the authorities.

Abina Coughlan said the deceased was her husband. He was 35 years of age. Peter Halloran, 4, Old Market Place, stated in reply to Head Constable Mc Guinness, that he was a stevedore. He started unloading the Elsena at 10am on Friday morning, and the accident occurred at 10.30. He was standing on the quay when he heard a crash; shouted to the winch man to stop, and to the men to get clear, as the mast was coming down. They seemed to be mesmerised, but seven of the men got clear. They were in the act of filling a bucket when he sang out to them. Two of them were pinned under the derrick.

30 August

MURDER ON BARRACK STREET

A very sad occurrence took place in a house situated near the base of Barrack Street hill, yesterday morning. The throat of a child, aged three months was gashed, apparently by a table knife, and died as a result some short time after. In the house dwelt a Mrs McCarthy, an aged woman, whose daughter was married to a Mr Moynihan, and they together with their child lived in the house. The man was away attending to his business, and alone in the house were Mrs McCarthy and Mrs Moynihan with her child. At 11 o'clock Mrs Moynihan went to a butcher's shop nearby. While away the child was entrusted to the care of the old woman, who during the absence of the child's mother took up a table knife and drew it across the child's throat. She then went out to a neighbour and confessed what she had done and the neighbour immediately acquainted the mother of the happening. The latter, distracted, hurried back to her house those in the butcher's shop instinctively realised that some tragic event had occurred, and followed and in a minute the street was black with people.

SEPTEMBER

PAY AND THE COST OF LIVING

The general cry is for more pay to meet the increased cost of living. The National Union of Clerks has arranged a series of conferences to be held throughout the country to voice the protest of clerical workers in salaried positions against the increasing cost of food. The union points out that while the average weekly wage-earner can, by organisation, secure wages increase or war bonus, the average salaried clerk is left with stationary wages and with little prospect of being able to maintain any position of respectability, in view of the high cost of living.

2 September

AGRICULTURAL PROVIDENCE

Labour is necessary to successful farming; it is useful to have some authentic information as to how the difficulty has been faced and met. Recently we published a summary of the livestock in Ireland from the figures supplied by the Department of Agriculture, and it was gratifying to know that during the past year the number of livestock and especially of breeding stock and young stock, had substantially increased. Though many inducements were offered to farmers, they refused to part with their stock unwisely, with the result that their herds have not been unduly denuded. The returns showed that there is an increase as compared with last year in the number of animals of all kinds, but what is more important than the increase in cattle generally is the official statement that there is a substantial increase in the number of breeding animals. The future of the cattle trade is thereby assured, and in addition to the increase in breeding classes and the young stock the one year olds have increased by five and a half per cent.

The total area under wheat is given as 76,438 acres, which is more than twice as much as was grown in 1914, and only slightly less than the area of last year. Oats occupy an area of 1,071,593 acres – practically the same as 1915. The land under barley is 150,063 acres – an increase of 6 per cent over last year. Potatoes, turnips, mangels, beet-root, and cabbage are all nearly up to last year's standard, which fact affords evidence of the enterprise and industry of the agricultural community. A remarkable increase is indicated in the area of land under flax. The total acreage is given as 91,454, which is an increase of 72 per cent as compared with 1915.

As a means of feeding an important Irish industry the cultivation of flax is the commended, and it is an indication of the growth of self-reliance to find that farmers here made such a notable effort to meet the demands of Irish mills by supplying them with a crop grown at home. The area under hay (1st year's, 2nd years' 3rd years' and permanent meadow) shows a slightly downward tendency, and pasture an almost imperceptible increase. It is perhaps impossible to expect a very marked increase in tillage during war time, when labour is difficult to procure, and that last year's standard (which showed an increase of over 3 per cent) should have been practically maintained this year is evidence of industry and determination to surmount difficulties. Agricultural Ireland has done remarkably well, all things considered, both in livestock and in crops, and providence ordains that fine weather will enable the balance of the harvest to be gathered in, the people who live on the land will have no reason to complain of the results of their labour.

3 September

SWEET HONEY

The sixteenth annual meeting of the Cork Beekeepers' Association was held at 2, Marlboro Street. Mr Michael Lynam, V P, occupied the chair. There was a fair attendance of members considering the very busy season and the scarcity of labour.

There is apparently a great scarcity of honey this year all over the British Isles. Three applications of large quantities of honey, both section and extracted, were placed before the members. One wholesale dealer desired to secure from 25 to 30 tons of run honey in 56lbs tins, a second wanted 75 dozen sections and as many 1lb bottles of extracted honey as could be sent, while a private individual supplied for 100 sections for home use. The secretary was instructed to inform these applicants that owing to the great loss of stocks during the past two unfavourable seasons very little Irish honey was likely to be exported this season.

THE FIGHT FOR LANGUAGE

At the inaugural meeting of the session held by the South parish Gaelic League Mr Seán Jennings, Chairman, presided. The meeting, which was held in the branch premises, An Grianan, Queen Street, was very largely attended.

Mr O'Murthuille, who was enthusiastically received, speaking in Irish, thanked the branch officials for inviting him to speak at that important meeting. He was very pleased to be privileged to speak to such a large and enthusiastic audience of Cork Gaels. Ireland had for a long time been endeavouring to decide whether she should cast aside all phases of Irish national patriotism and adopt an Imperialistic Ambassador or whether she had better stick to her own Gaelic, national civilisation. She found it hard to decide. Her position was equal to that of the ass in the story. The ass had two sheaves of corn given to him to strengthen him for a journey next day. He spent a whole night trying to decide which he should eat first, and died of hunger between them both. Ireland, too, would have expired between the two civilisations; in fact she could live only by sticking to her own. That she had decided to do, and now she was vigorously marching ahead to nationhood, largely due to the existence of the Irish language movement (applause). The history of Europe recorded the struggles that were fought by many small nations to ensure the safety of their languages. If Belgium, Poland, or Alsace and Lorraine had a right to fight for the freedom of their languages, by what right could Ireland be prevented, except by the unjust 'right' of might, and if such small nations as those had a right to fight for freedom, why shouldn't Ireland?

A MEETING OF RAILWAYMEN

A mass meeting of railwaymen was held in the Mechanics' Hall for the purpose of considering the action of the Executive Committee of National Union of Railwaymen in their recent demand for an increase of 10s per week for all railwaymen. Mr P Lynch, President of the Trades Council, occupied the chair.

The following resolution was unanimously carried: "That this meeting, representative of all grades employed on the railways in Cork, directs the attention of all concerned to the present high prices of food, in consequence of which the rank and file on the railways find it impossible to provide from their present earnings the bare necessaries of life. This meeting further desires to direct the attention of the Government to the fact that all reasonable and legitimate means have been exhausted to secure relief in the way of increased weekly war bonus or additional wages, without success. That the railway companies declare it to be impossible to meet our demands out of present rates and revenues. We are still suffering inequality of treatment as compared with the men employed on the railways in Great Britain, and as the Government have taken no effective steps to control or prevent the prevailing tendency of a still further rise in food prices, etc., we are resolved to support the decision of the National Union of Railwaymen in the demand for a 10s per week increase now before the companies of Great Britain and Ireland".

8 September

FATAL QUARREL

Castle Lane, off Blarney Street, Cork, was last night the scene of a tragedy. A quarrel between two men named William Hunt and John Dillon resulted in the almost instantaneous death of the former. It is alleged that following a dispute Dillon hit Hunt a few blows with his fist in the stomach. Hunt, who was about 72 years of age, staggered, and falling, apparently struck the ground with some force. Assistance was promptly rendered by some residents in the locality, and Hunt was removed to his house. It was believed, however, that if taken into the yard that the fresh air would enable him to recover, and he was taken to this portion of the premises, while a clergyman and doctor were being summoned. He however, never regained consciousness and death appears to have taken place a short time after the termination of the row.

The police on being informed about the occurrence took Dillon into custody, the arrest being effected by Constable O'Brien and Kelly, of the Shandon Street station, and he was lodged in the Bridewell. Other policemen of the same station, under the direction of Sergeant Neary, took possession of the deceased's house. Hunt was a general dealer, living in

Cattle lane, and Dillon, who is about thirty years of age, is described by the police as one who frequents fairs and race meeting for the purpose of gambling. About eight o'clock Dillon was in stable yard at Cattle lane, when Hunt entered it with a horse and cart. While the latter was performing the operation of untackling the animal from cart words passed between both men, ending in blows; and, as already stated, Hunt receiving one blow, it is believed, in the region of the heart, fell and death quickly followed. Dr P J Hayes, North Mall and a clergyman arrived on the scene a short time after the occurrence took place, but life was then extinct.

11 September

CORK'S NEW BISHOP

The most Rev Dr Cohalan was born at Kilmichael, Co. Cork, in 1858, and his early school days were spent at St. Vincent's Seminary in this city, a school which gave many eminent scholars to the church. Subsequently Dr Cohalan went to Maynooth, and in 1883 was a curate at Kilbritain. In the following year he was professor at St Finbarr's Seminary and chaplain to the Military Prison, Cork, after which he went to Tracton as curate. From 1886 to 1914 Dr Cohalan was Professor of Dogmatic and Moral Theology at Maynooth, and came from these to take up the duties of assistant Bishop of Cork, subsequently becoming Vicar Capitular, and now Bishop of the Diocese. Dr Cohalan's erudition and research have long since won him a distinguished place in letter, and he is widely recognised as a brilliant and profound scholar, whose

Cork Bishop Dr Daniel Cohalan.
(SOURCE: DIOCESE OF CORK AND ROSS)

contributions to Catholic literature possess a value and weight that no ordinary layman could accurately appraise. Included in Dr Cohalan's publications and works are "Trinity College its Income and Value to the Nation" "De Incarnatione" "De Deo Uno et Trino, De Deo Creatore, "De incarnatione", "Sanctissima Eucharista" and he is also the author of many valuable contributions to Catholic magazines and journals.

13 September

A QUESTION OF THE WAR BONUS

Cork Ratepayer's Association: Mr J C Rowe presided. Mr William Dorgan, solicitor said he called that a special meeting to consider a notice of motion which was on the agenda for a special meeting of the Corporation to be held on Friday, to give the labourers 3s a week as a bonus during war time. The men had already got two increases of wages and were paid better than builders' labourers in the city, and it could not be said that all the men by the Corporation were as efficient or worked as hard as the men employed by the ordinary employers in the city. The proposal, if carried, meant an increase of £2,000 a year on the rates, and the men would have 4s a week more than all the ordinary labourers. He thought that the Corporation should look at the matter from the employers' point of view as well as from that of the men. They all knew that the cost of everything had increased for the employers of labour as well as for the employees. The employers in addition had to pay 5s in the £ income tax. According to the standing orders increases could only be considered in July, and he submitted that the motion standing in the name of Mr J Horgan could not be considered. He held that though it was called a bonus it would be really an increase of wages.

Sir John Scott said they should recognise that the cost of living had gone up very much. But the Corporation ought to consider the matter carefully, and if they thought a moderate increase would meet the case they might fairly give a moderate increase. He suggested that they send a deputation to the Corporation meeting. Sir John Scott's suggestion was adopted and it was decided that all the members present await on the Corporation on Friday.

SAVING LIVES

Tomorrow the annual Flag Day Collection for the funds of the Lifeboat Association will be held in Cork, and few objects should meet with more whole hearted support from the citizens. No more noble or humane work could there be than that carried on by the Lifeboat Institution. The lifeboat crews in the various districts never stop to consider the terrible dangers which are there in the execution of their arduous and heroic work. Be the call from whom it may, the response is ever readily and willingly given. They do not hesitate to answer the call of those in distress. During the year 1915 through the work of the Institution no less than 671 lives and 61 boats and vessels have been saved, and 213 persons rescued as a precautionary measure from vessels in danger. 441 launches took place, while crews were assembled in readiness for service on 49 occasions. We owe a great deal to the brave fishermen and boatmen on our coasts who risk their lives for their fellow-men in distress, and it is not surely too much to ask that the institution which provides the boats for this noble rescue work should receive the generous aid of the public so that the most efficient and capable boats and material might be maintained and at hand to lessen the danger incurred by the heroes who man the lifeboats? To support the noble cause of the Lifeboat Institution is to afford aid and doubtless the response to tomorrow's appeal will be worthy of the cause for which it is made.

A FAIR CORPORATION WAGE

A special meeting of the Council was held to-day to consider a report of Committee of the Whole Council with reference to the proposed grant of a war bonus to the labourers in the employment of the Corporation. The Town Clerk read a resolution sent by the Cork Consumers' League asking the Corporation to grant a war bonus to the labourers. Mr J Horgan then moved the adoption of the minutes of the committee of the whole Council and said that it had been erroneously stated that the granting of the application would mean 3.97d in the £ on the rates.

DESIGNING THE FUTURE

Crawford Municipal School of Art: The First Term commences on Monday next the 18th September. Drawing, shading, painting from casts, common objects, and from life. Designing for various purposes, architecture, modelling in clay and casting etc. Wood carving, metal work, stone carving, embroidery, lace making, crochet, stencilling, etc. For further particulars apply at the School, Emmet Place.

Notice – Owing to the action of the County Council in withdrawing their annual grant to the Technical Instruction Committee, all students resident outside the City Boundary will be required to pay fees in excess of those specified in the Prospectus, unless such students, their parents or guardians, pay rates or rent in the City, which fact must be proved by production of receipts. Particulars of fees can be had on application. F B Giltinan, Secretary, Emmet Place, 14th Sept, 1916.

Crawford Municipal School of Art. (SOURCE: CORK CITY MUSEUM)

FREIGHTS, HIGH PRICES AND SHIP-BUILDING

As the question of freights has been so frequently pleaded as an excuse for the high prices of necessary commodities, and as the freight problem is entirely dependent on the available supply of tonnage, a necessary preliminary to securing a remedy for the existing state of affairs is to find out what tonnage is needed for the particular work for which it is required, and how much is available or can be made available. It has been suggested that the government could easily procure the necessary information as to how much tonnage is needed for the carriage of all staples required in both import and export by the commerce of Great Britain and Ireland, or for the carriage of certain necessaries of life.

Coal for instance is a commodity which it is believed could be considerably cheapened if the Government took the matter in hand and dealt with it in a business-like manner. The approach of the season when coal is used most extensively, owing to the long nights and cold days, is looked forward to by the poor with feelings of dread, as the present prohibitive prices make coal a commodity which is beyond the means of many. There has been something in the air of late relative to the possibility of the Government taking over the coal control, it has been hinted that all coal raised in Great Britain and Ireland may be sold and distributed under official supervision while the coal owners would continue the management of

Parnell Bridge, *c.* 1910. (SOURCE: CORK CITY MUSEUM)

the pits. It has been announced on official authority that such rumours are premature and misleading, though it is admitted that the Government is looking into the question with a view to improving the conditions of things.

21 September

THREE GALLANT CORK MUNSTERS

Two distinguished Conduct Medals, and one military medal were presented to three members of the Munster Regiment at the Camp Field, Tralee, for conspicuous bravery in the field. The three heroes are natives of Cork. They are – Company Sergeant Major J Tyner, 9th Munsters (854), Innshannon, Co. Cork, DCM; Private P Ring, 3rd Munsters (4958), Cork City, DCM and Sergeant A Skuce (3741), Skibbereen, Co Cork. The presentations were made by Colonel Johnson 2/4 Lincolns. Previous to the presentations the troops in the garrison, including the 2/4 Lincolns, and the Royal Munster Fusiliers, the latter under Captain H Townshend, of Shepperton, Cork, formed three sides of a square in the Camp Field, and in the centre the presentations took place.

Colonel Johnson, in making the presentations warmly congratulated the recipients on their gallant conduct, and expressed the hope that their splendid example would be followed, not only by the other men of the Munsters, but by his own battalion when they go to France. The first distinguished Conduct Medal was then presented to Company Sergeant – Major Tyner "for conspicuous gallantry when under heavy rifle and machine gun fire, he left his trench and assisted Second-Lieutenant Gleeson to bring in a wounded man, who was lying within ten yards of the enemy's entanglements". The second distinguished Conduct Medal was presented to Sergeant Albert Skuce, 9th Royal Munster Fusiliers, "who was on patrol in "No Man's Land" on the night of the 25th May last in company with Corporal Murphy, R M F when a raiding party of the enemy came out. He attacked and drove the enemy back. Murphy was shot through the knee and Sergeant Skuce picked him up and carried him back in safety to our lines. The third medal was presented to Private P Ring, 2nd Munsters, "for conspicuous gallantry during a raid when the leading bayonet man was wounded in the enemy's trenches Private P Ring took his rifle and with one other man held up the enemy for twenty minutes. He was badly wounded by a bomb, but stuck to his post till ordered to withdraw".

ENERGY AND DETERMINATION AT THE GAELIC LEAGUE

On being unanimously elected chairman, Seán Uí Tuama explained the object for which the committee was formed, viz: the re-organisation of the Gaelic League in Cork City and district. He felt sure that it only required a little energy on the part of Cork Gaelic Leagues not only to revive the old branches in the city and district, but to start new ones. The tide had now turned in their favour, and there was now more than ever before a tendency on the part of the people to give their sympathy with the language movement practical shape. There were in every district patriotic men and women who put this small nationality above all, and who only required a little encouragement, who only needed to see that they would not have to toll alone in order to make them active workers in the Irish Ireland Movement. It was the duty of those who were already in the Gaelic League to give such people as these the needed encouragement, and where necessary to contrive to help them in such matters as the securing of teachers, the holding of feiseanna and concerts, etc. This city and the district around it afforded Cork Gaelic Leagues a fine field for work of this kind. With very little trouble a sufficient number of Gaelic League branches could be started in Cork and its vicinity to enable them establish a District Committee. If a District Committee was established, it could easily have enough funds to enable it to secure the services of a competent man to act as teacher and organiser for the district and keep the League active in it. It now behoved members of the League in the City to set to work. With a little energy and determination on their part there should not be a single district round about without its branch of the Gaelic League by the middle of November at the very latest.

A CORPORATION AND A BISHOP

It is quite needless now to speak of the feeling of supreme satisfaction with which the citizens of Cork, and in particular the Catholic community, learned of the appointment of the Most Rev Dr Cohalan to the exalted office of Bishop of Cork. The public bodies, both of the city and county, have already voiced the popular sentiment in this regard, but the citizens in general have not been directly afforded the opportunity to give that striking evidence of their appreciation of his Lordship's appointment which they so earnestly desire. Doubtless, this fact has appealed to the Lord Mayor (Councillor T C Butterfield), and he has taken the timely and thoughtful step of convening a public meeting to be held in the Council Chamber, City Hall, at 12 o'clock on Thursday next. We are satisfied that the occasion will bring together one of the largest and most influential bodies of citizens that has yet assembled within the walls of the Council Chamber. Equally pleasing is the announcement made that the Lady Mayoress has invited a meeting

City Hall, *c.* 1910. (SOURCE: CORK CITY MUSEUM)

of the Catholic ladies of Cork to be held in the Lord Mayor's room on Tuesday next at noon. We are sure that the ladies will only too gladly seize the opportunity to give expression in fitting form to the fact they warmly share the popular feeling on his Lordship's entry into his high and holy office.

24 September

A SUCCESSFUL BRIGADE GALA

Under the auspices of the local companies of the Boy's Brigade and Church Lads' Brigade, a very enjoyable and successful swimming gala was conducted at the Municipal Baths on Friday evening. Every portion of the building was filled to its utmost capacity, and the loud and frequent applause, as well as the hearty laughter, testified to the high appreciation of the patrons. A very attractive programme was presented, and the large number of entries in every department demonstrated the great popularity of the fixture. Each event

Former buildings of Municipal Baths, demolished in 2004. (SOURCE: KIERAN MCCARTHY)

provided very keen competition, and the gala was certainly one of the most interesting and successful that has been conducted for many years. The arrangements were performed in a most satisfactory manner and the officers, as well as the committee in charge of the event, deserve to be heartily congratulated on the great success that attended their efforts.

HOW TO CHANGE A CLOCK

Lest changing of the clocks on next Saturday/Sunday night should be done in a careless or negligent manner, the government has taken the unusual step of issuing a notice to the public on the point. The Home Office does not undertake to instruct the Irish people on this manipulation of the time, for it is expected a service notice will be issued for this country in view of the recently passed Time (Ireland) Act 1916, which is now well known substitutes Greenwich for Dublin time as the "normal" time in Ireland. As a consequence of this Act the Irish will adjust their clocks not by one hour but only by 35 minutes. As this moving back process recklessly done is likely to cause injury to certain timepieces it may be no harm to quote the official warning that the hands of the ordinary striking clocks should not be moved backwards; the change of time should be made by putting forward the hands eleven hours (in Ireland for a period corresponding with the new time) and allowing the clock to strike fully at each hour". The hands we are further told, "should not be moved while the clock is striking". An alternative method in the case of pendulum clocks is to stop the pendulum for the required time. On Sunday and Monday next the public will therefore do well to remember the change in time and to bear in mind the alterations which have become necessary in railway time tables.

OCTOBER

4 October

PLACING A VALUE ON FISHERIES

Of the many industrial anomalies that glaringly stand out in this country, and the origin of which may be traced to inequitable treatment in the past, the Irish Deep Sea Fisheries occupy a prominent place. It appears to be true that much of the fish that is consumed in the South of Ireland reaches its destination via Grimsby, though large quantities of various kinds of fish are caught off the Southern Coast. If the Irish deep sea fisheries were properly organised and adequate facilities afforded for the transit of the fish inland, it is calculated that the value of the Irish fisheries should equal that of England. As it is, the value of Irish Fisheries is computed to be about a twentieth of that of England, and probably a tenth of that of Scotland. Possibly very few, if any, Irish Inland towns receive a regular supply of fresh fish, though no part of Ireland is more than sixty miles from the sea.

The reason of that extraordinary position of affairs is attributed to the desire that exists to hurry off by train for England any fish that is taken off the Irish Coast, or to cure it for export abroad. The home market is practically ignored, and so the measures that have been taken to promote an Irish industry that has boundless possibilities discard to a very great extent if not altogether, a valuable market that exists at our doors. It has been asserted that it is easier and cheaper to send fish caught off the Irish Coast to London, or Liverpool, or Manchester, than to towns centrally situated in Ireland, and while such non business-like methods prevail the Irish fish trade must languish and Irish fisheries continue to occupy a backward position instead of being a source of huge profit and a means of widespread employment.

A QUESTION OF SUBSCRIPTION

Of late there has been a marked tendency in a section of the British Press, buttressed by the Irish Tory Press, to urge that conscription should be applied to Ireland, and that Irishmen should be forced into the fighting ranks, whether they approve or not of that drastic form of procedure. For a country that has been largely depopulated as a consequence of the misgovernment that resulted from the Union it will be conceded by all unprejudiced persons that Ireland has already given freely to the best of her manhood and that men who voluntarily took up arms to fight for the sacred cause of freedom represent both in numbers and in valour a very considerable contribution. For Ireland is being made by an influential section of the British Press and by political opportunists of the Sir Edward Carson type that pay no consideration to Irish conditions or necessities, and put forward no valid argument in favour of military coercion for Ireland, except perhaps, that the Irishmen who have voluntarily gone forward have done so well and have shown such bravery in the field that the source which supplied them should be further tapped and the country drained while the fighting Irishman is forthcoming.

The late Lord Kitchener described Ireland's answer to the call to arms as "magnificent", and Mr Asquith was so impressed with Ireland's voluntary contribution to the war that in the House of Commons he opposed previous efforts to apply conscription to this country. The fact that Ireland has liberally given of her best becomes more clearly apparent when it is remembered that there are 400,000 farms in Ireland which continually require man-labour, but Sir Edward Carson and those who think with him evidently do not care two straws if the country be left derelict so long as they can gain a political advantage, even if by doing so they plunge the country into disorder.

KEYS TO THE FUTURE, RESULTS AT SOUTH PRESENTATION CONVENT SCHOOL

We show on another page the excellent results obtained by this well-known school in the various examinations for which the pupils are prepared. Such results speak for themselves but we cannot refrain from expressing the gratification it affords us to see that an institution which has done so much for the education of the children of the citizens continues on its triumphant course. The list of successes is an eloquent testimony to the thoroughness of the work done. In these days of keen competition, it is no easy task to win the much coveted exhibition prize or "place". Yet many such have been won by the pupils. The very large percentage of honours obtained is a pleasing feature, and the numerous pupil-teacher scholarships won by quite young students is very creditable. Irish receives special attention, as is evidenced by the large number of students obtaining honours in the language, which is to a great extent spoken in the school. A new feature in the curriculum is the commercial course, to which great importance is attached, and which is followed by a large number of pupils in all grades. The importance of this cannot be over estimated as it prepares girls for lucrative positions in the world of business. Many past pupils now fill important posts as secretaries, typists, and accountants. A large proportion of the students prepare for the profession of teaching and for them ample provision is made in the King's Scholarship and Matriculation Classes. Finding that the teaching profession is being overcrowded in Ireland there has been this year a peaceful invasion of England, when several girls entered English training colleges, secondary and primary. Nor are the other professions neglected, as many past students now at University College, Cork are following Arts, Medicine, Dentistry, or Science Courses. Among them may be mentioned the holders of the Honan Scholarships, Miss Mulcahy and Miss Keane. Miss Mulcahy has retained her scholarship by achieving the distinction of coming first among the first arts students with five first class honours while Miss Keane obtained her first medical Examination with first class honours in each of its four subjects. Miss Browne has gone successfully through her medical course, and is now in her last year. Miss May O'Connor, another past pupil, has just got her Second Medical, and obtained second class honours in Dentistry. Several of this year's Matriculation Class will proceed to University College when the session opens, and we wish them as full a measure of success as has attended their former fellow students.

10 October

GOOD AND SOUND WORK, CRAWFORD MUNICIPAL TECHNICAL COMMITTEE

Mr A F Sharman Crawford, Chairman, presided. The summary raises some important points re the numbers attending certain classes, viz, those in plumbing, typography, painting and decorating, gas manufacture and wireless telegraphy. As the committee are aware the last two subjects are not now taught in the Institute, and as regards the other three, there is a practical difficulty in the way of obtaining suitably qualified students in any considerable quantity for we are limited to the number of apprentices available in the city and neighbourhood. Thus, in typography, where at least four different classes have to be taught, we cannot obtain more than about 26 students, altogether, thus each class cannot be large. In plumbing we could do better than we do, but the reference in the summary to the apathy of the employers is here very true, and the committee might do worse than consider closing the class, unless the employers give more effective co-operation. This of course, is not to suggest that good and sound work is not being done in the class, but numbers are essential to the success of our scheme.

In domestic economy, the summary states that 'the teaching is generally sound, and in certain cases, highly satisfactory', but that 'too many students are crowded into the first classes during the early weeks of the year'. The numbers entering these classes have always been limited, and it is very hard to have to turn so many students away, but I have this session reduced somewhat the number allowed into each class, so that overcrowding cannot possibly occur. For the reason mentioned in the summary the class in high class cookery was discontinued by me last March, and it has not been revived. To the remaining comments - 1st, on the unnecessary wearing of jewellery in class, and 2nd, the necessary wearing of aprons and sleeves. I need only say that the former is a

Crawford Municipal Technical Institute, *c.* 1910, now the site of the Crawford College of Art and Design. (SOURCE: CORK CITY LIBRARY)

practice discouraged by our teachers who, however, have very seldom to speak about it, and the latter is already a rule of the Institute. He wished it to be understood that he took the summary in the spirit in which he understood it to be given, viz to be of help and assistance to the committee and staff, and as such it was always very welcome.

11 October

POVERTY IN THE CITY

The provision of cheap fuel for the poor of the city during the winter months is a matter which, as the Industrial Association properly suggests, ought to be seriously considered by the corporation without delay. Fuel of all kinds is likely to increase in price. Already it is far beyond the resources of the small wage earners, whose mode of livelihood – difficult enough before the war – has now become an intricate problem. There is another class – those who have no regular employment, and whose income does not exceed more than a few shillings each week – who have no possible chance of procuring sufficient food, not to speak of fuel, without the aid

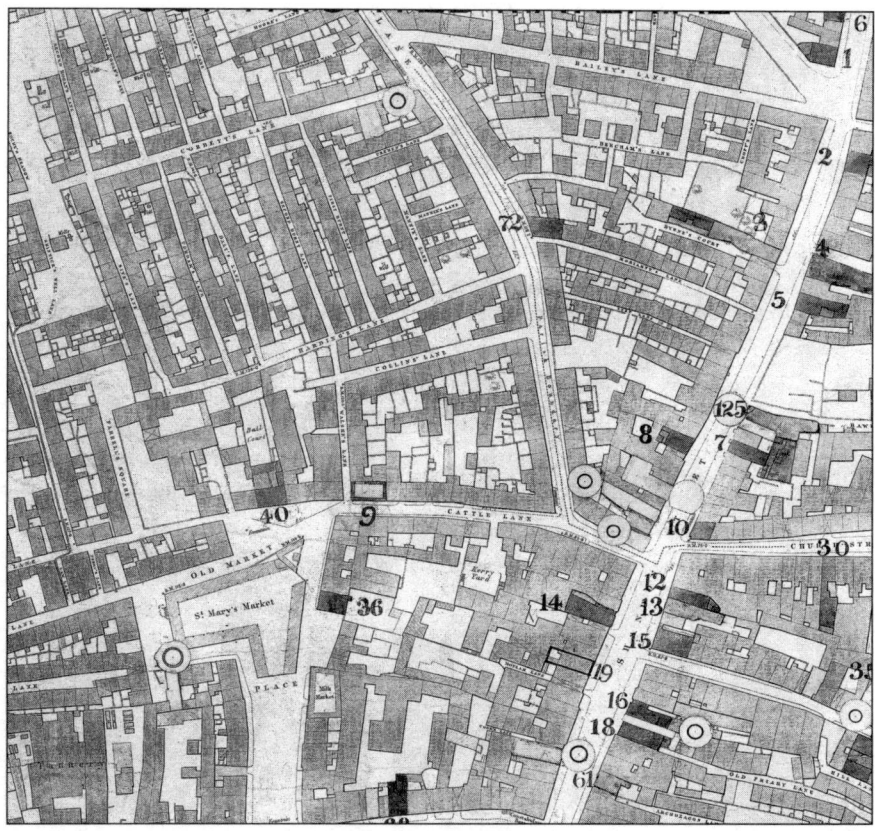

Laneways around Shandon Street, 1870. (SOURCE: CORK CITY LIBRARY)

of charitable assistance either from their own friends, a little better off than themselves, or from the societies in the city organised for the purpose of helping the necessities. Despite the increase of employment in some trades and the circulation of large sums as separation allowances, inquiry will show that much extreme poverty exists in Cork at the present time. That sad condition of things will become aggravated with the approach of winter unless organised public effort is made to ameliorate the lot of the genuine poor. We trust the Corporation at their meeting of Friday will decide on arranging for a conference in reference to the grave question raised by the Industrial Association and thus lead to something practical being done to prevent real suffering amongst the poor.

THE VENERATION OF FR MATHEW

The Father Mathew Anniversary Celebration was carried out on the usual grand scale. The Rev Fr Pious, President of the Hall bade the large audience a hearty *céad míle fáilte* to the celebrations that evening. More than a century and a quarter had passed since Father Mathew was born, and just 60 years ago, the people of Cork followed his remains to St Joseph's Cemetery. To few men was it given to have their names venerated and held in benediction. It was only to men of heroic deeds and renowned valour that such a need of praise was due. Father Mathew was a real hero and a great patriot, because he went forth to fight and to free his people from the slavery of intemperance. Today, for 60 years, his remains are in the tomb, but a grateful people cherish his memory and proclaim his noble deeds.

Fr Mathew Statue, St Patrick's Street, *c.* 1910. (SOURCE: CORK CITY MUSEUM)

DIALOGUES ON THE CONSCRIPTION QUESTION

The efforts of the die-hards to impose conscription on Ireland still continue, and Edward Carson, who apparently has constituted himself their leader, has seen fit to indict the Lord Lieutenant of Ireland for a speech the latter made on the question of Ireland's aid in the war. Lord Wimborne's statement was, in Sir Edward Carson's opinion, "harmful," because the former declared that Ireland has made a splendid contribution – a view which had previously been expressed by Lord Kitchener. Though Sir Edward Carson possesses some experience as a covenanter, and took the salute at a memorable march past in the North of Ireland when his ideas regarding rebellion were more robust that they are at present, he can hardly lay claim to be regarded as a military expert and as an authority of such weight as the late Lord Kitchener. The figures given by Lord Wimborne with reference to the number of men supposed to be available for military service in this country, though merely estimates, are yet sufficient to dispose satisfactorily of Sir Edward Carson's phantom army of half a million men. If the estimate made last year be correct, that there are in Ireland 562,000 males of military age, less the 157, 000 men already serving, one reaches a total of 405,000, which Lord Wimborne further diminished by the following deductions: – 90,000 farmers actually engaged in farm work, 50,000 men engaged on munitions and similar occupations, thus bringing the number down to 265,000. Further deductions for medical unfitness and for other causes brings that total to something which Lord Wimborne stated would be, roughly, between 100,000 and 200,000, his approximate estimate being 150,000.

HIGH STANDARDS AT ATHLETIC GROUNDS

The final of the County Hurling Championship which was played at the Cork Athletic Grounds yesterday was one of the most exciting games witnessed for a considerable time. It was not exactly that the game was of the high standard sometimes seen in a final, but that interest was kept at a high pitch from start to finish. This was due probably to the equality of the two teams, for at any period of the game there was little between them, and what little there was perhaps too much, for two more equal teams never faced each other. It was a fine game to look at, though there were many faults. Principal of those was the placing of the men on the winning side. Gorman, who was scoring for them, did remarkably well, but got practically no support, particularly in the second half, when invariably he had a couple of men to beat. There were, too, faults on the part of individuals on both sides, particularly when drawing on the ball. This was probably due to excitement, and indeed were it not for this factor the result might have been in favour of Shamrocks. They are certainly a remarkable team, for they have recently come into prominence, and bearing this in mind, the fact that they have run up for the hurling championship is a great tribute to them. They are deserving of the highest praise for the magnificent fight they made – a fight which has gained them a host of admirers. Midleton have always had a pretty useful team, and the combination that did battle yesterday have every reason to be proud, though it did look as if they played a better match against Blackrock. The football semi-final between Youghal and Collegians was a fairly interesting contest, though the last-named won rather easily. The attendance was of enormous proportions and the weather fine, but, as was to be expected, the sod was slightly on the soft side.

TRAGEDY ON THE TRAM

Mr Coroner William Murphy, solicitor, held an inquest at South Infirmary yesterday evening into the circumstances attending the death of the little girl Eileen Beale, aged 10½ years who died at the institution as a result of injuries received the previous day. Mr James J McCabe, LLB, solicitor appeared for the next of kin; Mr M Healy solicitor, MP, represented the Cork Tramway Co, and Mr Walsh, D.I., represented the police authorities. Edward Beale, mill worker, West Douglas, father of the deceased, gave evidence of identification. He last saw his daughter alive at 10 o'clock on Sunday morning, when she was in perfect health.

Mary Walsh (13), West Douglas, who was with deceased at the time of the occurrence said she, deceased, Mary Turner, Molly and Jane Kidney, and Jenny Watts, were playing near the tram terminus, about 3 o'clock. They were playing on the platform on the Cork end of the tram. The driver told them to get off the tram, and they all got off except the deceased. When Eileen Beale did not get off, he pushed her off, but she got on again. As she got on the tram, the bell rang and witness and others went away except deceased, towards the lower village. They heard a shout, and on looking back saw the deceased lying on the road. The tram was stopping at the time. The conductor lifted her up and took her into the clubroom.

John Mulcahy, Douglas, said that 3.15pm on Sunday he was coming out of the clubroom. James Walsh, who was with him shouted; "Oh, Lord, the child is dead". Witness then saw the two shoes come from under the tram off the child and the hind right hand wheel of the tram go over her. The driver stopped about a yard or half a yard from where the child lay, and witness and the conductor lifted the child into the room. The right leg was crushed between the ankle and the knee.

Dr Jeremiah Murphy said he was doing duty for Dr Lehane on Sunday. He saw deceased about 4.30 o'clock, when she was practically dying. Both legs were broken at the thigh, and there was a compound fracture near the ankle of the right leg. There was no other serious injury, though there were some abrasions. She died at 5pm. Death being due to shock. Everything possible was done for the child.

PACKAGES TO THE FRONT

We have been favoured with a copy of the report for the six months ending last June of the committee in charge of the Royal Munster Fusiliers Prisoners of War Fund. The figures contained in the report are remarkable. No fewer than 14,964 parcels were despatched to the prisoners during the six months, and these parcels contained useful articles of diet. Which go to supplement the scanty fare allowed to the brave men? Parcels are packed and despatched three times a week. Each prisoner receives 5s worth of food per week, in addition to the four pounds of bread which he receives from Switzerland. The committee also had at their disposal for despatch to Germany numerous gifts in kind. These gifts included articles of warm clothing, which are greatly appreciated by the prisoners. An interesting feature of the report is the reproduction of letters of thanks from several of the prisoners acknowledging the regular receipt of the parcels, and expressing in their own simple way appreciation of the efforts made on their behalf.

THE LEGACY OF ST FINBARR

The Collegiate Chapel of St Finn barr, which will be attached to the Honan Hostel adjoining University College, is rapidly approaching completion, and will be solemnly opened for service on the 5th prox.

In May of last year the foundation stone of the building was blessed and laid by the late Most Rev Dr O'Callaghan, and since then the work of building has gone on steadily; each month showing a distinct advance. Almost from the very first it was apparent to even a very casual observer that the new chapel was intended to be a real work of art. And now that the outside work is finished, everybody will admit that the architect planned a very handsome structure in the Hiberno-Romanesque style which prevailed in this country nine centuries ago. Comparatively few examples of the style have come down to the present time. The most famous is Cormac's Chapel on the Rock of Cashel. Recently some new churches

Honan Chapel today. (PICTURE: KIERAN MCCARTHY)

have been erected in the Hiberno-Romanesque, amongst which St Finn barr's Chapel will stand out as a very perfect specimen. It is singularly appropriate that Mr James F McMullen should adopt this style for a place which will be intimately associated, though not officially connected with University College.

In the same spot St Finn Barr many centuries ago established the great monastery where hundreds upon hundreds of earnest students were instructed in all the learning of the period. Then came changes and in course of time the famed monastic school was untenanted. Other centuries passed by bringing their own peculiar vicissitudes, until once more another educational establishment was raised upon the same ground. This in the course of a little more than one generation developed into a constituent college of the National University of Ireland and all who are most interested in higher education of the South of Ireland look forward to the day when it will be elevated to the dignity of an independent university. Side by side with University College was established a hostel for Catholic Students, now known as the Honan Hostel, while now through the munificence of the late Miss Honan and her executor, Sir John R O'Connell of Dublin, a beautiful place of worship has been provided for the residents of the Hostel and other Catholic students of University College.

FROM FRONGOCH WITH ADVICE

Sir, I have just returned from Frongoch Internment Camp. It occurs to me that others wishing to visit friends there might be glad to know how to manage and what are the rules governing the admission of the interned men's friends.

The notice recently published has unintentionally misled many. It is not possible for one person to visit eight men. Two men may be visited by each person, and eight only can be visited in all, each day, by four persons, allowing two men to each visitor. That I understand is how the notice should be read. The hour of the visit is written on the permit, but it is inevitable that there should be occasional alteration.

In making application to the censor at Frongoch, it is well to leave a clear week from the date of writing to the date of starting, so that there may be no doubt of receiving the permit to visit the different men before starting, otherwise difficulties may arise, and a long journey be taken in vain.

I found the best plan as to route as follows: Leave by North Wall boat 9.45 evening. On arrival at Holyhead wait for the train leaving at 2.55; for the train which goes on at once does not stop at Chester. Chester is reached 4.48 where in a warm waiting room, the time is spent until 8.55, when the train leaves for Bala, changing at Bala Junction. There is a good refreshment room at Chester. From Bala there is a train on to Frongoch. But, as the distance is only two miles and a half, one can go into the town and get lodging. By going over on Wednesday night one is enabled to visit friends on Thursday and on Friday, by spending a night in Bala. It is a pleasant walk from Bala to Frongoch.

The great point on reaching Frongoch is to obey rules absolutely, not only for one's own sake but far more for the sake of those whom one is visiting. You will gain nothing by trying to look through the wired enclosure, or by attempting to greet men who are being marched about on the road or inside. And, remember you may compromise them. It is a little difficult to know where to wait. There is a post office just above the camp, where it is possible to sit down and where tea can be got. In wet weather a refuge is very welcome. Visiting hours are 2-6.

Albinia Broderick

PILOTAGE SCHEMES

The discussion which took place at yesterday's meeting of the Cork Harbour Board in reference to the local pilotage scheme revealed a state of things which is far from satisfactory. As a body the Cork Harbour pilots are a skilled and daring lot of men. Their duties for the greater part of the year are trying and exacting. The worse the weather the greater the need for them to be on their stations. Without properly equipped boats it is impossible to expect an efficient service. The day has gone by when the lightly built sailing vessel can compete with the modern motor or steam boat.

Promptness is an essential of any system of pilotage which is to command respect. Pilots may be willing but unless supplied with the proper kind of boat for their work, their readiness to act goes for nothing. Without entering into the details set out in the report of yesterday's discussion, it is plain that several members are not satisfied with the way in which the system is working at present. It is rightly suggested that the pilots are entitled to have their views respected by the Board. Their livelihood depends on the success of the system, and so does the future of the Port of Cork. It is eminently desirable to remove all grounds for complaint against the present system, and to provide the pilots with vessels, the seaworthiness of which will be beyond question.

Roches Point, Cork Harbour, c. 1910. (SOURCE: CORK CITY MUSEUM)

WAR AND THE EMANCIPATION OF WOMEN

Now the war has been the means of breaking down musty and decadent obstacles to the emancipation of women. We have actually been invited to pass along avenues which we had long and anxiously been waiting for an opportunity to tread; paths long closed against us – a most fortunate thing for the county that we were ready. Where would the old world girl have been in this crisis? Weeping, no doubt, But this is the day for women to work, not weep. And yet during the past fifteen years we have been jeered at for our ambition, which always soared beyond the manipulation of the crochet needle.

For more than a decade we have suffered the sneers of a powerful and unscrupulous opposition in our efforts to become intelligent beings, and real, live units of this workaday world, however, these things are now only a relic of the past. A new atmosphere has been created and at long last women begin to live. Men have never been able to understand women, though this is hardly to be wondered at since we are only just beginning to be ourselves. Men, generally have been surprised at our "splendid women," as Mr Lloyd George calls us. But the women have not been surprised. We always knew we could accomplish the things for which we have been appraised, and do them well. It is no compliment when deeds occasion surprise. The greater surprise is that before this was the minority power or in other words, the male portion of the community, were prepared, and even anxious, to hold in check, perpetually, the energy, ambition, brains and fingers of women. What a past decade of waste! A country can only reach its high water mark when all God's creatures are allowed equal opportunity of expressing their particular desires and aims. Equality of opportunity should be the birth right of every male and female. Some will make little use of it; others much; but however great or small it should be a rule of civilisation.

CELEBRATING THE
COLLECTIONS OF IRISH MUSIC

In the Father Mathew Hall, Queen Street, on Friday night, Dr Annie Patterson, under the auspices of the South Parish Gaelic League, delivered a very interesting lecture on "Irish Music and How to Study it". There was a good attendance. Miss M McSwiney, BA, presided and introduced the lecturer.

Dr Patteron, who was very cordially received, expressed her regret that she could not address them in the language of the country but she would endeavour to speak to them through its music. As a first example of what Irish music was like she would ask her quartet of two male and two female voices to sing "when through life unblessed we roam." When this was rendered the lecturer said she would deal briefly with the various material available for students of Irish music. A number of collections had been made of old Irish tunes. The famous antiquary, Dr Petrie, made a very important and representative collection. Bunting was, however one of the first to note down Irish tunes for the purpose of preserving them, and he had the great advantage of taking down the tunes direct from some of the old Irish harpers. He made an excellent collection, which was largely drawn upon by Moore for his melodies. She would like to say a good deal about Moore, but it was a rather controversial matter, as some blamed Moore for altering some of Bunting's tunes in order to fit them to his melodies. However, they had to take Moore as they found him. Sir Henry Stanford also did a good deal for Irish music by his arrangement of pieces.

A great collector of Irish music was Captain O'Neill, of Chicago, who though far away from Ireland, took a great interest in old Irish music. He made a speciality of old clan march tunes. The late Dr P W Joyce, a county Limerick man, made a very notable collection. The lecturer further directed attention to the Feis Ceoil collection of tunes. Altogether something like six thousand pieces of old Irish Music had been collected, but in many cases there was overlapping, through different versions of the same tune being given. There were still many pieces uncollected and unpublished, which were well worth attention. The lecturer then played a selection of traditional airs from the various collections referred to and including "The March of Maguire" (Stanford).

NOVEMBER

1 November

GOD'S ACRE AND THE NORTH INFIRMARY

Sir – The Christian-like practical sympathy evidenced all round to those who are suffering from this fearful war has been a bright spot amidst the wailings of the broken hearted and afflicted and the encircling gloom. The wounded heroes, who are daily arriving, are justly entitled to a first charge upon the nation's tenders care and, thank God, they are receiving it all round. Royal palaces are open for their reception and those of royal blood cheerfully administer to their wounds and wants. Here in this city all that noble hearts can do is cheerfully undertaken by ladies and gentlemen whose exertions are beyond all praise. Our city hospitals are open night and day for their reception, and doctors and nuns spare no pains to relieve them. Some of our institutions are more highly favoured than others in the way of recreation grounds. The South Infirmary has a large space available and the Mercy Hospital, with the adjoining Dyke Parade and Fitzgerald's Park, has many advantages. The North Infirmary has practically no space where those poor fellows can retire for recreation – a few yards at most with three garden seats, is all that is available at present, and yet why should this be so when the expansive graveyard adjoining the buildings, beautifully situated and enclosed on all sides, needs only that a door, already fixed in the dividing wall should be open, and permission granted for their admission. Surely there should be no objection to this being done, and done at once?

One week with willing workers would arrange walks without disturbing a single grave, and there is ample space for comfortable seats all-round the enclosure, where these glorious defenders can have what they enjoy so much – a smoke and a chat with their comrades after their struggles for our liberty. At present their freedom is curtailed and the passages outside the wards are not suitable and to have to walk to the city must be uncomfortable, and leaves them open the door to God's Acre? St Paul's Churchyard, London, and others to mention are fixed with seats, and it is considered no desecration for the weary and heavy laden sons of the toil to take refuge there from the excitement of the busy centre. I am sure the broad-minded, tender-hearted Bishop, who since his advent here has shown such concern for the poor and afflicted of every class, and the zealous and kind rector of the parish will see that no narrow-minded influence shall keep closed this door of mercy to these blood-stained warriors of the cross and civilization – Yours faithfully Alfred M Cole, 21 Wellington Road, Cork, 30.10.1916.

5 November

UNITY AND CO-OPERATION, HONAN CHAPEL OPENS

The opening of St Finn Barr's Chapel at the University College yesterday constitutes a further notable feature in the progress of the institution. One cannot read the report of the proceedings at yesterday's opening ceremony without being struck by the weighty words which fell from his lordship the Bishop of Ross, who was the preacher of the occasion. Associated with his lordship in the ceremony were his Grace the Archbishop of Cashel, his Lordship the Most Rev Dr Cohalan,

Interior of Honan Chapel today. (SOURCE: KIERAN MCCARTHY)

each of whom takes a deep and abiding interest in the progress of University College. It was appropriate that the Bishop of Ross should trace in some detail the story of St Finn Barr's association with Cork as a seat of learning, for by the re-opening of the chapel yesterday the Saint's ideal was once again restored – the linking together of the Church with the College. Incidentally his Lordship referred to the recent pronouncement at the Protestant Synod by Bishop Dowse, in which he expressed a strong desire for unity and cooperation between Catholics and Protestants in the promotion of the good and prosperity of our common country.

7 November

MODERN CRAFTSMANSHIP AT THE HONAN CHAPEL

The above illustration shows the Monstrance which is now completed. It is a beautiful example of modern craftsmanship. It stands 3ft 2in in height from base to top of cross. The shaft is 1ft 4ins in height and the lunette 14½in diameter. The octagonal shaft from its spreading base to the terminating feature supporting the lunette is of fine proportions. The eight pierced panels in the lower portion of the base are of varying designs, embodying the interlaced or strap work pattern common to the art of this country. They are not copies or plagiarisms of the early work. This interlaced pattern is introduced into each of the various fittings aiming at harmonious and continuous effect in the whole scheme when completed. The upper portion of the base is circular in form

Illustration of detail on monstrance, Honan Chapel, 7 November 1916.
(SOURCE: *CORK EXAMINER*)

with four enamel bosses somewhat similar to those on the base, each being surrounded by pierced strap work panels of different designs. The terminating feature supporting the lunette takes the form of two grotesque animals with intertwining tails. The lunette is quite original in design, the common star or ray being here replaced by a broad outer band or pierced interlaced ornament divided into panels by circular piercings or cross formation. An inner and narrower band of pierced work surrounds the glass fronted receptacle in which the wafer rests. This inner band is also divided into panels, but in this case by bosses of blue enamel, which tend to concentrate the eye on the centre of the lunette. A cross of generous proportions surmounts the whole. The arms of this cross are enclosed within a circle and are emphasised by enamels of diamond shape set into the extremities. The monstrance is executed in silver, weighing about 220 ounces, and is heavily gilt. On the base is an inscription incorporating the names of the donors, donors' executor, designer, and the craftsman. This article has been designed by Professor William A Scott, of 45 Mountjoy Square, Dublin, and the craftwork has been executed by Messrs Edmond Johnson.

8 November

DIFFICULTIES IN CORK PILOTAGE SERVICES

Sir – A considerable amount of attention has been drawn of late to the present unsatisfactory conditions of the pilotage service of our harbour, and the recent admissions of the unseaworthy state some of the pilot boats, has come as a surprise to many. Some twenty or more years ago the Harbour Board took over the entire control of pilots and their boats and a comparison of the conditions existing then and now may not be out of place. At that time the pilots made their way to sea in boats of which they were sometimes the owners or part owners, and other times they shared the earnings with the boat owners. These boats usually had a dual occupation as in addition to piloting they were also engaged in fishing or were what is known as "slop chest boats," viz., selling at sea to homeward bound ships articles of clothing etc. The pilots themselves were not then as now all living in Queenstown. Kinsale, Glandore, Cape Clear, to mention a few places all had then in their community, pilots holding a "branch" or license for Cork Harbour.

There was no pooling of earnings. The greater number of ships a man brought in, the more money went into his pocket and the pockets of the owner and crew of this boat. This state of affairs naturally led to a keen rivalry in getting to ships first. The Queenstown pilots complained that they were not competing on level terms with the western men, who were on the spot, when a ship was making the land, and not to travel all the way from Queenstown to the Fastnet at great discomfort, expense, and sometimes risk. On the other hand, the Queenstown pilots were, I fancy, more in the know from information from shipping agents as to times of departure of ships, and knew pretty well when to expect them. The boats of that time were badly found in gear, etc. Racing for ships was a common occurrence, and "carrying on" followed. With bad gear, accidents were bound to happen, and the wonder is that they were so scarce. The members of the Harbour Board of the time were acquainted with these and other facts, and after consideration, decided to take over the control of boats and pilots, and establish things on a better footing. Some of the existing boats were brought at liberal prices, and after being repaired and refitted were sent to sea. Some of them, I think, were broken up. A number of stations were adopted, such as one at the Fastnet, one at Galley Head, one at the Old Head, and one at the Harbour, and it was deemed an impossibility for any ship to come in and make a complaint against what was looked on as a perfect system. The pilots had at last got good boats. Their earnings were pooled, and each man got his share of the common fund. A pilot master was appointed to take complete control and see that everything was in working order. The boats were expected to keep to sea in practically all weathers. The pilots all lived in Queenstown, and those of them who withdrew from the service were compensated. It gradually became apparent that the earnings of the fleet were not enough to support the number of stations, and they were cut down, and at present the harbour station alone remains.

Harbour Rock

AN ESTEEMED ACADEMIC, CRAWFORD MUNICIPAL TECHNICAL INSTITUTE

In electing Mr D Madden, AIC, ARC Sc I, to the post of head of the Chemistry department in the Crawford Municipal Technical Institute Cork, the committee has conferred a well-deserved honour on a young Corkman of conspicuous ability and sound personal and scientific qualifications. An old pupil of North Monastery, where he pursued a remarkably brilliant secondary course, carrying off first class exhibitions and medals for highest place in all of Ireland in mathematics and science, in all grades of the Intermediate, Mr Madden was one of the most popular of a distinguished group of talented pupils. He played with great success an important part in the Centenary Pageant 1911. He was awarded the "Harrington" gold medal for highest score in chemistry, for which so many keen young scientists at Our Lady's Mount competed. At the conclusion of his course at North Monastery, Mr Madden carried off in open competition a science and technological scholarship (value £275), tenable at Royal College of Science, Dublin. His four years' course at this institution was marked by the highest honours, especially in chemistry and mathematics, and after specialising in the Faculty of Applied Chemistry under such distinguished teachers as Professors G T Morgan. D Sc, FRS, and A O'Farrelly, MA, FCS he obtained the Associate Diploma of the Royal College of Science, being placed first of his year in chemistry, appointed demonstrator in chemistry at University College, Galway, in February, 1916, Mr Madden obtained by examination in July, 1916, the Associateship of the Institute of Chemistry of Great Britain and Ireland – a hall mark in the domain of practical chemistry – and was appointed by the Department of Agriculture and Technical Instruction for Ireland instructor in advanced chemistry for teachers' summer courses. A genial colleague and an enthusiastic worker Mr Madden is a thoroughly trained and a gifted teacher, who will prove an efficient lecturer in the post which her merits have won for him in his native city. His very many friends wish him every success in his new sphere.

INSTALLATION OF A NEW BISHOP

His Lordship [Bishop Cohalan] left his residence in the South Terrace about 11 o'clock, and escorted by the Men's Confraternity of the Holy Family attached to St. Finbarr's, to the number of about 1,000 men, all wearing the ribbon and medal of the Confraternity, and with their spiritual director. Rev T Noonan C.C headed by the Barrack-Street No. 1 Brass and Reed National Prize Band, and accompanied by the Emmet Pipers' Band proceeded to the Cathedral via South Terrace George's Quay, Parliament Bridge, Prince's Street, St Patrick's Street, St Patrick's Bridge, Camden Quay, John Redmond Street, and Roman Street. He was accompanied in his open carriage by Rev P Mc Sweeney. CC, St Finbarr's South, and his progress through these crowded thoroughfares at once signalised the strength of the ties that bind the Most Rev Dr Cohalan to his flock. The persons who lined the streets reverentially bowed their salutations to their Bishop, who imparted his blessing as he drove along.

At St Patrick's Bridge the triumphal procession was intercepted by the Butter Exchange Brass and Reed Band, and at the junction of the Bridge with the quay a banner spanned over the roadway and on his way the sincere prayer of all inscribed "Long life and happiness to our good Bishop". The way thence to the Cathedral was avenued by the boys of the Christian Brothers' School, North Monastery, who were marshalled by Mr T O'Sullivan drill instructor, most of whom bore the colours of the school flag staffs, the men of the Sick Poor Society, North Parish, and the Confraternity of the Cathedral. Roman Street was arched with flags and bunting and gaily decorated; at the beginning of the street the device "Welcome to our Bishop" expressed the general sentiment. The Cathedral Presbytery, and Cathedral Place, and St. Mary's Hall also bore indications of triumphant felicitations at the glad event.

FITZGERALD'S PARK ALLOTMENTS

The suggestion made at yesterday's meeting of the Fitzgerald Park Committee to utilise a portion of the spare space at the western end of the grounds for the cultivation of potatoes to provide additional food for the poor has a good deal to recommend it. But if on consideration it is not found feasible to grow potatoes on the ground indicated that should not deter these members from pressing forward their scheme in other directions. Unless the proposal for potato growing in the Park obtain unanimous support it is perhaps better to secure ground elsewhere for the same purpose. It has been frequently suggested that all waste ground within the city should be cultivated for the benefits of the poor. A society is in existence for the promotion of vegetable growing schemes in connection with such plots, and financial aid can be obtained for the hiring of such plots for the cropping of vegetables. If the scheme were adopted in Cork it would have the effect of providing an additional food supply which would be greatly valued by the poor, and would form an object lesson for the people which could not fail to have beneficial results.

Gates to Fitzgerald's Park, *c.* 1910. (SOURCE: *CORK EXAMINER*)

SERIOUS FLOODS

Accompanied by very heavy rains a severe storm passed over Cork during Thursday night and continued yesterday. About two o'clock the strong wind abated somewhat, and veering round from the southeast to the west, the heavy rains disappeared. For the remainder of the afternoon and evening slight showers were experienced, and the conditions were the reverse of those in evidence during the night and early morning.

During the forenoon, afternoon, and evening large crowds congregated along the quays and bridges overlooking the river at the North Channel, and evinced a great interest in the terrific rush of water towards the harbour, as well as the many articles that were borne along by that rush of water. Numerous cattle, sheep and pigs were seen in the water, while large trees, evidently blown down in districts adjoining the Lee in the suburbs, and furniture small boars, mangolds, turnips, potatoes, hot house frames, garden-seats, baulks of timber, corrugate iron and innumerable articles were carried away in the great flood. A large number of their articles were the green coloured seats from the Fitzgerald Park, where the flooding must have done a great deal of damage and caused much loss. All these circumstances demonstrated the immense severity of the storm, and the suffering, especially in the homes of the poor people, must have been intense. This suffering was very acute in the low-lying districts, where the thoroughfares were impassable owing to the depth of water covering them. In many instances access to the city was cut off, and with the water rushing into the houses, the misery of the occupants was terrible. Towards evening, conditions were not so serious, but the effects of the floods will be keenly felt for some time.

FORDS COMES TO CORK

The "Irish Times" says; – a special meeting of the Cork Corporation has been summoned for next Wednesday to consider a notice which has been given by the Lord Mayor; – "that the Standing Orders be suspended in order that a certain proposal be considered and agreed

FORDSON Farm Tractor.

FORDSON Farm Tractor.

THE DAWN OF A NEW ERA FOR THE FARMER!

FORDSON

THE UNIVERSAL FARM TRACTOR.

The Fordson Tractor means to the Farmer what the Ford Motor Car has been to the civilized world.

It is the Simplest of all Tractors to work, the Easiest to Maintain, and the most Satisfactory of all Power Machines.

The "Fordson" will displace three or four horses on the Farm, and will plough your three-horse land up to an acre per hour.

 *If you have Land to Plough we will do it for you, and thus demonstrate for you the above claim.*

Munster Motor Company, Limited,

ARDCAIRN, BALLINTEMPLE, CORK.

Advertisement for Fordson tractor production, Cork 1917.
(SOURCE: CORK CITY LIBRARY)

to". The proposal is from R Woodhead, of 91 Lord Street, Southport, on behalf of undisclosed principles for the purchase of a factory of the freehold of Cork Park, of the building site on the Marian, and of portion of the public roadway on the Marian, and a portion of the public roadway on Victoria quay, at a price of £10,000 with the stipulation that the building to be created shall cost at least £290,000, that at least 2,000 adult males shall be employed in the factory when it shall have been completed, and that a fair wage clause shall be inserted in all building contracts, and that a minimum wage of 1s an hour shall be paid to all adult males to be employed in the factory when completed.

This notice does not appear sensational at first glance, but it is strongly rumoured in the city that the Ford Motor Company are acquiring a large tract of land on either side of the Lee at deep water to start a branch of their world-wide industry in Cork. On the northern bank of the river for half a mile there extend the yards of the Cork Harbour Commissioners, which were formerly the site of shipbuilding yards conducted by the Pike family three quarters of a century ago, and it is rumoured that it is in contemplation to acquire this site as well as a very large plot on the South Bank extending for half a mile along deep water and running back through Cork Park Racecourse for a great depth. It is stated that the idea is to build a factory on either side of the river, and utilise portion of Cork Park for a model village for the workers such as has been established by Messrs. Bradbury, Lever Bros, and other great firms. The Cork Corporation and Cork Industrial Development Association are endeavouring to carry through this great project with all expedition, as it will immensely increase the industrial prosperity of the city, and citizens of high standing outside these bodies are giving the matter their active support.

23 November

FORDS AND THE CORPORATION OF CORK

The Town Clerk read the correspondence, which included:- (1) A letter from the meeting of Transport Workers held in the City Hall on Tuesday night, calling on the Corporation and other public bodies to facilitate the scheme; and (2) from Mr Maguire, secretary of the University College Engineering Society also asking the Corporation

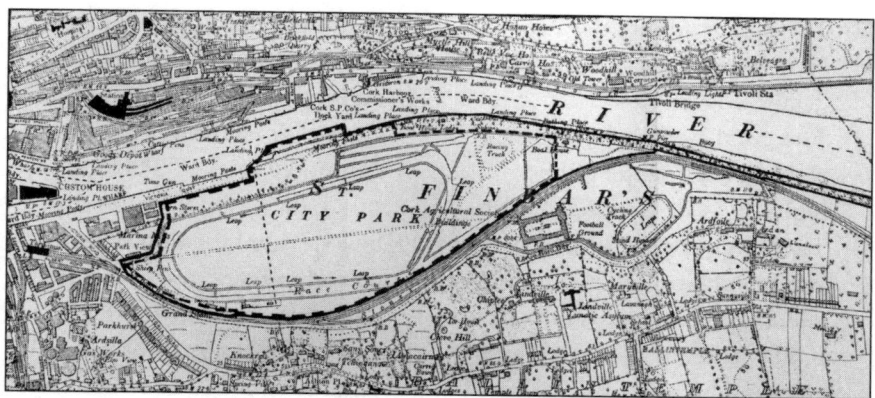

Map of proposed Ford complex on Cork City Park Racecourse, 1916. (SOURCE: CORK CITY LIBRARY)

to facilitate the scheme and thereby provide much-needed employment for students of the College, very many of whom had to leave their native city. The Lord Mayor rose with very great pleasure to propose the resolution which stood in his name. He did not intend to say very much about it, but he should say that he considered that Cork was extremely fortunate in having this offer made to it. He might also say that he considered it an epoch making offer, and he hoped nothing would be said or done there that day that would give any excuse to anybody for withdrawing these proposals. He did not anticipate any such thing because he knew the sense of the Corporation on the matter, and he knew, even though one might want this thing or the other thing and may want to have clauses put in, he thought that in the hands of their able solicitor the interest of the citizens of Cork would be safeguarded by Mr Barry Galvin.

He would now move that the standing orders be suspended.

Mr Curtis seconded and the motion was agreed to unanimously. The Town Clerk read the heads of agreement to be made between the Cork County Borough Council (hereinafter called the "vendor") of the one part, and Richard Woodhead of No. 91 Lord Street, Southport (hereinafter called the "purchaser") of the other:

(1) Subject to such statutory or other sanctions as may be necessary and subject also to the provisions hereinafter contained, the vendor will sell and the purchasers will purchase the freehold of all land as shown on accompanying plan marked "A" and coloured pink thereon, and also such portion of the land and roadway coloured blue thereon as may be in its possession.

(2) The plan is admittedly approximate as to scale and details.

(3) The purchasers shall have the right to enclose the public highway as shown on said plan.

(4) The purchaser shall construct and maintain (until taken over and adopted by the vendor) a public highway as marked and coloured brown in said plan.

(5) The vendor's willingness to sell is influenced by representations made by the purchaser as hereunder detailed, and notwithstanding any agreements or arrangements made to the vendor by the purchaser, the said lands shall revert to the vendor absolutely if any of the conditions stipulate hereunder are not complied with at such time or within such period as may be mutually agreed, or failing agreement, setting by an arbitrator. The conditions above-mentioned are:-

(a) The purchaser is acting for a principal and in no way as an intermediary for the purpose of re-sale or personal profit.

(b) The said lands will be used for the purpose of creating commercial, shipping and manufacturing premises and offices and generally in connection with industry or the housing of industrial workers.

(c) The estimated cost of such buildings, etc, to be immediately erected on said lands is computed at £400,000, but a sum of at least £200,000 shall be expended thereon within a period of three years from the completion of the transfer.

(d) The manufacture to be carried on in such premises will occupy at least 2,000 adult males.

(e) A minimum wage of one shilling (1s) per hour will be paid to all such adult males so employed.

(f) A fair wage clause in the usual terms will be inserted by the purchaser in any contracts which may be made for the erection of the said premises, etc.

(g) The vendor shall give to the purchaser a certificate that the conditions herein stipulated have been complied with so soon as possible after the vendor is satisfied the due fulfilment has been made.

(5) The price to be paid by the purchaser to the vendors for the transfer of said lands, etc., is agreed at ten thousand pounds (£10,000); payment to be made at to £250 within seven days after this agreement has been approved by the vendors; as to £1,750 upon signing of formal contract embodying the terms herein outlined, and as to the balance

upon completion of the transfer of said lands, etc., to the purchaser or such other party as he may appoint.

(6) The purchaser may, on or before, December 31st 1916, notify the vendors of his intention not to proceed with the transaction herein provided for, in which use he shall forfeit the said sum of £250, but otherwise shall be under no liability whatever in respect of this agreement.

(7) The vendors shall use every possible means to complete the transfer of the said lands, etc., as soon as possible, but the purchaser shall have no claim upon the vendors if for any legal reason a default or failure is made. If within two years from the date hereof the vendors have not completed the said transfer then the purchaser may claim and the vendors shall make return of any money paid by the purchaser as herein provided.

(8) The vendors' costs of obtaining statutory sanction hereinbefore referred to shall be borne by the purchaser.

Agreed this seventeenth day of November, 1916

27 November

NEW WORLDS, LOST NATIONS

At the present time Ireland is looking forward to seeing the Home Rule Act put into operation within a reasonable period. This will mean the completion of the national political programme, and for attaining it the Constitutional agitation must get credit. This does not however, preclude Irishmen from honouring such noble spirits as the men who were executed at Salford on the 23rd November 1867 made the greatest sacrifice that men can make for their country. Year after year the anniversary of the execution of Allen, Larkin and O'Brien has been celebrated throughout Ireland, and in most of the lands where Irishmen have made their homes. There have been many momentous changes since then. One might say, in the words of the poet. "New worlds have risen, we have lost old nations". The changes at home in Ireland are no less sweeping and significant. The Irish farmer has been raised from the condition of a serf to that of a free man possessing the right of ownership of the soil which he tills. The Irish rural labourer has been provided with a decent house in which to live and the workers in our towns have advanced far in material prosperity. The country as a whole has likewise advanced and continues to progress. It might be said by those who hold that worldly wealth and thriving commerce are incompatible with national ideals that the patriots of the past would be soon forgotten under present conditions. But the Irish are a grateful race, and do not readily forget well meant, even if unsuccessful efforts on behalf of their country any more than they forget generous services and measures of redress.

Nowhere has the memory of the Manchester martyrs been more consistently honoured than in Cork. This year unusual circumstances obtained but the Memorial Committee decided not to let the occasion pass without a demonstration, though many were rather doubtful as to the likelihood of a successful procession taking place. It could not, perhaps, be expected that the anniversary procession held yesterday would compare in size with the processions which were held in the city in years gone by, but taken all round, it was not unworthy of the memory of the dead. As in previous years, the procession was unattended by members of the trades bodies, Gaelic Athletic and other associations and citizens in general. The procession was not, however strictly speaking, organised in bodies, and those who marched in it did so principally as individual citizens. At intervals in the procession the principal bands played national airs. The procession was headed by the Cork Workingmens's No. 2 Brass Bank. Second place was given to the Volunteers' Pipers Band, and then the Barrack Street No. 1 Prize Brass and Reed Band, the Belvelly War Pipers, the Little Island Young Mens's Society Fife and Drum Band, Emmet Pipers Band, Quarry Lane Band, Cork Butter Exchange Band.

The processionists formed on the Western Road and marched via South and North Main Street, Pope's Quay, Camden Quay, Patrick Street, the Grand Parade, South Mall and Parnell Bridge to the City Hall, where a public meeting was held. At the National Monument the bands took up the "Dead March" which they played to the City Hall.

CAMPAIGNING FOR CORK'S INDUSTRIAL DEVELOPMENT

There are many satisfactory indications that Cork Industrial Development Association, after a protracted period of struggle and adversity, has come into its own, and that it has by perseverance and energy overcome prejudices, and won the confidence and goodwill of all classes in the community. Someone has written that to offer advice is always dangerous, but that to offer good advice is fatal. The Cork Industrial Development Association offered good advice to the people – advice which was disinterested and useful – and for that reason the Association was from time to time subjected to adverse criticism. Few persons like to be told how they ought to spend their money, and few manufacturers or shopkeepers like to be advised how they should conduct their business, or advertise or display their goods. An Association which set itself out to advise the public regarding its expenditure, and to urge that Irish made goods should be purchased in preference to imported articles, could scarcely fail to meet with the disapproval of individuals whose trade interest did not run exactly on Irish lines. Similarly, some shopkeepers, unable to take a long view, regarded the efforts of the Industrial Association to secure preferential treatment for Irish goods (with regard to their display and otherwise) as being of the nature of interference with their personal methods of doing business, but gradually the Industrial Development Association wore down such prejudices and proved that its action was always disinterested and its advice given solely in the interests of the community at large. It encouraged the people to look for Irish made goods, which are in variably of excellent value; it showed that the development of Irish industries meant the growth of employment, which provided an antidote for emigration, and finally the Industrial Development Association, by persistence of effort, has educated public opinion to believe that self-reliance is a virtue worthy of being cultivated by all classes both for the advantage of the community as a whole as well as for the individual interests that comprise it.

DECEMBER

5 December

AMUSEMENTS AT AOH

The Amusements Committee of the Cork City Divisions AOH have well-earned the gratitude of the general body of members because their assiduity in arranging entertainment gives delightful opportunity for social enjoyment, intellectual treats in the way of lectures and essays; and the provision of musical evenings marks the passing of some very happy hours. On Sunday evening, in the well-appointed Lecture Hall, Morrison's Island, members and their friends shared the pleasure of a really excellent concert under the efficient conductorship of Professor Theo Gmur. The programme introduced some new friends and with those whose great talents have given them a popularity that makes them old, compiled vocal and instrumental items and recitations, which charmed the overflow audience. The original 19 numbers were multiplied to over 38 by reason of an insistence on encores. This was a flattering proof of the respective abilities of the contributors, but none greater than each deserved – it was but a just recognition of mere merit.

6 December

THE GOOD SENSE OF THE PEOPLE

The Right Honorable Mr Justice Pim in his address to the Cork Grand Jury, when opening the Munster Winter Assizes, adduced remarkable figures in support of his pleasurable statement as to the reduction in crime. He evidently believes that drink is the genesis of most crimes, but in particular the offences that constitute the Irish calendar. He said: comparing 1915 with 1914, there was shown one of the most remarkable decreases in the history of crime in Ireland and particularly drunkenness has decreased in the most extraordinary gratifying and pleasing way. Some people thought it was due, perhaps, to the increase in the price of liquor, others that it was due to the earlier closing of the public-houses, but his lordship preferred to think that it came from the good sense of the people, who recognised that over-indulgence in strong drink was a thing that must injure and does injure irreparably the whole population". He mentioned that "the decrease from 1914 to 1915 was 1,179 to 680 in the County of the City of Cork; in the County of Cork there was a decrease of from 3,374 to 2,800. He thought that was a matter of high importance and one on which they could congratulate themselves.

7 December

THE WEIGHTING OF GENDER

The innovation of women letter-carriers has reached Cork. On Wednesday thirty aspirants, under convoy of the regular male staff, started at 6am to learn the work, and finished at 9am. It is said that this introduction of post-women to Cork will not result in their permanent employment, and they will only take the place of the male auxiliaries, whose services are not available. They will be paid 5*d*. per hour during period of duty. It is hard to realise that there was such a dearth of men available for postal work. The authorities state these post-women will not be asked to handle heavy parcels, their duties being confined to letters and letter packets. At Christmas time postmen get enough of these and to spare. All can remember their heavy loads, made up of letters and packets. During Christmas the long hours and weights carried are excessive, and tire out strong men who are used to years of that work. Therefore, if the women are only to carry light loads, who is to bear the brunt of the load that was hitherto divided between the eighty male auxiliaries and the permanent staff?

8 December

THE REVOLUTIONISING OF THE CITY

At today's meeting of the Cork Borough Council a matter of very great importance connected with the Cork Park Project, which should in a little time revolutionise and ameliorate the social life of the city, is to be considered. It is a letter from Mr Richard Woodhead of the Trafford Engineering Co. Ltd, Manchester, addressed to the City Solicitor, in which Mr Woodhead states that it would facilitate operations if he were able to obtain an additional frontage of 500 feet of the Marina (for which he is prepared to pay £1,000), to be acquired in the same manner and subject to the same stipulations and conditions as set forth in his agreement with reference to the Park site. The additional plot required appears to be a strip which could extend from where the Harbour Commissioners' enclosure ends to the Shandon Boat House, and its breadth would be from the edge of the quay to the park. The Corporation if they consider the wishes of the citizens, will gladly fall in with Mr Woodhead's proposal, as indeed the representatives of any progressive community would gladly afford the utmost facilities for the establishment of a great industry in the area under their control.

The stretch of the Marina left – from the Shandon Boat Club to Blackrock – should be ample to meet the requirements of promenadors, and up till now the Marina has been a source of expenditure, which brought no revenue. It is hoped that there will be no haggling or suggestions of petty bargaining in connection with Mr Woodhead's £1,000 offer that may have the effect of retarding the progress of the gigantic undertaking, which everyone who has the city's welfare and interest at heart is anxious. The scheme of the Trafford Engineering Co, will, if it materialises, mean the expenditure of at least a quarter of a million sterling annually in Cork.

9 December

THE EDUCATION OF WOMEN

In connection with the application from lady students and the Munster Women's Graduate Association, for the admission of lady students to the hospital [South Infirmary] as resident pupils, the House Committee recommended as follows; Having discussed the application made at the last meeting by the deputation, consisting of Miss Foreman and Prof O'Sullivan, for the admission of resident women students, it was decided that in the absence of suitable accommodation it was suggested that women students be admitted as day boarders from 9.30am, until such an hour as may be agreed on by the committee, such students to assist in the work of the hospital in the same way as the male students, and to be provided with meals on payment of one guinea per week, if desired.

With regard to this matter the following letter was received from

Sir Bertram Windle, President of University College Cork:- "I have been favoured with a copy of the letter, which is being sent by the Munster branch of the Irish Association of Women graduates in connection with the admission of women graduates as residents in the South Infirmary. The number of women medical students is rapidly increasing and it will be enormously to their advantage to have an opportunity of seeing the practice of a great medical institution, as can only be seen by those living within its walls. If, therefore, your committee can at all find it possible to accommodate them I can only say that you will gain the gratitude of all those who are interested in the education of women".

11 December

SETTING STANDARDS AT THE NORTH MON

In many parts of England, the Education Committees and the Juvenile Employment Sub-committees are giving considerable attention to the many points they now consider as being essential to the equipment of the boys, so that later in life they will be intelligent, progressive units in the industrial machine. Mostly all of the authorities consider that the raising of the qualification for apprenticeship from 14 to 16 years is an absolute necessity, for it is not until the lads reach near to the former age that they take an intelligent interest in the true meaning of school work. It is being advocated that great effort should be made to induce the trades to accept apprenticeships for shorter periods than seven years, say five years, and to refuse to take apprenticeships before 16 years of age. As matters are, there is a continual drift into the trades from the secondary schools at the age of 14 because parents know that the trades will not keep open places from boys who stay until 15 or 16.

Many of the Education Committees are of the opinion that the industrial education is now inadequate for the training of the future tradesman, and the schemes on which several of these bodies are now concentrating their efforts are

Entrance to North Monastery Secondary School today. (PICTURE: KIERAN MCCARTHY)

the extension of the age for compulsory school attendance to 14 years, strengthening and developing the upper standards in the elementary schools, the institution of higher grade schools, to follow this up with some kind of specialised instruction which shall be directly designed to prepare them for the work they are to undertake on leaving school. What England really needs are schools, teachers and morale in every respect identical with all that is to be found at the North Monastery, Cork.

13 December

UNDER THE MATRON'S EYE

Yesterday afternoon, through the courtesy of Captain F Downie, Director of Munitions, no.10 Area, Ireland, Lieutenant Hinge, the Lord Mayor and a representative of the *Examiner* were conducted round the Cork National Shell Factory, where on arrival some of the 150 hands at present employed there were partaking of afternoon tea in the canteen, which is attended by a number of voluntary lady helpers, who include the Lady Mayoress. Having passed through the canteen our representative was taken round the different machines, at each of which a number of girls were employed. The gas heaters register a heat of 1,000 degrees centigrade, and into which the nose of each shell is inserted and heated to a great temperature before being place into dies, and then into a 25-ton bottling press, in which the nose of the shell is shaped and turned. The process was gone through in the presence of our representative, and while explaining the process of manufacture Captain Downie expressed regret that he was unable to obtain skilled labour in Cork and pointed out that the men who were working hard at the bottling press and gas heaters were men who were trained at the Dublin National Shell Factory, and that more skilled workmen would be required, for whom immediate employment would be available in making application to Captain Downie and proving their fitness and efficiency for employment. When in full working order, as it will be in a few weeks more, the factory will afford employment to 250 persons, who will work in three shifts under conditions which will be exceptionally favourable. Each shift will be under the superintendence of a matron who is a trained nurse, and who will look after the general health of the workers. The scale of the wages paid to the girl workers are

10s 6d per week of forty-five hours as probationers, and at the conclusion of the probationary period, they will take their places in one of the three eight-hour shifts, when their wages shall be according to the shift in which they are engaged, namely – those on the shift from 6am to 2pm will receive 2s 6d per day; 2s 9d per day if on 2pm to 10pm shift; and 3s 3d per day if on the shift from 10pm to 6am.

15 December

ILLUMINATIVE CHRISTMAS CARDS

The Ladies Committee of the Cork IDA received several inquiries as to where Irish Xmas Cards, both private and stock, can be obtained. Some time ago Messrs Guy and Co. of Cork specialised in such cards, advertised them widely, and in this paper the series was described, and several illustrations given of the designs. They concentrated in these cards their many years' expert knowledge of colour lithography, and certainly the results were beautiful. Encomiums were received from specialists in the art of printing, as far as Scandinavia they had a sale, many palaeographists making a collection of them for a reason that should have made the series welcome to Irishmen, but in particular to students of the Gaelic language. Many stationers did their best to sell, but they admitted that those from whom they expected better, supporters of the Language movement, waived them aside in favour of some tawdry sickly sentimental cards. Apart from the want of patriotism which went to lessen the earning power of Irishmen, did they realise that these cards are reproductions of some of the most beautiful letters in perfect work of illuminating that the world has ever seen – the Book of Kells. The publishers of these cards secured many hundreds of lovely copies of the most exquisite letter forms, the copying being the life-work of a true artist who loved the work, and whose particular sense of colours made his task an achievement never before accomplished by copyists. The uncial and half-uncial lettering of this great book was the beginning of the perfection of illuminative writings.

BOXING AT CORK OPERA HOUSE

A very successful boxing tournament was conducted at the Cork Opera House on Saturday night. Every portion of the spacious building was well filled, and the programme presented was most cordially received. There were seven contests, and though some were of short duration, the bouts proved very interesting. The officials at the ringside discharged their duties in a very satisfactory manner.

Desmond V Cunningham
There was a six-round contest between D Desmond (Cork) and M Cunningham (Mallow). The opening round was of a rather even character; through Cunningham, who was of the stronger build, did most of the leading. Some vigorous fighting was witnessed in the second round, but Cunningham was wild in his deliveries, and Desmond gained a slight advantage. In the third round Cunningham's strength began to assert itself, and doing all the attacking. Cunningham had much the better of batters. Each contestant fought in determined fashion in the fourth round, and Desmond, who used his left in quick and useful action on Cunningham's body, took the lead. Cleverness enabled Desmond to maintain his advantage in the fifth round, and towards its close Cunningham was sent down by a right swing, but he promptly recovered. The sixth round opened in favour of Cunningham, whose body work was most effective, but Desmond withstood the attacks, and towards the end of the round delivered a good deal of punishment. Desmond was declared the winner on points.

EDUCATION AND THE WELFARE OF CHILDREN

The important duties discharged by the [Cork] School Attendance Committee should never have been necessary if parents only realised their responsibility for the welfare of children. The attendance has considerably improved owing to the pressure that it is within the power of the committee to exert on parents and guardians. Things were indeed bad when the Committee took up working, but there has been a great improvement effected – that is to say that whilst things are really bad today, the condition of affairs have been worse. Out of a total of 14,560 on the school rolls the average showed a daily absence of 3,324 – roughly not far off a percentage of 23 per cent. Whilst many parents have a reasonable excuse for not sending children to school, it is easy to believe that the figures go to prove that many of the cases are due to absolute neglect on the part of the parents. The salutary fines recently inflicted should go a long way towards improving school attendance. Where there is a well proved case of non-attendance arising through the negligence of the parents it is hoped that the magistrates, bearing in mind the number of absentees shown in the report will try and diminish this wrong to the children by inflicting severe penalties on the defaulting parents.

19 December

SUICIDE AT FRONGOCH

The latest news of the prisoners at the South Camp, Frongoch, was that owing to their refusing to answer roll-call and assist in the identification of those liable to military service that they were heavily penalised, one of the punishments being the deprivation of medical treatment when necessary. There is now another sad act added to the tragic drama, the suicide whilst in a state of unsound mind of Dr Peters, of Bala the Medical Officer. At the inquest serious allegations were made against the prisoners. The *Manchester Guardian* says that from the evidence it appeared that Dr Peters has not been in robust health lately, and was much worried by the annoyance caused and what he described as the untruthful statements made by Irish prisoners at the camp. He intended to resign and had written his resignation but postponed delivering it until he could reply to the inquiries from the Home Office.

DISPATCHES AT CORK GRAMMAR SCHOOL

In the Assembly Rooms on Saturday the annual Speech Day of the Cork Grammar School took place. Right Rev Dowse presided and the prizes were distributed by the Right Hon Mr Justice Barton. Right Rev Dr Dowse expressed his pleasure to preside at the annual meeting, which he regarded as one of the most important institutions in the city. The boys trained in the school would soon have to take their part of the work in the world, and their ability to do so depended on the education they got in the school. They could look back to the records of the school with a good deal of encouragement, for the records were such as the school may be proud of, and in which the students may take credit. Students of the school were holding good and important positions and doing work second to none in connection with their country. There were 183 of their students in the army or navy. The Headmaster then read his annual report in which reference was made to distinctions won by students of the school in the field of battle. S K Furney, NL Joynt and Hugo Gregg won the military cross, GA Moore, the Military medal, and F E Furney and LVH Allport were mentioned in dispatches. By the request of the boys, the amount usually spent on their prizes was forwarded as a subscription from them to the British Red Cross.

YULETIDE GIVING AT THE BARRACKS

There were several animated scenes and much juvenile gaiety at the Victoria Barracks on Wednesday evening, when through the kindness of Lieutenant-Colonel A Canning, CMG, commanding the 3rd Leinsters, and Mrs Canning, an entertainment was given to the wives and children of the men of the several battalions of the regiment who are resident in Cork and vicinity. The function, which was worked up with marked care, commenced at 3.30 when tea was served in the YMCA Hut to about 600 women and children. The tables were laid in an attractive

Victoria Barracks, *c.* 1910. (SOURCE: CORK CITY MUSEUM)

manner by Mrs Reed, Mrs Hayes, Mrs Knight, and Mrs Kavanagh, and the good things provided were done full justice to. Afterwards all proceeded to the Gymnasium, which was tastefully and elaborately decorated with flags and bunting. Here an enormous Christmas tree laiden with toys in waiting, and a look at the expectant and joyous faces of the little ones demonstrated at once the efforts of the promoters had not been in vain. Captain HRH Ireland MC in the time-honoured ruddy robes and snowy hair and whiskers, acted as Father Christmas, and the toys were given away by Mrs Reed. There were almost 500 children present, and when it stated that each received a pleasure-giving article from the tree, it can be seen that the work of the promoters was not easy.

23 December

THE HOPE OF CHRISTMAS

Christmas is being ushered in with bitter frosts and winds that bite shrewdly, and for those who have been so favoured that luxury is still attainable, and for whom the Yule Log burns brightly, a duty exists that must be fulfilled if the Christian spirit is not to be ignored or forgotten in the welter of war. The Christmas time is always a trying one for the poor – this year it will be exceptionally so. Many bread-winners have passed to their reward, leaving behind them helpless dependents, and when poverty is added to grief the lot of those who have to bear both trials is one for charity and pity. There is abundant evidence that the different city charities are sorely pressed – the high prices of fuel and food have added to their burden – and the demand for assistance is heavy and persistent. It is certain that the charitably disposed public will, as far as possible, help to alleviate the distress that prevails, even if it be beyond the power of the kindliest to heal the sorrow that saddens so many homes. But despite the poverty and the sorrow which are so universal in Europe, and in which Ireland participates to a considerable degree, there are still abundant reasons for gratitude to Providence that this country has been saved from the direct ravages of war, and the homes of the people spared from the murderous bombs of the enemy air-raiders. Sorrow and poverty exist in plenty, but Ireland though she has undergone a bitter trial and nurses the memory of a great grief, will still lift up her eyes and look to the future with all the hope, which Christmas instils in the hearts of Irishmen.

26 December

RELEASE FROM FRONGOCH

Throughout Saturday and Sunday men from the County of Cork arrested after the troubles of Easter Week and confined in internment camps in England, but who were released last week, arrived in Cork. They were met by relatives and friends at the Glanmire terminus, and proceeded to their respective homes. Amongst the released prisoners were: south and south east – Seamus Hannigan, Mitchelstown, Peter Donovan, Clonakilty, Thomas Synott, Wexford, John Connors, Ferns, John Kavanagh, Ferns, Michael Doyle, Enniscorthy, John Lacey, Enniscorthy, M O'Connor, Enniscorthy, M Cahill, Enniscorthy, Lee Doyle, Enniscorthy, P Synnott, Enniscorthy, P Carmody, Millstreet, J Twomey, Millstreet, John O'Riordan, Macroom, Martin Kinery, Fermoy, Peter O'Donovan, Clonakilty. Mr Art O'Brien, Hon Sec of the Irish Relief Fund, London, is informed by the Home Office that instructions have been issued to the Governor of Reading Prison to release all Irish Prisoners there in time for them to be home for Christmas. One hundred and thirty men left Frongoch last night, and the remainder will probably follow today.

26 December

FOOT AND MOUTH RISK

The new embargo on the shipment of cattle from Ireland, except those intended for slaughter within 96 hours, will cause some uneasiness in trade circles. Owing to a case of suspected foot and mouth disease at York the authorities deemed it advisable to issue the new order, but it is hoped that its existence will be of short duration, as the experience gained a few years ago will enable those concerned to deal effectively not only with the alleged case but also with those animals with which the suspected animal has come in contact. The 96 hours order will not hold up the Irish trade in the same way as did the order of a few years ago. England now relies so largely for her supply of beef on Ireland that her Ministers will not be inclined to continue any restriction on the trade for a day longer than is absolutely necessary.

28 December

THE HAPPY DAY

What might now be termed an old-established custom at the Cork Opera House is to open the after-Christmas season with a George Edward's musical comedy. The name of the famous producer was always taken as sufficient guarantee that a work would be effectively staged, and that the orchestra and chorus would bring out all of its best points. George Edwards has passed away, but the business organisation which he founded continues, and is determined to keep the standard of production up to the old traditional level. Their latest success is "The Happy Day", which ran for several months in London, and has been presented in the chief provincial centres with equal success. It was welcomed to Cork yesterday afternoon by an audience which left very few seats vacant in the Opera House, and the eight o'clock performances were even more extensively patronised, very many being unable to obtain permission for want of room. The play, which is in two acts, is the work of Mr Seymour Hicks; the music is by Sydney Jones and Paul A Rubens, and the latter with Adrian Ross, contributes the lyrics. As to the plot it may be briefly told. Prince Charles of Galania, who might be a knight errant in the old days of chivalry, is to marry Princess Mary of Valaria, whom he has never seen. He meets the Princess, but thinks she is somebody else, and they arrange to meet again at a sort of Bohemian ball that forms part of the municipal celebrations.

AUTHOR BIOGRAPHIES

KIERAN MCCARTHY

For over twenty years, Kieran has actively promoted Cork's heritage with its various communities and people. He has led and continues to lead successful heritage initiatives through his community talks, city and county school heritage programmes, walking tours, newspaper articles, books and his work through his heritage consultancy business. For the past sixteen years, Kieran has written a local heritage column in the *Cork Independent* on the history, geography and its intersection of modern day life in communities in Cork city and county. He holds a PhD in Cultural Geography from University College Cork and has interests in ideas of landscape, collective memory, narrative and identity structures.

Kieran is the author of seventeen books: *Pathways Through Time, Historical Walking Trails of Cork City* (2001), *Cork: A Pictorial Journey* (co-written 2001), *Discover Cork* (2003), *A Dream Unfolding, Portrait of St Patrick's Hospital* (2004), *Voices of Cork: The Knitting Map Speaks* (2005), *In the Steps of St Finbarre,* *Voices and Memories of the Lee Valley* (2006), *Generations: Memories of the Lee Hydroelectric Scheme* (co-written, 2008), *Inheritance, Heritage and Memory in the Lee Valley, Co. Cork* (2010), *Royal Cork Institution, Pioneer of Education* (2010), and *Munster Agricultural Society, The Story of the Cork Showgrounds* (2010), *Cork City Through Time* (co-written, 2012), *Journeys of Faith, Our Lady of Lourdes Church Ballinlough, Celebrating 75 Years* (2013), *West Cork Through Time* (co-written, 2013), *Cork Harbour Through Time* (co-written,

2014), *Little Book of Cork* (2015), *North Cork Through Time* (co-written, 2015) and *Ring of Kerry, The Postcard Collection* (2015). In June 2009 and May 2014, Kieran was elected as a local government councillor (Independent) to Cork City Council. He is also a member of the EU's Committee of the Regions. More on Kieran's work can be seen at www.corkheritage.ie and www.kieranmccarthy.ie.

SUZANNE KIRWAN

S uzanne Kirwan was born in west Waterford close to the Comeragh Mountains. She holds a honours degree in Business Studies (SME) from Limerick Institute of Technology, and an Honours Degree in Law (BCL) from University College Cork. Suzanne has a keen interest in drama. She has won numerous awards for best actress on the amateur drama circuit. She was awarded a silver, bronze and gold medal by the London Academy of Music and Drama. During her free time Suzanne enjoys spending her time in the countryside with her golden retriever Katie, and show jumping. Suzanne is currently working on her second book.

Also from The History Press

IRELAND
AT WAR

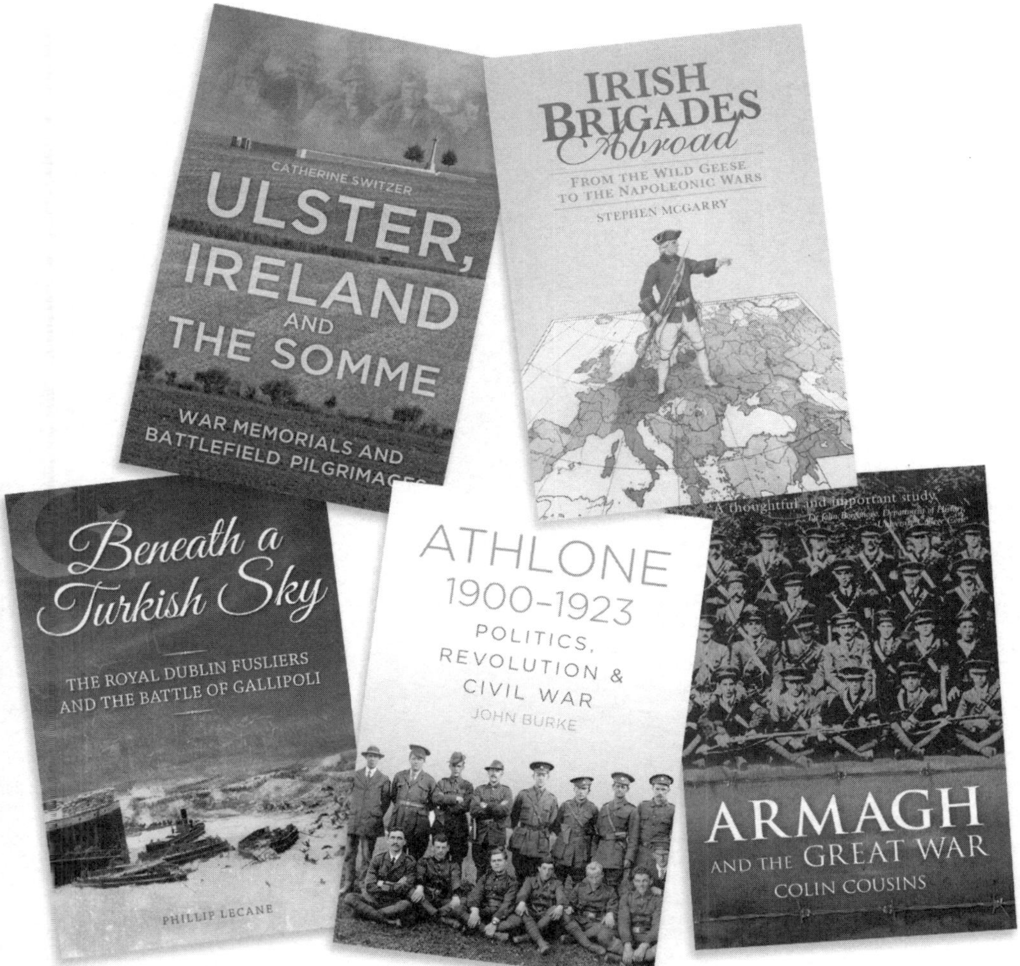

Find these titles and more at
www.thehistorypress.ie

The
History
Press
Ireland

How to Make a
BILLION
in 9 Steps

Richard Harpin

PIATKUS

PIATKUS

First published in Great Britain in 2025 by Piatkus

3 5 7 9 10 8 6 4 2

A CIP catalogue record for this book
is available from the British Library.

ISBN: 978-0-34944-644-8 (hardcover)
ISBN: 978-0-34944-538-0 (trade paperback)

Typeset by Hewer Text UK Ltd, Edinburgh
Printed and bound in Great Britain by Clays Ltd, Elcograf S.p.A.

Papers used by Piatkus are from well-managed forests and other responsible sources.

Piatkus
An imprint of
Little, Brown Book Group
Carmelite House
50 Victoria Embankment
London EC4Y 0DZ

The authorised representative
in the EEA is
Hachette Ireland
8 Castlecourt Centre, Dublin 15,
D15 XTP3, Ireland
(email: info@hbgi.ie)

An Hachette UK Company
www.hachette.co.uk

www.littlebrown.co.uk

To my children, for the days I didn't always make it home for bedtime, and to Kate for bringing them up so well. To my mother and brother for helping with my early business ventures. And to everyone who has worked at HomeServe for your hard work and commitment in building an amazing business.

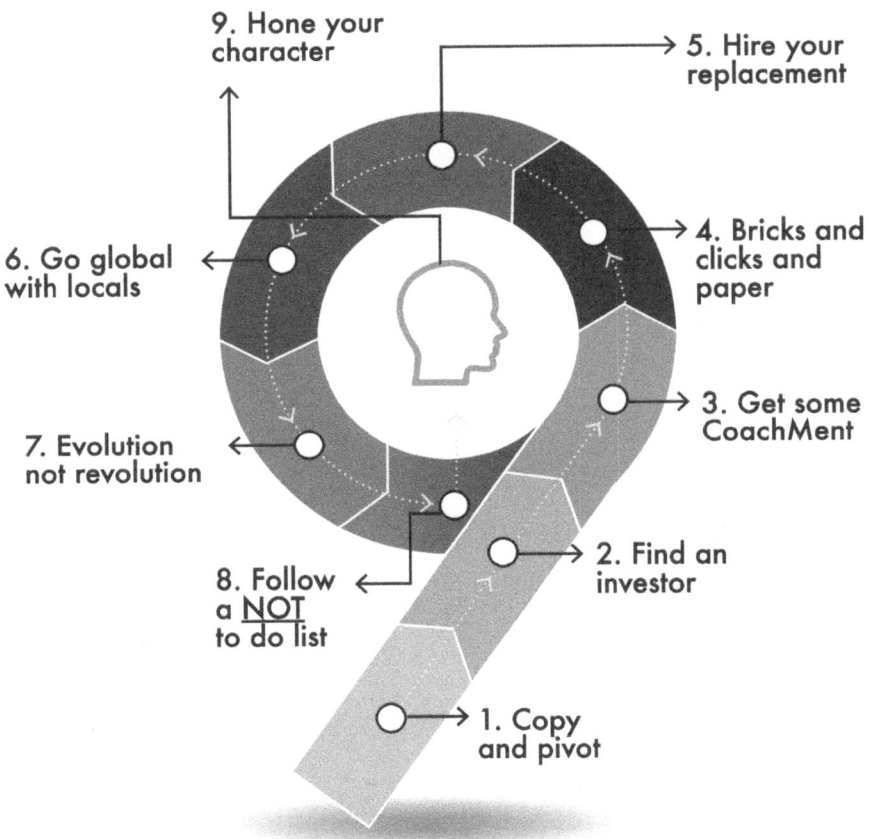

9. Hone your character

5. Hire your replacement

4. Bricks and clicks and paper

6. Go global with locals

3. Get some CoachMent

7. Evolution not revolution

2. Find an investor

8. Follow a <u>NOT</u> to do list

1. Copy and pivot

Contents